Design by Bill King, King Design & Print, Ipswich, Suffolk
Photography by Mark Ward, Elm Studios, Ipswich, Suffolk
Phototypesetting by Brian Rogers, Ipswich, Suffolk
Film origination by Halcyon Type & Design Ltd, Ipswich, Suffolk
Printed and bound in Great Britain by Print Wright Ltd, Ipswich, Suffolk
Production by Nick Tzimas and Bill King
Published and distributed by UK International Ceramics Ltd, 10 Wilford Bridge Spur, Melton, Woodbridge, Suffolk IP12 1RJ, England.

First Published 1991
Special Second Edition 1994
Third Edition 1996
Fourth Edition 2000

Bunnykins ® is a registered trade mark of Royal Doulton.

ISBN 0 9517772 9 7

© 2000. Text Louise Irvine
Listings Text © Nick Tzimas
Photographs and Listings © UKI Ceramics Ltd and Royal Doulton (UK) Ltd.

Acknowledgements for the Millennium Edition

We are delighted to be publishing the fourth edition of this book to celebrate the Millennium. The interest in Bunnykins figures has grown rapidly and collectors are constantly seeking new information on the subject. This new edition includes details of all the introductions and withdrawals until the end of 2000 and Nick Tzimas has produced a new rarity guide to Bunnykins figures.

Help in locating elusive models for all the editions has been provided by the specialist dealers Nick Tzimas, Richard Dennis and Derek and Jean Garrod. I am also indebted to executives at Royal Doulton for providing detailed information about Bunnykins figures, in particular George Bott, Nicola Nixon, Valerie Baynton, Ian Howe and Kerry Barcroft.

Bunnykins designers past and present have helped considerably with all the books and I am particularly grateful to Graham Tongue, Harry Sales and Walter Hayward. Several keen collectors have also provided useful information, in particular Tony Kenney, Leah Selig and Scott Reichenberg, who wrote the chapter on 'Collecting Bunnykins'.

I am grateful to Rachel Baker for typing the original manuscript and to Zoë Gilligan for her work on the second, third and fourth editions. My husband George continues to support the Bunnykins publications, editing my text and making helpful suggestions, while my son Ben's collection and interest grows with each new edition, showing me how much fun Bunnykins figures can be for all ages.

Louise Irvine

Products listed or shown were manufactured by Royal Doulton (UK) Limited. Royal Doulton and Bunnykins are registered trade marks and are used in the book with the kind permission of Royal Doulton (UK) Limited.

This book has been produced and published independently by UKI Ceramics Ltd.

Royal Doulton
BUNNYKINS FIGURES

by
LOUISE IRVINE

MILLENNIUM
EDITION

Published by
UK International Ceramics Ltd
10 Wilford Bridge Spur, Melton
Woodbridge, Suffolk IP12 1RJ
England

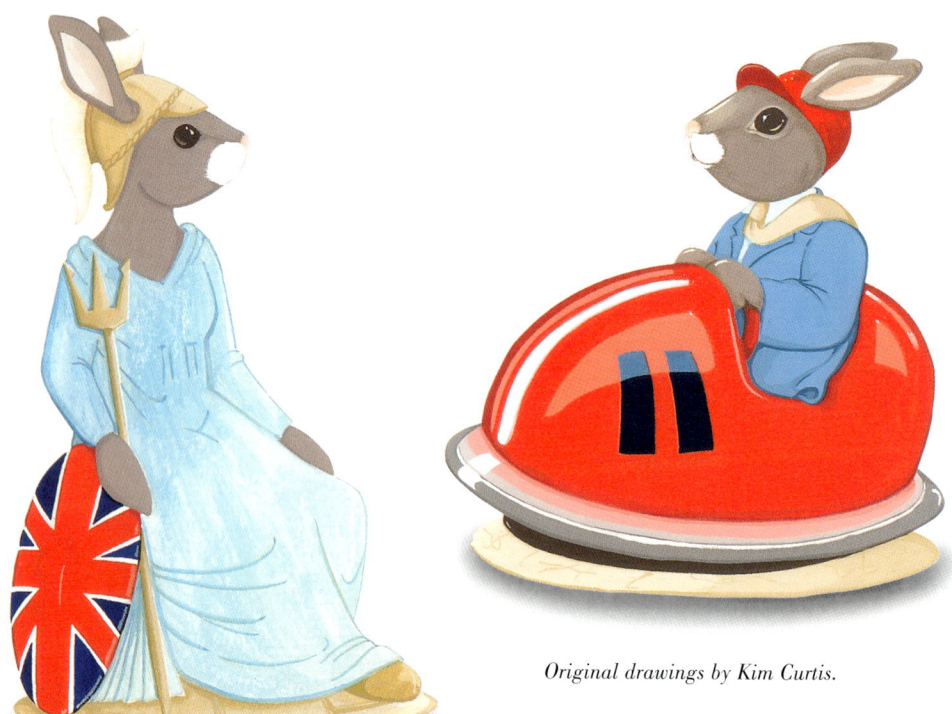

Original drawings by Kim Curtis.

About the Author

Louise Irvine is a freelance writer and lecturer with a special interest in ceramic history. For many years she worked as Director of Historical Promotions for Royal Doulton, initiating their International Collectors Club and organising exhibitions, notably 'The Doulton Story' at the Victoria and Albert Museum. She has written a variety of books and articles on Royal Doulton collectables and she travels extensively to lecture in the UK and overseas.

Publisher's Acknowledgements

We would like to thank Alan Porter, Graham Tongue, Harry Sales, Ian Howe, Derek and Jean Garrod, Bob and Irene Davidge, Leah Selig, Lee and Dee Cunningham and Scott Reichenberg.

We are also especially grateful to George Bott and Nicola Nixon, Sales Managers at Royal Doulton, for their help, co-operation and assistance in the publication of this book. Finally our special thanks to Louise Irvine and Paul Tzimas whose ideas and enthusiasm inspired this book.

Nick Tzimas

CONTENTS

	Page
THE STORY OF BUNNYKINS FIGURES	1
BUNNYKINS DESIGNERS & MODELLERS	11
HOW A BUNNYKINS FIGURE IS MADE	19
BUNNYKINS FIGURE COLLECTION	21
LIST OF BUNNYKINS FIGURES	49
LIST OF PRACTICAL BUNNYKINS	66
COLLECTING BUNNYKINS FIGURES BY SCOTT REICHENBERG	67
COLOUR VARIATIONS	72
RARITY GUIDE BY NICK TZIMAS	75
BUNNYKINS BACKSTAMPS	85
IN THE MARKET-PLACE BY NICK TZIMAS	89
PLACES TO VISIT	92
CLUBS AND MAGAZINES	93
FURTHER READING	93
INDEX TO FIGURE COLLECTION	94
COLLECTORS NOTES	96

Bunnykins Shaped Tableware c.1939

THE STORY OF BUNNYKINS FIGURES

SINCE 1934 generations of children around the world have delighted in the antics of the Bunnykins family at mealtimes and their fans multiplied when the irrepressible rabbits hopped off the tableware to inspire little figures. They were soon regarded as the ideal gift for decorating nurseries and bedrooms with parents and grandparents buying new models for birthdays, Christmas and other special occasions, particularly Easter which has long been associated with rabbits. In recent years adults have had as much fun as children collecting Bunnykins figures hence the need for this new reference book.

Barbara Vernon, the young nun who created Bunnykins, would no doubt be surprised to hear how collectable her designs have become as she had young children in mind when she sketched the original scenes in between her teaching duties at an English convent school. Her father, Cuthbert Bailey, was the general manager of Royal Doulton's factory in Stoke-on-Trent and it was he who recognised the potential of her bunny drawings. They were adapted for production on a range of nurseryware by

Barbara Vernon

Cuthbert Bailey

Original drawing by Barbara Vernon.

1

Royal Doulton artist Hubert Light who was also responsible for designing the familiar border design of running rabbits.

For the first five years only tableware and other functional items, such as night lights, were introduced but in 1939 the first Bunnykins figures appeared. **Billy, Mary, Reggie, Freddie, Farmer** and **Mother Bunnykins** were only loosely based on Barbara Vernon's characters. They seem to have more in

Early Bunnykins figures.

Rabbit in Hunting Dress HN101

common with the animal figures modelled by Art Director Charles Noke in the early 1900s, in particular the rabbit in hunting dress HN101. It is likely that the six original Bunnykins figures were also Noke's work as he was fascinated with the idea of endowing animals with human characteristics and created a succession of comical anthropomorphic figures, for example his **Granny Owl, Huntsman Fox,** and **Pedlar Wolf.**

The early Bunnykins figures did not remain in production for long because of the outbreak of World War Two and so they are very difficult to find today. Although the nurseryware range continued to develop after the war, in the capable hands of artist Walter Hayward, it was not until 1972 that figures once more joined the collection. By this time the John Beswick company had joined the Royal Doulton group and with the merger came new talents and expertise. The Beswick studios are well known for their animal studies and their Beatrix Potter figures have been avidly collected since 1947. One of the modellers responsible for bringing this new dimension to Beatrix Potter's illustrations was Albert Hallam and he used his considerable experience to revive Bunnykins figures. Nine new models were introduced in 1972 followed by three more the following year. At four inches tall they were considerably smaller than the original figures, the largest of which was over seven inches.

Walter Hayward

All the subjects were taken from Walter Hayward's nurseryware illustrations thus **Mrs Bunnykins 'Clean Sweep' DB6** derives from a spring cleaning scene found on large plates and **Buntie Bunnykins 'Helping Mother' DB2** is taken from a baking scene which appears on small plates, jugs, teapots etc. Sometimes there is little artistic licence and a dressmaking scene is changed to a knitting one to make **Busy Needles DB10**.

Although the subjects all derive from Walter Hayward's Bunnykins scenes, Barbara Vernon's influence is still apparent as the Mr. Bunnykins character, with his round spectacles and pipe, retains a strong resemblance to her father Cuthbert Bailey. He appears in figure form as **Mr. Bunnykins 'Autumn Days' DB5** and **Family Photograph DB1**.

The new Bunnykins figures were given different names. Gone were Freddie, Reggie and Mary from the thirties, instead there was Dollie appropriately playing with her dolly in **Playtime DB8** and Daisie making a daisy chain in **Spring Time DB7**. Billie remained constant, although spelt differently, and he is seen sledging with his new sister Buntie in **Sleigh Ride DB4**.

The next three Bunnykins figures were modelled by Alan Maslankowski who was briefly a resident modeller at the Beswick studios. His subjects were also all inspired

Albert Hallam

by nurseryware scenes with two, **Grandpa's Story** DB14 and **Sleepytime** DB15, originating from the same design 'Bedtime Story'. Alan left to work on a freelance basis in 1974 and it was a number of years before the next Bunnykins figures appeared. When they did it was with an entirely new look.

A nationwide competition in 1981 led to the naming of a new pop star rabbit **Mr. Bunnybeat 'Strumming'** DB16 which was produced by Harry Sales, the Design Manager of the Beswick studios. He became fascinated with the idea of topical Bunnykins characters reflecting current preoccupations and he began to jot down daily observations of people and events as

Harry Sales

inspiration for new figures. Another important ingredient in Harry's designs, his whimsical sense of humour, first emerged in a doodle of a rabbit taking off for the moon with a firework on his back! This absurd little character raised a smile amongst all his colleagues and clearly demonstrated that Bunnykins could also appeal to an adult audience.

Astro Bunnykins 'Rocket Man' DB20 was launched in 1982 and with him a new era for the rabbit family. For five years Harry was totally absorbed in the Bunnykins collection creating new characters from chance remarks and encounters. A classic example of this occurred while he was driving home one evening and noticed a rather portly gentleman trudging along the roadside in a state of near exhaustion, suitably dressed in jogging clothes complete with sweatband. He became **Jogging Bunnykins** DB22. More energetic characters followed, encouraged by

Bedtime Story plate designed by Walter Hayward.

Harry's own sporting interests, and he continued to see the funny side of life particularly in **Bogey Bunnykins** DB32 who is looking into the distance for his golf ball and it is at his feet! Another amusing sporting bunny helped celebrate the 1984 Olympics by carrying a very heavy Olympic torch.

1984 was a very important year for the Bunnykins family as they celebrated their Golden Jubilee. To mark the occasion the Royal Doulton Brass Band decided to record a single entitled 'The March of the Bunnykins' and this inspired Harry to create the **Oompah Band** DB23-27. The musical rabbits made their debut on British television to launch their new record before starring in Jubilee celebrations in other parts of the world. A special backstamp to commemorate this significant anniversary was printed on the bases of the **Oompah Band** and all the other Bunnykins figures in 1984.

Original drawing by Harry Sales

By the end of the Jubilee year Bunnykins figures were widely recognised as popular collectables for adults as well as desirable gifts for children. A **Bunnykins Collectors Book** was published with details of all the designs produced to date and this little publication features in one of Harry's last models, **Collector Bunnykins** DB54 which was made exclusively for members of the Royal Doulton International Collectors Club.

In the development of the Bunnykins range Harry Sales worked very closely with David Lyttleton who modelled the figures to his exact specifications. On occasion he also collaborated with Graham Tongue, who took over responsibility for the collection between 1986 and 1995. Graham had over twenty years experience at Beswick as a designer and modeller and whilst Studio Manager he was also involved in the development of a team of younger artists. Three of them, Warren Platt, Martyn Alcock and Amanda Hughes-Lubeck, were given the opportunity to model designs for the Bunnykins collection and together they are responsible for most of the current range.

Many of Graham's ideas for Bunnykins arose out of discussions with his wife Cheryl, a retired school teacher, and his figures were designed to appeal

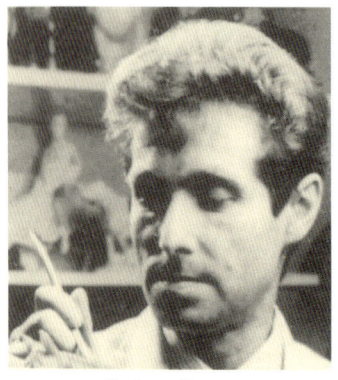

Graham Tongue

primarily to younger children. He incorporated educational or traditional values wherever possible thus youngsters were reminded to cross the road safely with the **Lollipopman DB65** or to say their prayers every night just like **Bedtime Bunnykins DB55**. This little rabbit in his pyjamas proved to be one of Graham's most successful designs, charming adults and children alike. He is a perfect illustration of the increased "humanisation" of the recent Bunnykins characters who have a wide range of expressive features and bodies more like people than rabbits.

Considerable research went into Graham's Bunnykins characters especially the authentic costumes they wear. For the **Brownie Bunnykins DB61** he consulted the Girl Guides Association for details of their uniform and badges and he invited a local policeman into the studio to pose for the **Policeman Bunnykins DB64**. Costumes and accessories have also been borrowed from a milkman and an engine driver in order to produce accurate models.

As well as developing his own ideas, Graham also adapted designs by other artists. In 1988, a few years after the retirement of Walter Hayward,

Working drawing by Graham Tongue.

The Oompah Band as featured in Colin Twinn's Nursery Rhyme book, 1988.

the Bunnykins nurseryware designer, a new artist was chosen to visualise the bunnies' exploits. Colin Twinn, an established children's illustrator, was asked to create a new Bunnykins family, giving each rabbit an individual personality for a series of books published by Frederick Warne. The new Bunnykins children William, Susan, Polly, Tom, Harry and Victoria are quite a handful for their mother and father as can be seen on the pages of the **Counting, ABC, Nursery Rhymes** and **Rhyming Games** books.

Some of Colin's illustrations were used on Bunnykins nurseryware and his delightful characters inspired several figures. Graham chose the most appropriate images of Polly, Tom and Harry from the **Counting** book and produced detailed drawings for Martyn Alcock to model. Existing figures were adapted for the rest of the family as they linked in so well with Colin's interpretation of the Bunnykins characters, thus **Tally Ho!** DB12, with a few changes, became **William Bunnykins** DB69. Colin's books continued to suggest new subjects for Bunnykins figures until 1990, for example the **Fisherman** DB84 and the **Cook** DB85, but Graham and his modellers were also kept very busy with special commissions. In 1986 **Uncle Sam Bunnykins** DB50 was made specially for the U.S.A. and **Australian Bunnykins** DB58 was produced to mark the Bicentenary of the country in 1988. Bunnykins figures have also been an important feature of the Childsworld artist demonstrations in the U.S.A. and new colourways have been devised for these events. In 1990 a special edition of the Bunnykins **Oompah Band**, renamed **Royal Doulton Collectors Band** DB86-DB90, was the star attraction of the U.K. Doulton Fair in London and this led the Managing Director, Nick Tzimas, to explore new possibilities for Bunnykins characters. He commissioned a Suffolk watercolour artist, Denise Andrews, to do some paintings of the band for some promotional leaflets and she became so interested in the subject that she read all the Bunnykins books and began to sketch the rabbits in her spare time.

Everybody was so impressed with her designs that she was asked to visualise a new series of sporting characters as well as a collection of traditional British personalities exclusively for sale by UK International Ceramics. All of her detailed designs were modelled by Royal Doulton's team of artists and this fruitful collaboration produced all time favourites, such as her set of cricketing characters and **Clown Bunnykins DB128**. Her **Jester Bunnykins DB161** and **Trick or Treat Bunnykins DB162** were very well received by collectors.

Denise Andrews

In 1994 Bunnykins celebrated their Diamond Jubilee with parties all over the world and special commemorative figures. Design Manager Graham Tongue created a charming Bunnykins figure carrying a cake entitled **60th Anniversary Bunnykins DB137**; **Cheerleader Bunnykins DB143** rooted for the anniversary in true American style, courtesy of UK International Ceramics; and an energetic **Aussie Surfer Bunnykins DB133** was commissioned exclusively for the Australian market.

1995 proved to be equally exciting with the launch of an animated film **Happy Birthday Bunnykins**, starring William Bunnykins, which was produced in Canada, and sold in video form. The Royal Doulton International Collectors Club celebrated its 15th anniversary by commissioning a new colourway of **Storytime** entitled **Partners in Collecting DB151** and several more special occasions figures were introduced, such as **Easter Greetings Bunnykins DB149**, **New Baby Bunnykins DB158** and **Mothers Day Bunnykins DB155**.

A brand new range of Bunnykins nurseryware began to appear in the shops during 1995, thanks to the talents of freelance illustrator, Frank Endersby, who later designed the first Bunnykins annual Christmas plates for the Collectors Club. Bunnykins designs also began to feature on many other types of merchandise following the establishment of Royal Doulton's new licensing department. Children's clothes, nursery bedding, silver giftware and boxed confectionery are just some of the products now to be found with Bunnykins motifs.

The late 1990s saw an increase in figure commissions from retailers around the world and national themes were particularly popular. The **Statue of Liberty** DB198 and **Pilgrim Bunnykins** DB212 were made especially for the American market whilst **Sydney Bunnykins** DB195 and the **Bunnykins Games** DB205-9 were produced for Australia. Meanwhile UK International Ceramics kept the Union Jack flying with Bunnykins representatives from Scotland DB180, Ireland DB178, Wales DB172 and England DB163 plus the impressive **Britannia Bunnykins** DB219 for the Millennium. **Tourist Bunnykins** DB190 travelled to all parts of the globe where there are members of the Collectors Club and Royal Doulton continued the holiday atmosphere with their **Bunnykins Figure of the Year** collection DB154, 166, 177 and 189.

The first Bunnykins tableau DB194 and the first Bunnykins toby jug were launched by UK International Ceramics in 1999 and both novelty items were greeted with enthusiasm by collectors. The **Fortune Teller** toby was designed by a new artist, Kim Curtis, who was introduced to Nick Tzimas in 1998. Already she has produced several successful designs for Bunnykins figures, notably **The Cowboy** DB201, **The Indian** DB202 and **The Jazz Band** DB182, 184, 185, 186 and 210.

Kim Curtis

No doubt, with all these exciting new developments, Bunnykins fans will continue to multiply, ensuring an even more buoyant collectors market in the new millennium.

Fortune Teller Bunnykins Toby Jug, D7157

BUNNYKINS DESIGNERS AND MODELLERS

OVER THE years a number of very talented artists have contributed to the success of the Bunnykins figure range, each adding distinctive qualities. In most cases the ideas are developed on paper by one artist and then modelled by another although many of the graphic designers are equally talented as modellers. The majority of artists associated with the DB range have been resident at the John Beswick Studio of Royal Doulton where all the Bunnykins figures are made. Details of the artists involved are given below in chronological order together with the dates of their careers with Royal Doulton.

Barbara Vernon   1934–1939

The original creator of Bunnykins was the daughter of Cuthbert Bailey, the Managing Director of Doulton in the 1930s. She has spent her life teaching in an English convent and the Bunnykins drawings were done in her spare time. Although she did not produce designs specifically for Bunnykins figures, her portrait of her father as a Bunnykins character with pipe and round spectacles influenced the figure of **Mr Bunnykins 'Autumn Days'** DB5.

Detail from a Barbara Vernon design which inspired Mr Bunnykins 'Autumn Days' DB5.

Hubert Light   1916–1948

It was Hubert Light's job to prepare Barbara Vernon's drawings for the lithographic production process and he occasionally added details to enhance the originals. He was responsible for designing the Bunnykins nurseryware backstamp and also the chain of running rabbits which features around the rims.

Charles Noke 1889–1941

As Art Director for Royal Doulton from 1913 until his retirement, Charles Noke was responsible for the development of many popular collectables, including figures, character jugs and animal studies. He particularly enjoyed modelling character animals and it is believed he produced the first Bunnykins figures **Mother, Farmer, Mary, Billy, Freddie** and **Reggie**.

The set of early Bunnykins figures.

Walter Hayward   1933–1984

As a tableware designer for Royal Doulton, Walter Hayward produced some of the company's best selling patterns but, after the Second World War, he was also given the responsibility of continuing the Bunnykins nurseryware range. Initially he adapted Barbara Vernon's designs but he soon developed his own style and produced more than 100 scenes, including some unique hand-painted commissions. He also illustrated some Bunnykins story books and gift cards. He never signed his work but the presence of a group of cheeky mice became his trademark. His nurseryware designs inspired the first 15 Bunnykins figures modelled by Albert Hallam and Alan Maslankowski.

Albert Hallam   1926–1975

Having joined the Beswick factory as an apprentice mould-maker at the age of 14, Albert Hallam became head mould-maker and then graduated to modelling. Initially he produced vases and bowls but by the late 1960s he was working on animal studies. He produced several figures for the Beatrix Potter range and, after the Beswick factory became part of the Royal Doulton group, his obvious talent for character animals led to the launch of a new Bunnykins figure range. He was responsible for modelling the first 12 figures in the DB range, all of which were based on nurseryware patterns by Walter Hayward.

Alan Maslankowski   1967–present

At the age of 15, Alan Maslankowski joined the Royal Doulton group as an apprentice modeller and the company arranged for him to attend classes at the Burslem School of Art. His training complete, he began producing animal models for the Beswick range as well as some Bunnykins figures: **The Artist DB13, Grandpa's Story DB14** and **Sleepytime DB15**, the last remaining in production for almost twenty years. Two more of his designs did not go into production — a female Bunnykins holding a mirror and a male Bunnykins with a picnic basket. For many years Alan worked on a freelance basis for the company but he is now a resident artist again, concentrating mainly on figures for the HN collection.

Harry Sales   1961–1986

Primarily a graphic artist, Harry Sales joined the John Beswick factory in 1960 and was appointed Design Manager in 1975. In that capacity, he was responsible for the development of all products made at the Beswick factory but he became particularly enthusiastic about Bunnykins, sketching new designs at every spare moment. He produced page after page of witty ideas and these provide a fascinating record of his fertile imagination. His particular contribution was the introduction of adult Bunnykins themes, especially sporting characters, which were very popular throughout the 1980s. Having contributed around 30 Bunnykins characters to the range, Harry left Royal Doulton in 1986 to pursue a freelance career.

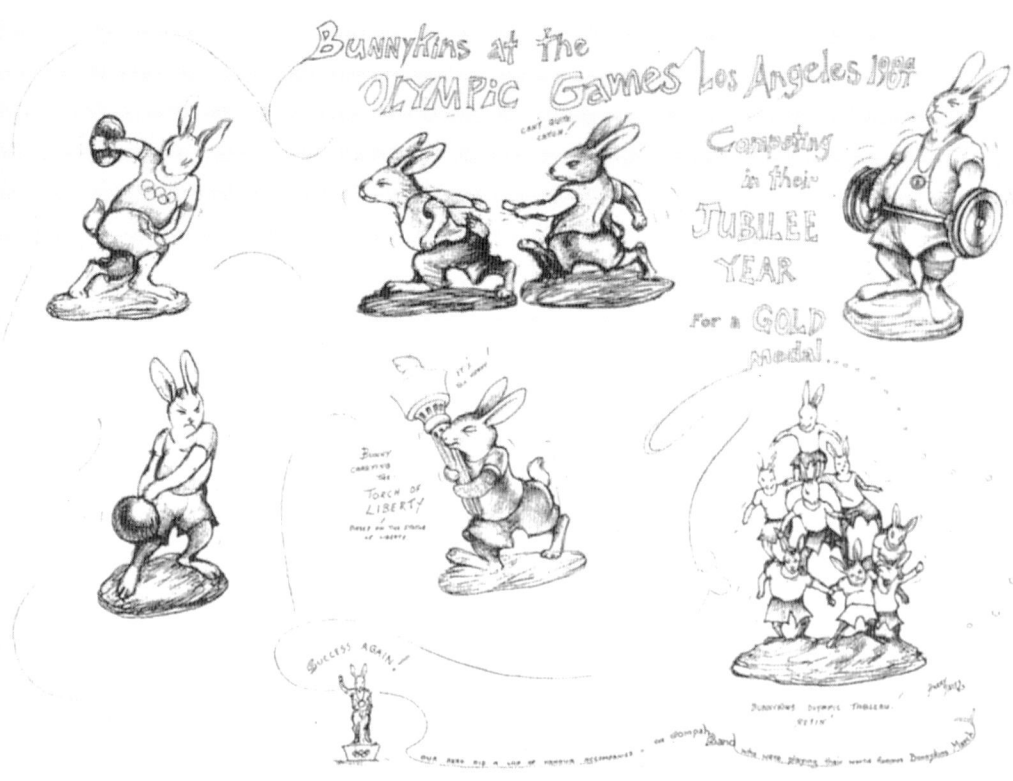

Original drawings by Harry Sales.

David Lyttleton   1973–1986

Having worked as an electrician, David Lyttleton joined the Beswick studio and studied for a technician's diploma. He produced models to Harry Sales designs and his work included Beatrix Potter and Bunnykins figures. He was responsible for modelling more than 20 Bunnykins figures before leaving the company in 1986.

Original drawing by Graham Tongue.

Graham Tongue   1966–1995

An experienced designer and modeller, Graham Tongue joined the John Beswick factory in 1966 becoming Head Modeller in 1973. He modelled several Bunnykins figures to Harry Sales designs in the early 1980s as well as a wide variety of naturalistic animal studies. He was appointed Design Manager in 1986, assuming responsibility for the Bunnykins range amongst others. To date he has produced around 30 designs which have been modelled by his team of assistants Warren Platt, Martyn Alcock and Amanda Hughes-Lubeck. Most of his characters have reflected childhood themes and preoccupations but, in addition to his own ideas, he also supervised all the special commissions by freelance artists who have explored a variety of themes. In 1995 Graham retired from his position as Design Manager but continues to model for Royal Doulton at his own studio.

Colin Twinn   Freelance

As an established illustrator of children's books, Colin Twinn was commissioned to design a series of Bunnykins books for the publishers Frederick Warne and a selection of scenes was adapted for use as nurseryware patterns between 1988 and 1992. The members of the new style Bunnykins family, which he created, were modelled as figures by Graham Tongue and his team and there was a lot of cross-fertilisation between the books and the DB range in the late 1980s.

Detail of Colin Twinn's illustration showing Lollipopman Bunnykins DB65.

Warren Platt   1985–present

It was a Youth Training Scheme that introduced Warren Platt to the Beswick Studio and he quickly demonstrated his natural abilities as a modeller. He studied at Stafford Art School and became a full-time modeller in 1986. He works primarily on the Beatrix Potter and Bunnykins ranges and to date he has modelled more than 20 figures for the DB range, including the very successful **Clown DB128** and **Sweetheart Bunnykins DB130**.

Martyn C.R. Alcock 1986–present

The youngest member of the John Beswick team, Martyn Alcock studied at the North Staffordshire Polytechnic whilst training as a modeller under Graham Tongue. He has modelled a number of figures for the Brambly Hedge mice collection and more than 20 characters for the Bunnykins DB range, including the unusual **Halloween Bunnykins DB132**.

Amanda Hughes-Lubeck 1988–1998

A graduate of the Sir Henry Doulton School of Sculpture, Amanda Hughes became a modeller at the John Beswick Studio because of her interest in animal sculpture. She tended to concentrate on wildlife studies although her collection of comical clown figures, the **Little Lovables**, proved very popular. She modelled 12 Bunnykins figures including **The Bride DB101**, which has been widely used as a wedding cake decoration. Following her marriage in 1993, she became known as Amanda Hughes-Lubeck. In 1995 she became Design Studio Head at Beswick, but left in 1998 to spend more time with her new baby. She continues to model for Royal Doulton at her own studio and some of her recent models include **Sydney Bunnykins DB195, Statue of Liberty Bunnykins DB198** and **Pilgrim Bunnykins DB212**.

Denise Andrews Freelance

Since graduating from the Suffolk School of Art, Denise Andrews has worked as a freelance artist, specialising in watercolours and pen and ink illustrations for books and magazines. She became involved in the Bunnykins world when Nick Tzimas, Managing Director of UKI Ceramics Ltd, asked her to produce some promotional drawings for the **Royal Doulton Collectors Band DB86–DB90** in 1990. She quickly assimilated the style of the Bunnykins characters and consequently was exclusively commissioned by the company to work on some new ideas for Bunnykins figures. 23 of her designs were modelled by the Beswick team, including the most successful **Trick or Treat Bunnykins DB162**.

Shane Ridge   1994–present

Since leaving school in 1978, Shane Ridge has had a varied career in the ceramic industry, with experience in mouldmaking, tableware and relief modelling. He also attended Stoke Polytechnic to further develop his skills. He joined the Royal Doulton group as a tableware modeller and transferred to the Beswick studio in 1994 where he is contributing to the Bunnykins and Beatrix Potter ranges. He was responsible for modelling many popular designs including the first tableau **Merry Christmas Bunnykins DB194**.

Frank Endersby   1994–present

This talented freelance illustrator was commissioned to create a new range of scenes for Bunnykins tableware in 1994. He produced twenty sets of drawings suitable for plates, bowls, mugs and beakers and the new nurseryware began to appear on the shop shelves in 1995. Endersby's wide experience as a children's book illustrator enabled him to capture the spirit of the early Bunnykins characters perfectly and he was also asked to design the first annual Bunnykins Christmas plate for members of the Royal Doulton Collectors Club in 1997.

Bunnykins plate designed by Frank Endersby

Kim Curtis   Freelance

Kim's studies began at Middlesex University where she took a foundation course in art and design. Her interest in book illustration then took her to the City Literary Institute and Falmouth School of Art and Design. She has a thriving business selling hand-painted gifts at craft fairs and she is also writing and illustrating her first children's book. Her talent for drawing anthropomorphic animals led to an introduction to Nick Tzimas of UK International Ceramics and he commissioned some Bunnykins designs in 1998. The result was the very successful **Bunnykins Jazz Band** which was launched in 1999. Kim has also produced designs for the **Minstrel Bunnykins DB211, England Athlete Bunnykins DB216 and Britannia Bunnykins DB219**.

HOW A BUNNYKINS FIGURE IS MADE

THE BUNNYKINS figure modellers work from detailed briefs and drawings provided by the designers and they manipulate the clay until they have successfully translated the original concept into three dimensions. The finished clay model is then taken to the mould maker who skillfully disects it in order to take plaster of Paris moulds of the various components. The average Bunnykins figure usually requires a seven part mould, three for the head and four for the body.

The master mould is used to cast prototype figures for discussion and colour trials. Ideally only four figures are taken at this stage as the plaster of Paris wears down with each impression and the master mould still needs to be used to produce the rubber case from which all the working moulds are made. Approximately 35 to 40 Bunnykins figures can be made from each plaster of Paris working mould and this is constantly monitored as excessive use would eliminate all the modeller's original detail.

Bunnykins figures are cast in earthenware using liquid clay, known as slip, which is poured into the assembled moulds through a hole in the top. As the clay dries out it forms a "skin" on the interior of the mould and when it has reached the required thickness the excess slip is poured out. The moulds are then taken apart to reveal the head or the body of a Bunnykins figure.

The clay is very fragile at this stage and it takes considerable skill to stick all the parts together without damaging them. Sometimes there are slight variations in the angle of the heads or accessories. (See variations on pages 72-74). When the clay has dried out the seams are sponged away, another delicate operation performed by the fettlers, and the figure is ready for its first firing. The kiln is fired to a temperature of 1195° and in the intense heat the figure shrinks by $1/12$th of its original size. It is then known as a 'biscuit' figure, because of its texture, and is ready for decorating.

The painters use a palette of ceramic colours, derived from metallic oxides, to achieve the rich colours of the Bunnykins costumes and fur. The paint is fired on at a temperature of 760° and then glazed before being fired again in a glost kiln, to a temperature of 1060°. It finally emerges with a shiny transparent glaze emphasizing the brilliance of the underglaze colours. Occasionally on-glaze colours are also added, for example the vivid red of Santa Bunnykins' costume or the bright blue jackets of the

Collectors Band. These colours also need to be fired on so that they sink into the glaze and remain permanent and there is a special, low temperature, enamelling kiln for this purpose.

Over the years the colours used on the Bunnykins figures have altered slightly in line with new research and collectors may notice some variations. It is worth remembering that each figure is individually decorated by skilled artists and inevitably there will be differences in interpretation but then that is the appeal of hand-painted products. (See variations on pages 72-74).

Collectors are welcome to tour the John Beswick studios of Royal Doulton and see the Bunnykins figures being made. For further details contact the Tours Organiser at John Beswick, Gold Street, Longton, Stoke-on-Trent. Telephone 01782 292292.

Painting Bunnykins figures.

THE BUNNYKINS FIGURE COLLECTION

DB1
Family
Photograph

DB2
Buntie Bunnykins
'Helping Mother'

DB3
Billie Bunnykins
'Cooling Off'

DB4
Billie and Buntie Bunnykins
'Sleigh Ride'

DB5
Mr. Bunnykins
'Autumn Days'

DB6
Mrs. Bunnykins
'Clean Sweep'

DB7
Daisie Bunnykins
'Spring Time'

DB8
Dollie Bunnykins
'Playtime'

DB9	DB10	DB11	DB12
Storytime	Busy Needles	Rise and Shine	Tally Ho!

DB13	DB14	DB15	DB16
The Artist	Grandpa's Story	Sleepytime	Mr. Bunnybeat 'Strumming'

DB17	DB18	DB19	DB20
Santa Bunnykins	Mr. Bunnykins	Mrs. Bunnykins	Astro Bunnykins
'Happy Christmas'	'At the Easter Parade'	'At the Easter Parade'	'Rocket Man'

DB21	DB22	DB28	DB28
Happy Birthday	Jogging	Olympic	Australian
Bunnykins	Bunnykins	Bunnykins	Colourway

DB23	DB24	DB25	DB26	DB27
Sousaphone Bunnykins	Trumpeter Bunnykins	Cymbals Bunnykins	Drummer Bunnykins	Drum-Major Bunnykins

DB29	DB30	DB31	DB32
Touchdown Bunnykins	Knockout Bunnykins	Downhill Bunnykins	Bogey Bunnykins

| **DB40**
Aerobic
Bunnykins | **DB41**
Freefall
Bunnykins | **DB42**
Ace
Bunnykins | **DB43**
Home Run
Bunnykins |

| **DB45**
King John | **DB46**
Queen Sophie | **DB47**
Princess Beatrice | **DB48**
Prince Frederick | **DB49**
Harry the Herald |

DB50	DB51	DB52	DB54
Uncle Sam Bunnykins	Mr. Bunnykins 'At the Easter Parade'	Mrs. Bunnykins 'At the Easter Parade'	Collector Bunnykins

DB55	DB56	DB57	DB58
Bedtime Bunnykins	Be Prepared Bunnykins	Schooldays Bunnykins	Australian Bunnykins

DB59	DB60	DB61	DB62
Storytime	Schoolmaster Bunnykins	Brownie Bunnykins	Santa Bunnykins Tree Ornament

DB63	DB64	DB65	DB66
Bedtime Bunnykins	Policeman Bunnykins	Lollipopman Bunnykins	Schoolboy Bunnykins

DB67	DB68	DB69	DB70
Family Photograph	Father, Mother & Victoria Bunnykins	William Bunnykins	Susan Bunnykins

DB71	DB72	DB73	DB74
Polly Bunnykins	Tom Bunnykins	Harry Bunnykins	Nurse Bunnykins

DB75	DB76	DB77	DB78
Fireman	Postman	Paperboy	Tally Ho!
Bunnykins	Bunnykins	Bunnykins	

DB79	DB80	DB81	DB82
Bedtime	Dollie Bunnykins	Billie & Buntie Bunnykins	Ice Cream
Bunnykins	'Playtime'	'Sleigh Ride'	Bunnykins

DB83	DB84	DB85
Susan Bunnykins as Queen of the May	Fisherman Bunnykins	Cook Bunnykins

DB86	DB87	DB88	DB89	DB90
Sousaphone Bunnykins	Trumpeter Bunnykins	Cymbals Bunnykins	Drummer Bunnykins	Drum-Major Bunnykins

DB91	DB92	DB93	DB94	DB95
King John	Queen Sophie	Princess Beatrice	Prince Frederick	Harry the Herald

DB96	DB97	DB98	DB99	DB100
Touchdown Bunnykins	Touchdown Bunnykins	Touchdown Bunnykins	Touchdown Bunnykins	Touchdown Bunnykins
Ohio State University	University of Michigan	Cincinnati Bengals	Notredame College	University of Indiana

DB101	DB102	DB103	DB104
Bride Bunnykins	Groom Bunnykins	Bedtime Bunnykins	Carol Singer Bunnykins

DB105	DB106	DB107	DB108	DB109
Sousaphone Bunnykins	Trumpeter Bunnykins	Cymbals Bunnykins	Drummer Bunnykins	Drum-Major Bunnykins

DB108　　　　　　PROTOTYPE　　　　　　DB26　　　　　　PROTOTYPE
　　　　　　　　　　　　　　　　　　50th Anniversary

DB110–114
Bunnykins Royal Family
Not issued

DB115
Harry
the Herald

33

DB116 Goalkeeper Bunnykins	**DB117** Footballer Bunnykins	**DB118** Goalkeeper Bunnykins	**DB119** Footballer Bunnykins

DB120 Goalkeeper Bunnykins	**DB121** Footballer Bunnykins	**DB122** Goalkeeper Bunnykins	**DB123** Soccer Player Bunnykins

DB124	DB125	DB126	DB127
Rock and Roll Bunnykins	Milkman Bunnykins	Magician Bunnykins	Guardsman Bunnykins

DB128	DB129	DB130	DB131
Clown Bunnykins	Clown Bunnykins	Sweetheart Bunnykins	Master Potter Bunnykins

DB132	DB133	DB134	DB135
Halloween Bunnykins	Aussie Surfer Bunnykins	John Bull Bunnykins	Mountie Bunnykins

DB136	DB137	DB142	DB143
Sergeant Mountie Bunnykins	60th Anniversary Bunnykins	Cheerleader Bunnykins	Cheerleader Bunnykins

DB144	DB145	DB146	DB147
Batsman Bunnykins	Bowler Bunnykins	Christmas Surprise Bunnykins	Rainy Day Bunnykins

DB148	DB149	DB150	DB151
Bathtime Bunnykins	Easter Greetings Bunnykins	Wicket Keeper Bunnykins	Partners in Collecting Bunnykins

DB152	DB153	DB154	DB155
Boy Skater	Girl Skater	Father	Mother's Day
Bunnykins	Bunnykins	Bunnykins	Bunnykins

DB156	DB157	DB158	DB159
Gardener	Goodnight	New Baby	Magician
Bunnykins	Bunnykins	Bunnykins	Bunnykins

DB160 Out for a Duck Bunnykins	**DB161** Jester Bunnykins	**DB162** Trick or Treat Bunnykins	**DB163** Beefeater Bunnykins

DB164 Juggler Bunnykins	**DB165** Ringmaster Bunnykins	**DB166** Sailor Bunnykins	**DB167** Mother and Baby Bunnykins

DB168	DB169	DB170	DB171
Wizard Bunnykins	Jockey Bunnykins	Fisherman Bunnykins	Joker Bunnykins

DB172	DB173	DB174	DB175
Welsh Lady Bunnykins	Bridesmaid Bunnykins	Sweetheart Bunnykins	Uncle Sam Bunnykins

DB176	DB177	DB178	DB179
Ballerina Bunnykins	Seaside Bunnykins	Irishman Bunnykins	Cavalier Bunnykins

DB180	DB181·	DB182	DB183
Scotsman Bunnykins	Doctor Bunnykins	Banjo Player Bunnykins	Fireman Bunnykins

DB184	DB185	DB186	DB187
Clarinet Player	Double Bass Player	Saxophone Player	Boy Skater
Bunnykins	Bunnykins	Bunnykins	Bunnykins

DB188	DB189	DB190	DB191
Judge	Mother	Tourist	Piper
Bunnykins	Bunnykins	Bunnykins	Bunnykins

DB192	DB193	DB194
Santa's Helper Bunnykins	Detective Bunnykins	Merry Christmas Bunnykins

DB195	DB196	DB197	DB198
Sydney Bunnykins	Angel Bunnykins	Mystic Bunnykins	Statue of Liberty Bunnykins

43

DB199	DB201	DB202	DB203
Airman Bunnykins	Cowboy Bunnykins	Indian Bunnykins	Businessman Bunnykins

DB204	DB210	DB211	DB212
Morris Dancer Bunnykins	Trumpet Player Bunnykins	Minstrel Bunnykins	Pilgrim Bunnykins

DB208	DB205	DB206	DB207	DB209
Basketball Player Bunnykins	Runner Bunnykins	Swimmer Bunnykins	Gymnast Bunnykins	Soccer Player Bunnykins

DB213	DB214	DB215	DB216
Sundial Bunnykins	Lawyer Bunnykins	Sightseer Bunnykins	England Athlete Bunnykins

DB217
Old Balloon Seller
Bunnykins

DB218
Fortune Teller
Bunnykins

DB219
Britannia
Bunnykins

The Bunnykins Jazz Band Figures.

DB33 **DB38**

DB37

DB34

DB35

DB53 **DB36**

DB39

Bunnykins Music Boxes

47

D6966
London City Gent Bunnykins Teapot

D6996
USA President Bunnykins Teapot

D7027
Aussie Explorer Bunnykins Teapot

D7126
Geisha Girl Bunnykins Teapot

48

LIST OF BUNNYKINS FIGURES

CERTIFICATES AND ENGRAVED EDITION NUMBERS

IN 1991, Royal Doulton introduced a certificate of authenticity to accompany **Rock and Roll Bunnykins** DB124 and the individual number of the limited edition was engraved on the base of the figure. Since 1997 engraved numbers have appeared on most limited edition pieces and this is indicated in the DB listings by the text 'special numbered edition' or 'numbered limited edition'.

Since 1995 all UK International Ceramics commissions have been accompanied by a certificate of authenticity and Royal Doulton has issued certificates with the **Bunnykins of the Year** series, the **Bunnykins Games** set and some RDICC exclusives. There is now a reference in the DB listings if a certificate was issued with the figure, 'Special backstamp and certificate'.

DB1 **Family Photograph**
From a design by Walter Hayward, number LF15
Modelled by Albert Hallam
Introduced: 1972   Withdrawn: 1988
See DB67 for different colourway and DB68 for revised model

DB2 **Buntie Bunnykins 'Helping Mother'**
From a design by Walter Hayward, number SF19
Modelled by Albert Hallam
Introduced: 1972   Withdrawn: 1993

DB3 **Billie Bunnykins 'Cooling Off'**
From a design by Walter Hayward, number HW23R
Modelled by Albert Hallam
Introduced: 1972   Withdrawn: 1987

DB4 **Billie and Buntie Bunnykins 'Sleigh Ride'**
From a design by Walter Hayward, number HW141
Modelled by Albert Hallam
Introduced: 1972   Withdrawn: 1997
See DB81 for different colourway

DB5 **Mr. Bunnykins 'Autumn Days'**
From a design by Walter Hayward, number LF128
Modelled by Albert Hallam
Introduced: 1972   Withdrawn: 1982

DB6 **Mrs. Bunnykins 'Clean Sweep'**
From a design by Walter Hayward, number LF14
Modelled by Albert Hallam
Introduced: 1972   Withdrawn: 1991

DB7 **Daisie Bunnykins 'Spring Time'**
From a design by Walter Hayward, number HW25
Modelled by Albert Hallam
Introduced: 1972   Withdrawn: 1983

DB8 **Dollie Bunnykins 'Playtime'**
From a design by Walter Hayward, number HW115R
Modelled by Albert Hallam
Introduced: 1972   Withdrawn: 1993
See DB80 for different colourway

DB9   Storytime
      From a design by Walter Hayward,
      number HW23
      Modelled by Albert Hallam
      Introduced: 1972   Withdrawn: 1997
      See DB59 for different colourway

DB10 Busy Needles
      From a design by Walter Hayward,
      number HW26
      Modelled by Albert Hallam
      Introduced: 1973   Withdrawn: 1988
      See DB70 for revised model

DB11 Rise and Shine
      From a design by Walter Hayward,
      number HW26R
      Modelled by Albert Hallam
      Introduced: 1973   Withdrawn: 1988

DB12 Tally Ho!
      From a design by Walter Hayward,
      number HW140R
      Modelled by Albert Hallam
      Introduced: 1973   Withdrawn: 1988
      See DB33 for music box, DB69 for revised model and DB78 for different colourway

DB13 The Artist
      From a design by Walter Hayward,
      number SF20
      Modelled by Alan Maslankowski
      Introduced: 1975   Withdrawn: 1982

DB14 Grandpa's Story
      From a design by Walter Hayward,
      number SF130
      Modelled by Alan Maslankowski
      Introduced: 1975   Withdrawn: 1983

DB15 Sleepytime
      From a design by Walter Hayward,
      number SF130
      Modelled by Alan Maslankowski
      Introduced: 1975   Withdrawn: 1993

DB16 Mr. Bunnybeat 'Strumming'
      Designed by Harry Sales
      Modelled by David Lyttleton
      Introduced: 1982   Withdrawn: 1988
      See DB38 for music box and DB124 for different colourway

DB17 Santa Bunnykins 'Happy Christmas'
      Designed by Harry Sales
      Modelled by David Lyttleton
      Introduced: 1981   Withdrawn: 1996
      See DB34 for music box and DB62 for Christmas tree ornament

DB18 Mr. Bunnykins 'At the Easter Parade'
      Designed by Harry Sales
      Modelled by Graham Tongue
      Introduced: 1982   Withdrawn: 1993
      See DB51 for different colourway

DB19 Mrs. Bunnykins 'At the Easter Parade'
      Designed by Harry Sales
      Modelled by David Lyttleton
      Introduced: 1982   Withdrawn: 1996
      See DB39 for music box and DB52 for different colourway

DB20 Astro Bunnykins 'Rocket Man'
      Designed by Harry Sales
      Modelled by David Lyttleton
      Introduced: 1983   Withdrawn: 1988
      See DB35 for music box

DB21 Happy Birthday Bunnykins
      Designed by Harry Sales
      Modelled by Graham Tongue
      Introduced: 1983   Withdrawn: 1997
      See DB36 for music box

DB22 Jogging Bunnykins
      Designed by Harry Sales
      Modelled by David Lyttleton
      Introduced: 1983   Withdrawn: 1989
      See DB37 for music box

Bunnykins Oompah Band
Designed by Harry Sales
Modelled by David Lyttleton
Introduced: 1984   Withdrawn: 1990

DB23   **Sousaphone Bunnykins**
See DB86 and DB105 for different colourways

DB24   **Trumpeter Bunnykins**
See DB87 and DB106 for different colourways

DB25   **Cymbals Bunnykins**
See DB88 and DB107 for different colourways

DB26   **Drummer Bunnykins**
The drums on figures produced in 1984 are inscribed '50th Anniversary', later ones are inscribed 'Bunnykins Oompah Band'
See DB89 and DB108 for different colourways

DB27   **Drum-Major Bunnykins**
See DB90 and DB109 for different colourways

DB28   **Olympic Bunnykins**
Designed by Harry Sales
Modelled by David Lyttleton
Introduced: 1984   Withdrawn: 1988
This figure was not available in the U.S.A. A green and gold version was produced exclusively for Australia in 1984

DB29   **Touchdown Bunnykins**
Designed by Harry Sales
Modelled by David Lyttleton
Introduced: 1985   Withdrawn: 1988
50 figures were commissioned in maroon and gold team colours by Regina China shop in 1985 to promote a match at Boston College, U.S.A. *See page 68.*
See DB96-DB100 for different colourways

DB30   **Knockout Bunnykins**
Designed by Harry Sales
Modelled by David Lyttleton
Introduced: 1985   Withdrawn: 1988

DB31   **Downhill Bunnykins**
Designed by Harry Sales
Modelled by Graham Tongue
Introduced: 1985   Withdrawn: 1988

DB32   **Bogey Bunnykins**
Designed by Harry Sales
Modelled by David Lyttleton
Introduced: 1985   Withdrawn: 1992

DB33   **Tally Ho Music Box**
From a design by Walter Hayward, number HW140R
Modelled by Albert Hallam
Introduced: 1985   Withdrawn: 1993
The music played is 'Rock A Bye Baby'
See DB12 and DB78 for figures and DB69 for revised model

DB34   **Santa Bunnykins Music Box**
Designed by Harry Sales
Modelled by David Lyttleton
Introduced: 1985   Withdrawn: 1991
The music played is 'White Christmas'
See DB17 for figure and DB62 for Christmas tree ornament

DB35   **Astro Bunnykins 'Rocket Man' Music Box**
Designed by Harry Sales
Modelled by David Lyttleton
Introduced: 1985   Withdrawn: 1989
The music played is 'Fly Me to the Moon'
See DB20 for figure

DB36   **Happy Birthday Bunnykins Music Box**
Designed by Harry Sales
Modelled by Graham Tongue
Introduced: 1985   Withdrawn: 1991
The music played is 'Happy Birthday To You'
See DB21 for figure

DB37   **Jogging Bunnykins Music Box**
Designed by Harry Sales
Modelled by David Lyttleton
Introduced: 1987   Withdrawn: 1989
The music played is 'King of the Road'
See DB22 for figure

DB38   **Mr. Bunnybeat 'Strumming' Music Box**
Designed by Harry Sales
Modelled by David Lyttleton
Introduced: 1987   Withdrawn: 1989
The music played is 'Hey Jude'
See DB16 for figure

DB39   **Mrs. Bunnykins 'At the Easter Parade' Music Box**
Designed by Harry Sales
Modelled by David Lyttleton
Introduced: 1987   Withdrawn: 1991
The music played is 'Easter Parade'
See DB19 and DB52 for figures

DB40   **Aerobic Bunnykins**
Designed by Harry Sales
Modelled by David Lyttleton
Introduced: 1985   Withdrawn: 1988

DB41   **Freefall Bunnykins**
Designed by Harry Sales
Modelled by David Lyttleton
Introduced: 1986   Withdrawn: 1989

DB42   **Ace Bunnykins**
Designed by Harry Sales
Modelled by David Lyttleton
Introduced: 1986   Withdrawn: 1989

DB43   **Home Run Bunnykins**
Designed by Harry Sales
Modelled by David Lyttleton
Introduced: 1986   Withdrawn: 1993

DB44   **Ballet Bunnykins**
Designed by Harry Sales
Modelled by David Lyttleton
This figure was not put into production

Bunnykins Royal Family
Designed by Harry Sales
Modelled by David Lyttleton
Introduced: 1986   Withdrawn: 1990

DB45   **King John**
See DB91 for different colourway

DB46   **Queen Sophie**
See DB92 for different colourway

DB47   **Princess Beatrice**
See DB93 for different colourway

DB48   **Prince Frederick**
See DB94 for different colourway

DB49   **Harry the Herald**
See DB95 and DB115 for different colourways

DB50   **Uncle Sam Bunnykins**
Designed by Harry Sales
Modelled by David Lyttleton
Introduced: 1986   Still current
The figure is only available in the U.S.A.
See DB175 for different colourway

DB51   **Mr. Bunnykins 'At the Easter Parade'**
Designed by Harry Sales
Modelled by David Lyttleton
Introduced: 1986 only
This new colourway was commissioned by Royal Doulton U.S.A. for sale at special events in 1986
See DB18 for different colourway

DB52   **Mrs. Bunnykins 'At the Easter Parade'**
Designed by Harry Sales
Modelled by David Lyttleton
Introduced: 1986 only
This new colourway was commissioned by Royal Doulton U.S.A. for sale at special events in 1986
See DB19 for different colourway and DB39 for music box

DB53   **Carol Singer Music Box**
Designed by Harry Sales
Modelled by David Lyttleton
Introduced: 1986   Withdrawn: 1990
The music played is 'Silent Night'
See DB104 for figure

DB54   **Collector Bunnykins**
Designed by Harry Sales
Modelled by David Lyttleton
Introduced: 1987 only
The figure was commissioned by the Royal Doulton International Collectors Club exclusively for its members
Special backstamp

DB55 **Bedtime Bunnykins**
Designed by Graham Tongue
Modelled by David Lyttleton
Introduced: 1987 Withdrawn: 1998
See DB63, DB79 and DB103 for different colourways

DB56 **Be Prepared Bunnykins**
Designed by Graham Tongue
Modelled by David Lyttleton
Introduced: 1987 Withdrawn: 1996

DB57 **Schooldays Bunnykins**
Designed by Graham Tongue
Modelled by David Lyttleton
Introduced: 1987 Withdrawn: 1994

DB58 **Australian Bunnykins**
Designed by Harry Sales
Modelled by Warren Platt
Introduced: 1988 only
This figure was produced to celebrate the bicentenary of Australia and was exclusive to that country
Special backstamp

DB59 **Storytime**
From a design by Walter Hayward, number HW23
Modelled by Albert Hallam
Introduced: 1987 only
This new colourway was commissioned by Royal Doulton U.S.A. for sale at special events in 1987
See DB9 for different colourway

DB60 **Schoolmaster Bunnykins**
Designed by Graham Tongue
Modelled by Warren Platt
Introduced: 1987 Withdrawn: 1996

DB61 **Brownie Bunnykins**
Designed by Graham Tongue
Modelled by Warren Platt
Introduced: 1987 Withdrawn: 1993

DB62 **Santa Bunnykins 'Happy Christmas' Christmas Tree Ornament**
Designed by Harry Sales
Modelled by David Lyttleton
Introduced: 1987 only
This ornament was commissioned by American Express in a special edition of 1,551
Special backstamp
See DB17 for figure and DB34 for music box

DB63 **Bedtime Bunnykins**
Designed by Graham Tongue
Modelled by David Lyttleton
Introduced: 1987 only
This new colourway was produced for sale at D.H. Holmes, New Orleans, Louisiana
Special backstamp
See DB55, DB79 and DB103 for different colourways

DB64 **Policeman Bunnykins**
Designed by Graham Tongue
Modelled by Martyn Alcock
Introduced: 1988 Withdrawn: 2000

DB65 **Lollipopman Bunnykins**
Designed by Graham Tongue
Modelled by Martyn Alcock
Introduced: 1988 Withdrawn: 1991

DB66 **Schoolboy Bunnykins**
Designed by Graham Tongue
Modelled by Martyn Alcock
Introduced: 1988 Withdrawn: 1991

DB67 **Family Photograph**
From a design by Walter Hayward, number LF15
Modelled by Albert Hallam
Introduced: 1988 only
This new colourway was commissioned by Royal Doulton U.S.A. for sale at special events in 1988
Special backstamp
See DB1 for different colourway and DB68 for revised model

DB68 **Father, Mother & Victoria Bunnykins**
Based on the design for
Family Photograph DB1
Modelled by Martyn Alcock
Introduced: 1988 Withdrawn: 1996
This subject was remodelled and renamed to link in with Colin Twinn's new Bunnykins family illustrations

DB69 **William Bunnykins**
Based on the design for Tally Ho! DB12
Modelled by Martyn Alcock
Introduced: 1988 Withdrawn: 1993
This subject was remodelled and renamed to link in with Colin Twinn's new Bunnykins family illustrations

DB70 **Susan Bunnykins**
Based on the design for
Busy Needles DB10
Modelled by Martyn Alcock
Introduced: 1988 Withdrawn: 1993
This subject was remodelled and renamed to link in with Colin Twinn's new Bunnykins family illustrations

DB71 **Polly Bunnykins**
Designed by Graham Tongue
Modelled by Martyn Alcock
Introduced: 1988 Withdrawn: 1993
This subject was based on Colin Twinn's illustration in the 'Counting' book

DB72 **Tom Bunnykins**
Designed by Graham Tongue
Modelled by Martyn Alcock
Introduced: 1988 Withdrawn: 1993
This subject was based on Colin Twinn's illustration in the 'Counting' book

DB73 **Harry Bunnykins**
Designed by Graham Tongue
Modelled by Martyn Alcock
Introduced: 1988 Withdrawn: 1993
This subject was based on Colin Twinn's illustration in the 'Counting' book

DB74 **Nurse Bunnykins**
Designed by Graham Tongue
Modelled by Martyn Alcock
Introduced: 1989 Still current
The red cross on the uniform was changed to green in 1994

DB75 **Fireman Bunnykins**
Designed by Graham Tongue
Modelled by Martyn Alcock
Introduced: 1989 Still current
See DB183 for different colourway

DB76 **Postman Bunnykins**
Designed by Graham Tongue
Modelled by Martyn Alcock
Introduced: 1989 Withdrawn: 1993

DB77 **Paperboy Bunnykins**
Designed by Graham Tongue
Modelled by Martyn Alcock
Introduced: 1989 Withdrawn: 1993

DB78 **Tally Ho!**
From a design by Walter Hayward, number HW140R
Modelled by Albert Hallam
Introduced: 1988 only
This new colourway was produced for sale at Macy's, U.S.A.
Special backstamp
See DB12 for different colourway, DB33 for music box and DB69 for revised model

DB79 **Bedtime Bunnykins**
Designed by Graham Tongue
Modelled by David Lyttleton
Introduced: 1988 only
This new colourway was produced for sale at Belks, U.S.A.
Special backstamp
See DB55, DB63 and DB103 for different colourways

DB80 Dollie Bunnykins 'Playtime'
From a design by Walter Hayward, number HW115R
Modelled by Albert Hallam
Introduced: 1988 only
This new colourway was produced for sale at Higbees, D.H. Holmes, Hornes, Strawbridge and Clothier, U.S.A.
Special backstamp for each shop
See DB8 for different colourway

DB81 Billie & Buntie Bunnykins 'Sleigh Ride'
From a design by Walter Hayward, number HW141
Modelled by Albert Hallam
Introduced: 1989 only
This new colourway was commissioned by Royal Doulton U.S.A. for sale at special events in 1989
Special backstamp
See DB4 for different colourway

DB82 Ice Cream Bunnykins
Designed by Graham Tongue
Modelled by Warren Platt
Introduced: 1990 Withdrawn: 1993
This subject was based on Colin Twinn's illustration in the 'Counting' book

DB83 Susan Bunnykins as Queen of the May
Designed by Graham Tongue
Modelled by Martyn Alcock
Introduced: 1990 Withdrawn: 1992
This subject was based on Colin Twinn's illustration in the 'Counting' book

DB84 Fisherman Bunnykins
Designed by Graham Tongue
Modelled by Warren Platt
Introduced: 1990 Withdrawn: 1993
This subject was based on Colin Twinn's illustration in the 'Rhyming Games' book

DB85 Cook Bunnykins
Designed by Graham Tongue
Modelled by Warren Platt
Introduced: 1990 Withdrawn: 1994
This subject was based on Colin Twinn's illustration in the 'ABC' book

Royal Doulton Collectors Band
Designed by Harry Sales
Modelled by David Lyttleton
Introduced: 1990 Now sold out
The renamed colourway of the Bunnykins Oompah Band was commissioned by U.K. Fairs Ltd. in a special edition of 250 sets for sale at the 8th Annual U.K. Doulton Fair, London

DB86 Sousaphone Bunnykins
See DB23 and DB105 for different colourways

DB87 Trumpeter Bunnykins
See DB24 and DB106 for different colourways

DB88 Cymbals Bunnykins
See DB25 and DB107 for different colourways

DB89 Drummer Bunnykins
The drum is inscribed 'Royal Doulton Collectors Band'
Special backstamp only on the drummer
See DB26 and DB108 for different colourways

DB90 Drum-Major Bunnykins
See DB27 and DB109 for different colourways

Bunnykins Royal Family
Designed by Harry Sales
Modelled by David Lyttleton
Introduced: 1990 Now sold out
This new colourway was commissioned by U.K. International Ceramics Ltd. in a special edition of 250 sets

DB91 King John
Special backstamp only on King John
See DB45 for different colourway

DB92 Queen Sophie
See DB46 for different colourway

DB93 Princess Beatrice
See DB47 for different colourway

DB94 Prince Frederick
See DB48 for different colourway

DB95 Harry the Herald
A Union Jack is emblazoned on his tabard instead of the initial 'B' on DB49
See DB49 and DB115 for different colourways

Touchdown Bunnykins
Designed by Harry Sales
Modelled by David Lyttleton
Introduced: 1990   Now sold out
Five new colourways in various U.S. University football team colours were commissioned by Gourmet Antiques in a special edition of 200 for each team
See DB29 for different colourway

DB96 Touchdown Bunnykins
Ohio State University Grey/Orange

DB97 Touchdown Bunnykins
University of Michigan Yellow/Blue

DB98 Touchdown Bunnykins
Cincinnati Bengals Orange/Black

DB99 Touchdown Bunnykins
Notre Dame College Green/Yellow

DB100 Touchdown Bunnykins
University of Indiana White/Red

DB101 Bride Bunnykins
Designed by Graham Tongue
Modelled by Amanda Hughes-Lubeck
Introduced: 1991   Still current

DB102 Groom Bunnykins
Designed by Graham Tongue
Modelled by Martyn Alcock
Introduced: 1991   Still current

DB103 Bedtime Bunnykins
Designed by Graham Tongue
Modelled by David Lyttleton
Introduced: 1991 only
This new colourway was commissioned by Royal Doulton U.S.A. for sale at special events in 1991
Special backstamp
See DB55, DB63 and DB79 for different colourways

DB104 Carol Singer Bunnykins
Designed by Harry Sales
Modelled by David Lyttleton
Introduced: 1991   Now sold out
This figure was commissioned by U.K. International Ceramics Ltd. in a special edition of 1,000
Special backstamp
See DB53 for music box

Royal Doulton Collectors Band
Designed by Harry Sales
Modelled by David Lyttleton
Introduced: 1991   Now sold out
The renamed colourway of the Bunnykins Oompah Band was commissioned by U.K. International Ceramics Ltd. in a special edition of 250 sets

DB105 Sousaphone Bunnykins
See DB23 and DB86 for different colourways

DB106 Trumpeter Bunnykins
See DB24 and DB87 for different colourways

DB107 Cymbals Bunnykins
See DB25 and DB88 for different colourways

DB108 Drummer Bunnykins
The drum is inscribed 'Royal Doulton Collectors Band' in green lettering
Special backstamp only on the drummer
See DB26 and DB89 for different colourways

DB109 Drum-Major Bunnykins
       See DB27 and DB90 for different colourways

DB110- Bunnykins Royal Family
DB114   Not issued

DB115 Harry the Herald
       Designed by Harry Sales
       Modelled by David Lyttleton
       Introduced: 1991   Now sold out
       This new colourway was commissioned by Lambeth Productions in a special edition of 300 exclusively for sale at the International Doulton Collectors weekend in Toronto, Canada
       Special backstamp

       Goalkeeper Bunnykins
       Designed by Denise Andrews
       Modelled by Warren Platt
       Introduced: 1991   Now sold out
       Four different colourways were commissioned by U.K. International Ceramics Ltd. in a special edition of 250 in each colour.

       Footballer Bunnykins
       Designed by Denise Andrews
       Modelled by Warren Platt
       Introduced: 1991   Now sold out
       Four different colourways were commissioned by U.K. International Ceramics Ltd. in a special edition of 250 in each colour.

DB116 Goalkeeper Bunnykins
       Green/Black colourway
       Special backstamp

DB117 Footballer Bunnykins
       Green/White colourway
       Special backstamp

DB118 Goalkeeper Bunnykins
       Red/Black colourway
       Exclusively for sale in England
       Special backstamp

DB119 Footballer Bunnykins
       Red colourway
       Exclusively for sale in England
       Special backstamp

DB120 Goalkeeper Bunnykins
       Yellow/Black colourway
       Exclusively for sale at the 9th Annual U.K. Doulton Fair, London
       Special backstamp

DB121 Footballer Bunnykins
       White/Blue colourway
       Exclusively for sale at the 9th Annual U.K. Doulton Fair, London
       Special backstamp

DB122 Goalkeeper Bunnykins
       Grey/Black colourway
       Special backstamp

DB123 Soccer Player Bunnykins
       This Blue/White colourway of the footballer was renamed for the U.S.A.
       Special backstamp

DB124 Rock and Roll Bunnykins
       Designed by Harry Sales
       Modelled by David Lyttleton
       Introduced: 1991   Now sold out
       This renamed colourway of Mr. Bunnybeat 'Strumming' was commissioned by Royal Doulton U.S.A. in a numbered limited edition of 1,000 to celebrate the opening of the Cleveland Hall of Fame
       Special backstamp and certificate
       See DB16 for different colourway

DB125 Milkman Bunnykins
       Designed by Graham Tongue
       Modelled by Amanda Hughes-Lubeck
       Introduced: 1992   Now sold out
       This figure was commissioned by U.K International Ceramics Ltd. in a special edition of 1,000
       Special backstamp

DB126 Magician Bunnykins
Designed by Graham Tongue
Modelled by Warren Platt
Introduced: 1992   Now sold out
This figure was commissioned by
Pascoe & Co and Charles Dombeck

DB127 Guardsman Bunnykins
Designed by Denise Andrews
Modelled by Warren Platt
Introduced: 1992   Now sold out
This figure was commissioned by
U.K. International Ceramics Ltd.
in a special edition of 1,000
Special backstamp

DB128 Clown Bunnykins
Designed by Denise Andrews
Modelled by Warren Platt
Introduced: 1992   Now sold out
This figure was commissioned by
U.K. International Ceramics Ltd.
in a special edition of 750
Special backstamp
See DB129 for different colourway

DB129 Clown Bunnykins
Designed by Denise Andrews
Modelled by Warren Platt
Introduced: 1992   Now sold out
This colourway was commissioned by
U.K. International Ceramics Ltd.
in a special edition of 250 for sale at the
10th Annual U.K. Doulton Fair, London
Special backstamp
See DB128 for different colourway

DB130 Sweetheart Bunnykins
Designed by Graham Tongue
Modelled by Warren Platt
Introduced: 1992   Withdrawn: 1997
This figure was first released by
Royal Doulton U.S.A. at the International
Collectibles Exposition at South Bend
Indiana, July 1992 and went on
general release in June 1993
See DB174 for different colourway

DB131 Master Potter Bunnykins
Designed by Graham Tongue
Modelled by Warren Platt
Introduced: 1992   Withdrawn: 1993
This figure was commissioned by the
Royal Doulton International Collectors
Club exclusively for its members
Special backstamp

DB132 Halloween Bunnykins
Designed by Graham Tongue
Modelled by Martyn Alcock
Introduced: 1993   Withdrawn: 1997
This figure was pre-released in the U.S.A.
in July 1993 and launched internationally
in July 1994

DB133 Aussie Surfer Bunnykins
Designed by Graham Tongue
Modelled by Martyn Alcock
Introduced: 1994   Withdrawn: 1999
This figure was commissioned exclusively
for Royal Doulton Australia to celebrate
the 60th Anniversary of Bunnykins
Special backstamp

DB134 John Bull Bunnykins
Designed by Denise Andrews
Modelled by Amanda Hughes-Lubeck
Introduced: 1993   Now sold out
This figure was commissioned by
U.K. International Ceramics Ltd.
in a special edition of 1,000
Special backstamp

DB135 Mountie Bunnykins
Designed by Graham Tongue
Modelled by Warren Platt
Introduced: 1993   Now sold out
This figure was commissioned by
Lambeth Productions in a
special edition of 750 for sale at
the International Doulton Weekend
in Toronto
Special backstamp
See DB136 for different colourway

DB136 Sergeant Mountie Bunnykins
Designed by Graham Tongue
Modelled by Warren Platt
Introduced: 1993   Now sold out
This model with sergeant stripes was
commissioned by Lambeth Productions
in a special edition of 250
for sale exclusively at the
International Doulton Weekend in Toronto
Special backstamp
See DB135 for different colourway

DB137 60th Anniversary Bunnykins
Designed by Graham Tongue
Modelled by Martyn Alcock
Introduced: 1994 only
This figure was produced to celebrate the
60th Anniversary of Bunnykins
and was only available in 1994

DB138-
DB141 Not issued

DB142 Cheerleader Bunnykins
Designed by Denise Andrews
Modelled by Warren Platt
Introduced: 1994   Now sold out
This figure was commissioned by
U.K. International Ceramics Ltd.
in a special edition of 1,000
Special backstamp
See DB143 for different colourway

DB143 Cheerleader Bunnykins
Designed by Denise Andrews
Modelled by Warren Platt
Introduced: 1994   Now sold out
This figure was commissioned by
U.K. International Ceramics Ltd.
in a special edition of 1,000 for the
Doulton Fairs in England to celebrate the
60th Anniversary of Bunnykins
Special backstamp
See DB142 for different colourway

DB144 Batsman Bunnykins
Designed by Denise Andrews
Modelled by Amanda Hughes-Lubeck
Introduced: 1994   Now sold out
This figure was commissioned by
U.K. International Ceramics Ltd.
in a special edition of 1,000
Special backstamp

DB145 Bowler Bunnykins
Designed by Denise Andrews
Modelled by Warren Platt
Introduced: 1994   Now sold out
This figure was commissioned by
U.K. International Ceramics Ltd.
in a special edition of 1,000
Special backstamp

DB146 Christmas Surprise Bunnykins
Designed by Graham Tongue
Modelled by Warren Platt
Introduced: 1994   Still current
This figure was first released by
Royal Doulton U.S.A. in July 1994
and went on general release in
January 1995
See DB192 for different colourway

DB147 Rainy Day Bunnykins
Designed by Graham Tongue
Modelled by Warren Platt
Introduced: 1994   Withdrawn: 1997

DB148 Bathtime Bunnykins
Designed by Graham Tongue
Modelled by Warren Platt
Introduced: 1994   Withdrawn: 1997

DB149 Easter Greetings Bunnykins
Designed by Graham Tongue
Modelled by Warren Platt
Introduced: 1995   Withdrawn: 1999
This figure was first released by Royal
Doulton U.S.A. in 1995 and went on
general release in January 1996.

DB150 **Wicket Keeper Bunnykins**
Designed by Denise Andrews
Modelled by Amanda Hughes-Lubeck
Introduced: 1995   Now sold out
This figure was commissioned by
U.K. International Ceramics Ltd.
in a special edition of 1,000
Special backstamp

DB151 **Partners in Collecting**
From a design by Walter Hayward,
number HW23
Modelled by Albert Hallam
Introduced: 1995 only
This new colourway of **Storytime** was
commissioned by the Royal Doulton
International Collectors Club for sale at
their 15th Anniversary Convention in
Williamsburg, Virginia and then through
their club magazine exclusively for
members.
Special backstamp
*See DB9 and DB59 for different
colourways*

DB152 **Boy Skater Bunnykins**
Designed by Graham Tongue
Modelled by Martyn Alcock
Introduced: 1995   Withdrawn: 1998
See DB187 for different colourway

DB153 **Girl Skater Bunnykins**
Designed by Graham Tongue
Modelled by Martyn Alcock
Introduced: 1995   Withdrawn: 1997

DB154 **Father Bunnykins**
Designed by Martyn Alcock
Modelled by Martyn Alcock
Introduced: 1996 only
This is the first of the series
'Bunnykins of the Year'
Special backstamp and certificate

DB155 **Mother's Day Bunnykins**
Designed by Graham Tongue
Modelled by Shane Ridge
Introduced: 1995   Still current

DB156 **Gardener Bunnykins**
Designed by Warren Platt
Modelled by Warren Platt
Introduced: 1996   Withdrawn: 1998

DB157 **Goodnight Bunnykins**
Designed by Graham Tongue
Modelled by Shane Ridge
Introduced: 1995   Withdrawn: 1999

DB158 **New Baby Bunnykins**
Designed by Graham Tongue
Modelled by Graham Tongue
Introduced: 1995   Withdrawn: 1999

DB159 **Magician Bunnykins**
Designed by Graham Tongue
Modelled by Warren Platt
Introduced: 1998
This figure was commissioned by John
Sinclair in a special edition of 1,500
Special backstamp
See DB126 for different colourway

DB160 **Out for a Duck Bunnykins**
Designed by Denise Andrews
Modelled by Amanda Hughes-Lubeck
Introduced: 1995   Now sold out
This figure was commissioned by
U.K. International Ceramics Ltd.
in a special edition of 1,250
Special backstamp and certificate

DB161 **Jester Bunnykins**
Designed by Denise Andrews
Modelled by Shane Ridge
Introduced: 1995   Now sold out
This figure was commissioned by
U.K. International Ceramics Ltd.
in a special edition of 1,500
Special backstamp and certificate

DB162 **Trick or Treat Bunnykins**
Designed by Denise Andrews
Modelled by Amanda Hughes-Lubeck
Introduced: 1995   Now sold out
This figure was commissioned by
U.K. International Ceramics Ltd.
in a special edition of 1,500
Special backstamp and certificate

DB163 Beefeater Bunnykins
Designed by Denise Andrews
Modelled by Amanda Hughes-Lubeck
Introduced: 1996   Now sold out
This figure was commissioned by
U.K. International Ceramics Ltd.
in a special edition of 1,500
Special backstamp and certificate

DB164 Juggler Bunnykins
Designed by Denise Andrews
Modelled by Warren Platt
Introduced: 1996   Now sold out
This figure was commissioned by
U.K. International Ceramics Ltd.
in a special edition of 1,500
Special backstamp and certificate

DB165 Ringmaster Bunnykins
Designed by Denise Andrews
Modelled by Warren Platt
Introduced: 1996   Now sold out
This figure was commissioned by
U.K. International Ceramics Ltd.
in a special edition of 1,500
Special backstamp and certificate

DB166 Sailor Bunnykins
Designed by Graham Tongue
Modelled by Shane Ridge
Introduced: 1997 only
This is the second figure in the
'Bunnykins of the Year' series
Special backstamp and certificate

DB167 Mother and Baby Bunnykins
Designed by Shane Ridge
Modelled by Shane Ridge
Introduced: 1997   Still current

DB168 Wizard Bunnykins
Designed by Denise Andrews
Modelled by Shane Ridge
Introduced: 1997   Now sold out
This figure was commissioned by
UK International Ceramics Ltd. and was
the first to be issued by this company in a
special numbered edition of 2,000
Special backstamp and certificate

DB169 Jockey Bunnykins
Designed by Denise Andrews
Modelled by Martyn Alcock
Introduced: 1997   Now sold out
This figure was commissioned by
UK International Ceramics Ltd. in a
special numbered edition of 2,000
Special backstamp and certificate

DB170 Fisherman Bunnykins
(Second Version)
Designed by Graham Tongue
Modelled by Shane Ridge
Introduced: 1997   Withdrawn: 2000

DB171 Joker Bunnykins
Designed by Denise Andrews
Modelled by Martyn Alcock
Introduced: 1997   Now sold out
This figure was commissioned by
UK International Ceramics Ltd. in a
special numbered edition of 2,500
Special backstamp and certificate

DB172 Welsh Lady Bunnykins
Designed by Denise Andrews
Modelled by Warren Platt
Introduced: 1997   Now sold out
This figure was commissioned by
UK International Ceramics Ltd. in a
special numbered edition of 2,500
Special backstamp and certificate

DB173 Bridesmaid Bunnykins
Designed by Graham Tongue
Modelled by Amanda Hughes-Lubeck
Introduced: 1997   Withdrawn: 1999

DB174 Sweetheart Bunnykins
Designed by Graham Tongue
Modelled by Warren Platt
Introduced: 1997
This figure was commissioned for sale at
UK Fairs in a special numbered edition
of 2,500
Special backstamp
See DB130 for different colourway

DB175 Uncle Sam Bunnykins
Designed by Harry Sales
Modelled by David Lyttleton
Introduced: 1997
This figure was commissioned by
Pascoe & Co. in a special numbered
edition of 1,500 to commemorate the
10th anniversary of the
New England Doulton Club
Special backstamp
See DB50 for different colourway

DB176 Ballerina Bunnykins
Designed by Graham Tongue
Modelled by Graham Tongue
Introduced: 1998   Still current

DB177 Seaside Bunnykins
Designed by Martyn Alcock
Modelled by Martyn Alcock
Introduced: 1998 only
This is the third figure in the
'Bunnykins of the Year' series
Special backstamp and certificate

DB178 Irishman Bunnykins
Designed by Denise Andrews
Modelled by Martyn Alcock
Introduced: 1998   Now sold out
This figure was commissioned by
UK International Ceramics Ltd. in a
special numbered edition of 2,500
Special backstamp and certificate

DB179 Cavalier Bunnykins
Designed by Graham Tongue
Modelled by Graham Tongue
Introduced: 1998
This figure was commissioned by
Pascoe & Co. and Seaway China in a
special numbered edition of 2,500
Special backstamp

DB180 Scotsman Bunnykins
Designed by Denise Andrews
Modelled by Graham Tongue
Introduced: 1998   Now sold out
This figure was commissioned by
UK International Ceramics Ltd. in a
special numbered edition of 2,500
Special backstamp and certificate

DB181 Doctor Bunnykins
Designed by Martyn Alcock
Modelled by Martyn Alcock
Introduced: 1998   Still current

DB182 Banjo Player Bunnykins
Designed by Kim Curtis
Modelled by Shane Ridge
Introduced: 1998   Now sold out
This figure is part of the 'Jazz Band'
collection which was commissioned by
UK International Ceramics Ltd. in a
special numbered edition of 2,500
Special backstamp and certificate

DB183 Fireman Bunnykins
Designed by Graham Tongue
Modelled by Martyn Alcock
Introduced: 1998
This figure was commissioned by
Pascoe & Co. in a special numbered
edition of 3,500
Special backstamp
See DB75 for different colourway

DB184 Clarinet Player Bunnykins
Designed by Kim Curtis
Modelled by Shane Ridge
Introduced: 1998   Now sold out
This figure is part of the 'Jazz Band'
collection which was commissioned by
UK International Ceramics Ltd. in a
special numbered edition of 2,500
Special backstamp and certificate

DB185 Double Bass Player Bunnykins
Designed by Kim Curtis
Modelled by Shane Ridge
Introduced: 1998   Now sold out
This figure is part of the 'Jazz Band'
collection which was commissioned by
UK International Ceramics Ltd. in a
special numbered edition of 2,500
Special backstamp and certificate

DB186 Saxophone Player Bunnykins
Designed by Kim Curtis
Modelled by Shane Ridge
Introduced: 1998   Now sold out
This figure is part of the 'Jazz Band'
collection which was commissioned by
UK International Ceramics Ltd. in a
special numbered edition of 2,500
Special backstamp and certificate

DB187 Boy Skater Bunnykins
Designed by Graham Tongue
Modelled by Martyn Alcock
Introduced: 1998
This figure was commissioned by
Colonial House of Collectibles in a
special numbered edition of 2,500
Special backstamp
See DB152 for different colourway

DB188 Judge Bunnykins
Designed by Caroline Dadd
Modelled by Shane Ridge
Introduced: 1999
This figure was commissioned by
the Royal Doulton International
Collectors Club as a membership gift
Special backstamp

DB189 Mother Bunnykins
Designed by Caroline Dadd
Modelled by Martyn Alcock
Introduced: 1999
This is the fourth figure in the
'Bunnykins of the Year' series
Special backstamp and certificate

DB190 Tourist Bunnykins
Designed by Caroline Dadd
Modelled by Martyn Alcock
Introduced: 1 January until 11 April 1999
This figure was commissioned by
the Royal Doulton International
Collectors Club exclusively
for its members
Special backstamp and certificate

DB191 Piper Bunnykins
Designed by Martyn Alcock
Modelled by Martyn Alcock
Introduced: 1999
This figure was commissioned by
Pascoe & Co. and Seaway China in a
special numbered edition of 3,000
Special backstamp

DB192 Santa's Helper
Designed by Graham Tongue
Modelled by Warren Platt
Introduced: 1999
This figure was commissioned by
Pascoe & Co. in a special numbered
edition of 2,500
Special backstamp
See DB146 for different colourway

DB193 Detective Bunnykins
Designed by Kim Curtis
Modelled by Warren Platt
Introduced: 1999   Now sold out
This figure was commissioned by
UK International Ceramics Ltd. in a
special numbered edition of 2,500
Special backstamp and certificate

DB194 Merry Christmas Bunnykins Tableau
Designed by Caroline Dadd
Modelled by Shane Ridge
Introduced: 1999
The first ever Bunnykins tableau
was commissioned by
UK International Ceramics Ltd. in a
limited numbered edition of 2,000
Special gold backstamp and certificate

DB195 Sydney Bunnykins
Designed by Dalglish, Bryant,
Bartholomeucz
Modelled by Amanda Hughes-Lubeck
Introduced: 1999   Now sold out
This figure was commissioned by
Dalbry Antiques in a special numbered
edition of 2,500
Special backstamp and certificate

DB196 Angel Bunnykins
Designed by Caroline Dadd
Modelled by Martyn Alcock
Introduced: 1999   Still current

DB197 Mystic Bunnykins
Designed by Martyn Alcock
Modelled by Martyn Alcock
Introduced: July to December 1999
Special backstamp

DB198 Statue of Liberty Bunnykins
Designed by Caroline Dadd
Modelled by Amanda Hughes-Lubeck
Introduced: 1999
This figure was commissioned by
Pascoe & Co. in a special numbered
edition of 3,000
Special backstamp

DB199 Airman Bunnykins
Designed by Caroline Dadd
Modelled by Shane Ridge
Introduced: 1999
This figure was produced by
Royal Doulton in a numbered limited
edition of 5,000

DB200 Sundial Bunnykins
Millennium Tableau
Designed by Caroline Dadd
Modelled by Shane Ridge
This figure was not put into production

DB201 Cowboy Bunnykins
Designed by Kim Curtis
Modelled by Martyn Alcock
Introduced: 1999   Now sold out
This figure was commissioned by
UK International Ceramics Ltd. in a
special numbered edition of 2,500
Special backstamp and certificate

DB202 Indian Bunnykins
Designed by Kim Curtis
Modelled by Martyn Alcock
Introduced: 1999   Now sold out
This figure was commissioned by
UK International Ceramics Ltd. in a
special numbered edition of 2,500
Special backstamp and certificate

DB203 Businessman Bunnykins
Designed by Caroline Dadd
Modelled by Martyn Alcock
Introduced: 1999
This figure was produced by
Royal Doulton in a numbered limited
edition of 5,000

DB204 Morris Dancer Bunnykins
Designed by Caroline Dadd
Modelled by Shane Ridge
Introduced: 2000 only
This figure was made for sale at special
events in the UK
Special backstamp

Bunnykins Games
Designed by Romanda Groom
Modelled by Shane Ridge
Introduced: 1999
This set was commissioned by Royal
Doulton Australia in a limited edition of
2,500
There is one individually numbered
certificate for the complete set of
Bunnykins Games
Special backstamp

DB205 Runner Bunnykins
DB206 Swimmer Bunnykins
DB207 Gymnast Bunnykins
DB208 Basketball Player Bunnykins
DB209 Soccer Player Bunnykins
(Second version)

DB210 Trumpet Player Bunnykins
Designed by Kim Curtis
Modelled by Shane Ridge
Introduced: 2000
This figure is part of the 'Jazz Band'
collection which was commissioned by
UK International Ceramics Ltd. in a
numbered limited edition of 2,500
Special backstamp and certificate

DB211 Minstrel Bunnykins
Designed by Caroline Dadd
Modelled by Martyn Alcock
Introduced: 1999   Now sold out
This figure was commissioned by
UK International Ceramics Ltd. and was
the first to be issued by this company in a
numbered limited edition of 2,500
Special backstamp and certificate

DB212 Pilgrim Bunnykins
Designed by Amanda Hughes-Lubeck
Modelled by Amanda Hughes-Lubeck
Introduced: 1999
This figure was commissioned by
Pascoe & Co. in a special numbered
edition of 2,500
Special backstamp

DB213 Sundial Bunnykins
Designed by Martyn Alcock
Modelled by Martyn Alcock
Introduced: 2000
This is the fifth figure in the
'Bunnykins of the Year' series,
the first on the theme of 'Time'
Special backstamp and certificate

DB214 Lawyer Bunnykins
Designed by Martyn Alcock
Modelled by Martyn Alcock
Introduced: 2000
This figure was commissioned by the
Royal Doulton International Collectors
Club as a membership gift
Special backstamp

DB215 Sightseer Bunnykins
Designed by Martyn Alcock
Modelled by Martyn Alcock
Introduced: 1 January to 23 April 2000
This figure was commissioned by the
Royal Doulton International Collectors
Club exclusively for its members
Special backstamp and certificate

DB216 England Athlete Bunnykins
Designed by Kim Curtis
Modelled by Shane Ridge
Introduced: 2000   Now sold out
This figure was commissioned by
UK International Ceramics Ltd. in a
numbered limited edition of 2,500
Special backstamp and certificate

DB217 Old Balloon Seller Bunnykins
From a design by Leslie Harradine
number HN1315
Modelled by Amanda Hughes-Lubeck
Introduced: 2000
This figure was commissioned by
Pascoe & Co. and Seaway China
in a special numbered edition of 2,000
Special backstamp

DB218 Fortune Teller Bunnykins
Designed by Warren Platt
Modelled by Warren Platt
Introduced: April to September 2000
Special backstamp

DB219 Britannia Bunnykins
Designed by Kim Curtis
Modelled by Shane Ridge
Introduced: 2000
This figure was commissioned by
UK International Ceramics Ltd. in a
numbered limited edition of 2,500
Special backstamp and certificate

LIST OF PRACTICAL BUNNYKINS

D6010 Teapot
Modelled by Charles Noke
Introduced: 1939   Withdrawn: by 1945

D6034 Egg Cup
Modelled by Charles Noke
Introduced: 1939   Withdrawn: by 1945

D6040 Sugar Sifter
Modelled by Charles Noke
Introduced: 1939   Withdrawn: by 1945

D6056 Sugar Bowl
Modelled by Charles Noke
Introduced: 1939   Withdrawn: by 1945

D6057 Cream Jug
Modelled by Charles Noke
Introduced: 1939   Withdrawn: by 1945

D6615 Bunnybank (first version)
Introduced: 1967   Withdrawn: 1977

D6615 Bunnybank (second version)
Introduced: 1979   Withdrawn: 1981
This version is ³/₄ inch taller and has a larger coin slot

D6966 London City Gent Teapot
Modelled by Martyn Alcock
Introduced: 1994
This teapot was commissioned by John Sinclair in a special edition of 2,500
This is the first in the 'Bunnykins Teapots of the World' series
Special backstamp

D6996 USA President Teapot
Modelled by Shane Ridge
Introduced: 1995
This teapot was commissioned by John Sinclair in a special edition of 2,500
This is the second in the 'Bunnykins Teapots of the World' series
Special backstamp

D7027 Aussie Explorer Teapot
Modelled by Shane Ridge
Introduced: 1996
This teapot was commissioned by John Sinclair in a special edition of 2,500
This is the third in the 'Bunnykins Teapots of the World' series
Special backstamp

D7126 Geisha Girl Teapot
Modelled by Martyn Alcock
Introduced: 1998
This teapot was commissioned by John Sinclair in a special edition of 2,500
This is the fourth in the 'Bunnykins Teapots of the World' series
Special backstamp

D7157 Fortune Teller Bunnykins Toby Jug
Designed by Kim Curtis
Modelled by Warren Platt
This toby jug was commissioned by UK International Ceramics Ltd. in a numbered limited edition of 1,500
Special backstamp and certificate

COLLECTING BUNNYKINS FIGURES
SCOTT REICHENBERG

OVER THE past few years I have been asked repeatedly how I became involved in the Bunnykins world. It all began by accident...

Rabbit items have always been around our house as my mother has collected them since she was a child. I was brought up to appreciate rabbits in all shapes and sizes, including the live ones running through the woods nearby. Anyone who has tried to catch a rabbit will know they do not sit still for very long and this has been my experience with Bunnykins too!

Bunnykins figures became regular birthday and anniversary gifts for my mother after the DB range was introduced in 1972 and I helped look out for interesting pieces for her collection. When Royal Doulton Australia brought out various Bunnykins items for the Bicentenary celebrations in 1988, I contacted a couple of Australian collectors to see if they could help me locate these exclusive pieces. In return I asked them if I might help them find anything that was not available 'down under'. It was this innocent question that led me down the bunny trail looking under every leaf.

'Collector' Bunnykins DB54, 'Australian' Bunnykins DB58, and 'Olympic Australian' Bunnykins DB28.

'Cooling off' Bunnykins DB3, 'Mountie' Bunnykins DB135, and 'Rise and Shine' Bunnykins DB11.

Go hunting for Bunnykins and you will find lots of other people following the same trail and, as with any collectable item, supply and demand are usually two different things. Take the 1930s Bunnykins figures, for example. Everyone would love to own these impressive models but unfortunately there were not enough produced at the time. The phenomenal success of the limited edition **Sergeant Mountie Bunnykins** DB136, which sold out within an hour of its launch, is proof that more and more serious collectors are joining the Bunnykins hunt.

However, there are still plenty of collecting opportunities in the current range and, since the mid 1980s, numerous special

'Touchdown Bunnykins' DB29 in maroon and gold colours commissioned by Regina China Shop in 1985 to promote a match at Boston College, U.S.A.

68

commissions have stimulated the market. There's also the challenge of hunting for all the recently retired pieces that are no longer waiting patiently to be caught. By the end of 1999, Royal Doulton had discontinued over 180 Bunnykins figures and they are quickly hopping from the secondary market into collectors' cabinets

Collectors of Bunnykins figures often also look out for examples of the amusing children's dinnerware to accessorise their displays. With around 230 different scenes on a wide variety of shapes, it is easy to get caught up in the chase for as many designs as possible. Early discontinued designs by Barbara Vernon and Walter Hayward are becoming increasingly hard to find but it is comparatively easy to pick up the retired scenes by Colin Twinn.

Another growing area of Bunnykins collecting is all the ephemera and character merchandise, by that I mean the many licensed products featuring our favourite rabbits which have been made by various manufacturers. Books, stationery, puzzles, placemats, calendars and growth charts are just some of the different items that can be found with Bunnykins designs on them and it is fun to see how methods of advertising and the public's perceptions have changed during the last sixty years.

A prototype of Uncle Sam Bunnykins with a yellow bow tie which was auctioned for charity in the U.S.A. in 1992.

One of the most rewarding aspects of my pursuit of Bunnykins has been the many friendships formed with other collectors. What began as a mere business transaction in 1988 has turned into an all consuming hobby, writing and telephoning collectors around the world, swapping information and seeking new pieces. I have never actually met many of the collectors that I have come to know, due to the miles between us, but that has not stopped me from getting to know them well. I believe any Bunnykins collector is a friend waiting to be met and you will soon have an international network of fellow enthusiasts who will be happy to discuss Bunnykins collecting experiences with you as long as you like. It is the excitement of the chase that particularly appeals to me. When I can say that I hunted all over for a particular piece and many years later found it at a nominal price tucked away in the corner of a shelf it becomes all the more valuable to me.

William Bunnykins in an unpainted white jacket sometimes appears in the market place.

Soldier Bunny Bank. First version 1967-c1977 and second version 1979-1981.

Some time ago, whilst hunting around a large antiques and collectables show, I was asked by a young woman what sort of things I collected. When I replied that I was an avid Bunnykins collector, she burst into laughter at the very thought of a grown man collecting anything of the sort. If only she knew how many serious adult collectors there are out there, hunting these little rabbits, I believe she would be amazed. Regardless of age or gender, Bunnykins appeal to the child in all of us and we appreciate something very unique in the world of collecting. Today, more than ever before, there is a wealth of published information on the subject. Absorbing all the facts in this book will help you in your hunt for these elusive little rabbits. Remember, rabbits do multiply! Happy hunting!

A colour variation of Milkman Bunnykins DB125 with silver topped milk bottles

Nurse Bunnykins DB74 with green crosses.

COLOUR VARIATIONS

*Two different colour variations of
Freefall Bunnykins DB141.*

*Two different colour variations of
Daisie Bunnykins DB7.*

*Brownie Bunnykins DB61
with painted and unpainted belt.*

*Buntie Bunnykins DB2
with different head positions.*

*Polly Bunnykins DB71 with
painted and unpainted skipping ropes.*

*Different colour variations of
'Cooling Off' Bunnykins DB3.*

*Jogging Bunnykins DB22
showing yellow or white teeshirt.*

*Lollipopman Bunnykins DB65
with different style signs.*

Collector Bunnykins DB54 with the magnifying glass in different positions.

Billie and Buntie Bunnykins DB4 with differently painted blue dress.

Bathtime Bunnykins DB148 with colour variations to the bases and position of the heads.

60th Anniversary Bunnykins DB137 with different position of heads and colour of dresses.

RARITY GUIDE
NICK TZIMAS

THIS guide has been compiled in response to frequent requests from collectors and is intended to provide an indication of relative scarcity. It must be stressed that the comparative rarity of Bunnykins figures is a matter of opinion and these assessments are based on my personal experience of the Bunnykins market, particularly the dramatic developments of the last fifteen years.

Until the Bunnykins Golden Jubilee in 1984, only 28 figures had been issued and all were easily obtainable, even the four models withdrawn in 1982/3. This all changed in 1984 with the start of special colourways for exclusive distribution, followed by regular withdrawals from the range and the first limited editions in 1990. Today, there are more than 230 figures to find, many of which are discontinued or fully subscribed limited editions.

Bunnykins figures now appear regularly at auction and Doulton dealers carry stocks of discontinued models. Saleroom results and prices at antique shows and markets have been monitored and then related to purchases and collector demand to produce these estimates. Other criteria include: introduction dates; production periods; international availability and edition sizes.

After much deliberation, figures have been assigned one of six rarity categories. As this is a controversial subject, no doubt some collectors will have different ideas based on the elusiveness of particular models in different parts of the world. The fact that a figure has been designated 'common' need not detract from its desirability. Some of the most appealing subjects fall into this category as they were best selling models with wide aesthetic appeal. In the end rarity is determined by what collectors want and the prices they are prepared to pay, not by dealers and price guides.

Note: These rarity categories are for standard figures without colour, model or backstamp variations.

RARITY CATEGORIES

A: EXTREMELY RARE
B: VERY RARE
C: RARE
D: LESS COMMON
E: COMMON
F: STILL IN PRODUCTION

BUNNYKINS FIGURES

DB42　Ace Bunnykins
Issued: 1986-1989
Rarity: D

DB40　Aerobic Bunnykins
Issued: 1985-1988
Rarity: D

DB199　Airman Bunnykins
Issued: 1999　Now sold out
Limited Edition of 5,000
Rarity: D

DB196　Angel Bunnykins
Issued: 1999　Still current
Rarity: F

DB13　Artist, The
Issued: 1975-1982
Rarity: C

DB20　Astro Bunnykins 'Rocket Man'
Issued: 1983-1988
Rarity: D

D7027　Aussie Explorer Teapot
Issued: 1996　Now sold out
Special Edition of 2,500
Rarity: D

DB133　Aussie Surfer Bunnykins
Issued: 1994-1999
Rarity: E

DB58　Australian Bunnykins
Issued: 1988 only
Rarity: B

DB176　Ballerina Bunnykins
Issued: 1998　Still current
Rarity: F

DB182　Banjo Player Bunnykins
Issued: 1998　Now sold out
Special Edition of 2,500
Rarity: D

DB208　Basketball Player Bunnykins
Issued: 1999
Limited Edition of 2,500
Rarity: F

DB148　Bathtime Bunnykins
Issued: 1994-1997
Rarity: E

DB144　Batsman Bunnykins
Issued: 1994　Now sold out
Special Edition of 1,000
Rarity: C

DB56　Be Prepared Bunnykins
Issued: 1987-1996
Rarity: E

DB55　Bedtime Bunnykins
Issued: 1987-1998
Rarity: E

DB63　Bedtime Bunnykins
Issued: 1987 only
Rarity: C

DB79　Bedtime Bunnykins
Issued: 1988 only
Rarity: A

DB103　Bedtime Bunnykins
Issued: 1991 only
Rarity: D

DB163　Beefeater Bunnykins
Issued: 1996　Now sold out
Special Edition of 1,500
Rarity: B

DB3　Billie Bunnykins 'Cooling Off'
Issued: 1972-1987
Rarity: C

DB4　Billie and Buntie Bunnykins 'Sleigh Ride'
Issued: 1972-1997
Rarity: E

DB81   Billie and Buntie Bunnykins
'Sleigh Ride'
Issued: 1989 only
Rarity: D

D6001   Billy Bunnykins
Issued: 1939
Rarity: A

DB32   Bogey Bunnykins
Issued: 1985-1992
Rarity: C

DB145   Bowler Bunnykins
Issued: 1994   Now sold out
Special Edition of 1,000
Rarity: C

DB152   Boy Skater Bunnykins
Issued: 1995-1998
Rarity: E

DB187   Boy Skater Bunnykins
Issued: 1998
Special Edition of 2,500
Rarity: D

DB101   Bride Bunnykins
Issued: 1991   Still current
Rarity: F

DB173   Bridesmaid Bunnykins
Issued: 1997-1999
Rarity: E

DB219   Britannia Bunnykins
Issued: 2000
Limited Edition of 2,500
Rarity: F

DB61   Brownie Bunnykins
Issued: 1987-1993
Rarity: D

D6615   Bunnybank *(first version)*
Issued: 1967-1977
Rarity: C

D6615   Bunnybank *(second version)*
Issued: 1979-1981
Rarity: D

DB86-90   Bunnykins Collectors Band
Issued: 1990   Now sold out
Rarity: A

DB105-DB109   Bunnykins Collectors Band
Issued: 1991   Now sold out
Rarity: A

DB23-27   Bunnykins Oompah Band
Issued: 1984-1990
Rarity: C

DB45-49   Bunnykins Royal Family
Issued: 1986-1990
Rarity: C

DB91-95   Bunnykins Royal Family
Issued: 1990   Now sold out
Special Edition of 250 sets
Rarity: A

DB2   Buntie Bunnykins
'Helping Mother'
Issued: 1972-1993
Rarity: D

DB203   Businessman Bunnykins
Issued: 1999   Now sold out
Limited Edition of 5,000
Rarity: D

DB10   Busy Needles
Issued: 1973-1988
Rarity: C

DB104   Carol Singer Bunnykins
Issued: 1991   Now sold out
Special Edition of 1,000
Rarity: B

DB179   Cavalier Bunnykins
Issued: 1998   Now sold out
Special Edition of 2,500
Rarity: D

DB142   Cheerleader Bunnykins
Issued: 1994   Now sold out
Special Edition of 1,000
Rarity: C

DB143	Cheerleader Bunnykins Issued: 1994 Now sold out Special Edition of 1,000 Rarity: C	DB181	Doctor Bunnykins Issued: 1998 Still current Rarity: F
DB146	Christmas Surprise Bunnykins Issued: 1994 Still current Rarity: F	DB8	Dollie Bunnykins 'Playtime' Issued: 1972-1993 Rarity: D
DB184	Clarinet Player Bunnykins Issued: 1998 Now sold out Special Edition of 2,500 Rarity: D	DB80	Dollie Bunnykins 'Playtime' Issued: 1988 only Rarity: C
DB128	Clown Bunnykins Issued: 1992 Now sold out Special Edition of 750 Rarity: C	DB185	Double Bass Player Bunnykins Issued: 1998 Now sold out Special Edition of 2,500 Rarity: C
DB129	Clown Bunnykins Issued: 1992 Now sold out Special Edition of 250 Rarity: B	DB31	Downhill Bunnykins Issued: 1985-1988 Rarity: C
DB54	Collector Bunnykins Issued: 1987 only Rarity: B	DB149	Easter Greetings Issued: 1995-1999 Rarity: E
DB85	Cook Bunnykins Issued: 1990-1994 Rarity: D	D6034	Egg Cup Issued: 1939-1945 Rarity: A
DB201	Cowboy Bunnykins Issued: 1999 Now sold out Special Edition of 2,500 Rarity: C	DB216	England Athlete Bunnykins Issued: 2000 Now sold out Limited Edition of 2,500 Rarity: C
D6057	Cream Jug Issued: 1939-1945 Rarity: A	DB1	Family Photograph Issued: 1972-1988 Rarity: D
DB7	Daisie Bunnykins 'Spring Time' Issued: 1972-1983 Rarity: C	DB67	Family Photograph Issued: 1988 only Rarity: C
DB193	Detective Bunnykins Issued: 1999 Now sold out Special Edition of 2,500 Rarity: C	D6003	Farmer Bunnykins Issued: 1939 Rarity: A

DB154	Father Bunnykins Issued: 1996 only Rarity: D	D6024	Freddie Bunnykins Issued: 1939 Rarity: A
DB68	Father, Mother and Victoria Bunnykins Issued: 1988-1996 Rarity: D	DB41	Freefall Bunnykins Issued: 1986-1989 Rarity: C
DB75	Fireman Bunnykins Issued: 1989 Still current Rarity: F	DB156	Gardener Bunnykins Issued: 1996-1998 Rarity: E
DB183	Fireman Bunnykins Issued: 1998 Special Edition of 3,500 Rarity: E	D7126	Geisha Girl Teapot Issued: 1998 Special Edition of 2,500 Rarity: E
DB84	Fisherman Bunnykins Issued: 1990-1993 Rarity: C	DB153	Girl Skater Bunnykins Issued: 1995-1997 Rarity: E
DB170	Fisherman Bunnykins *(Second Version)* Issued: 1997-2000 Rarity: E	DB116	Goalkeeper Bunnykins Issued: 1991 Now sold out Special Edition of 250 Rarity: B
DB117	Footballer Bunnykins Issued: 1991 Now sold out Special Edition of 250 Rarity: B	DB118	Goalkeeper Bunnykins Issued: 1991 Now sold out Special Edition of 250 Rarity: B
DB119	Footballer Bunnykins Issued: 1991 Now sold out Special Edition of 250 Rarity: B	DB120	Goalkeeper Bunnykins Issued: 1991 Now sold out Special Edition of 250 Rarity: B
DB121	Footballer Bunnykins Issued: 1991 Now sold out Special Edition of 250 Rarity: B	DB122	Goalkeeper Bunnykins Issued: 1991 Now sold out Special Edition of 250 Rarity: B
DB218	Fortune Teller Bunnykins Issued: April to September 2000 Rarity: D	DB157	Goodnight Bunnykins Issued: 1995-1999 Rarity: E
D7157	Fortune Teller Bunnykins Toby Jug Issued: 1999 Now sold out Limited Edition of 1,500	DB14	Grandpa's Story Issued: 1975-1983 Rarity: C

DB102   Groom Bunnykins
Issued: 1991   Still current
Rarity: F

DB127   Guardsman Bunnykins
Issued: 1992   Now sold out
Special Edition of 1,000
Rarity: B

DB207   Gymnast Bunnykins
Issued: 1999
Limited Edition of 2,500
Rarity: F

DB132   Halloween Bunnykins
Issued: 1993-1997
Rarity: E

DB21   Happy Birthday Bunnykins
Issued: 1983-1997
Rarity: D

DB73   Harry Bunnykins
Issued: 1988-1993
Rarity: C

DB115   Harry The Herald
Issued: 1991   Now sold out
Special Edition of 300
Rarity: B

DB43   Home Run Bunnykins
Issued: 1986-1993
Rarity: C

DB82   Ice Cream Bunnykins
Issued: 1990-1993
Rarity: D

DB202   Indian Bunnykins
Issued: 1999   Now sold out
Special Edition of 2,500
Rarity: C

DB178   Irishman Bunnykins
Issued: 1998   Now sold out
Special Edition of 2,500
Rarity: C

DB161   Jester Bunnykins
Issued: 1995   Now sold out
Special Edition of 1,500
Rarity: B

DB169   Jockey Bunnykins
Issued: 1997   Now sold out
Special Edition of 2,000
Rarity: C

DB22   Jogging Bunnykins
Issued: 1983-1989
Rarity: D

DB134   John Bull Bunnykins
Issued: 1993   Now sold out
Special Edition of 1,000
Rarity: B

DB171   Joker Bunnykins
Issued: 1997   Now sold out
Special Edition of 2,500
Rarity: C

DB188   Judge Bunnykins
Issued: 1999 only
Rarity: D

DB164   Juggler Bunnykins
Issued: 1996   Now sold out
Special Edition of 1,500
Rarity: D

DB30   Knockout Bunnykins
Issued: 1985-1988
Rarity: C

DB214   Lawyer Bunnykins
Issued: 2000 only
Rarity: F

DB65   Lollipopman Bunnykins
Issued: 1988-1991
Rarity: C

D6966   London City Gent Teapot
Issued: 1994   Now sold out
Special Edition of 2,500
Rarity: D

DB126	Magician Bunnykins Issued: 1992 Now sold out Rarity: C		DB135	Mountie Bunnykins Issued: 1993 Now sold out Special Edition of 750 Rarity: B
DB159	Magician Bunnykins Issued: 1998 only Special Edition of 1,500 Rarity: B		DB16	Mr. Bunnybeat 'Strumming' Issued: 1982-1988 Rarity: C
D6002	Mary Bunnykins Issued: 1939 Rarity: A		DB18	Mr. Bunnykins 'At The Easter Parade' Issued: 1982-1993 Rarity: C
DB131	Master Potter Bunnykins Issued: 1992-1993 Rarity: C		DB51	Mr. Bunnykins 'At The Easter Parade' Issued: 1986 only Rarity: A
DB194	Merry Christmas Bunnykins Tableau Issued: 1999 Special Edition of 2,000 Rarity: F		DB5	Mr. Bunnykins 'Autumn Days' Issued: 1972-1982 Rarity: C
DB125	Milkman Bunnykins Issued: 1992 Now sold out Special Edition of 1,000 Rarity: B		DB19	Mrs. Bunnykins 'At The Easter Parade' Issued: 1982-1996 Rarity: C
DB211	Minstrel Bunnykins Issued: 1999 Now sold out Limited Edition of 2,500 Rarity: D		DB52	Mrs. Bunnykins 'At The Easter Parade' Issued: 1986 only Rarity: A
DB204	Morris Dancer Bunnykins Issued: 2000 only Rarity: D		DB6	Mrs. Bunnykins 'Clean Sweep' Issued: 1972-1991 Rarity: C
D6004	Mother Bunnykins Issued: 1939 Rarity: A		DB33	Music Box – Tally Ho Issued: 1985-1993 Rarity: C
DB189	Mother Bunnykins Issued: 1999 only Rarity: D		DB34	Music Box – Santa Bunnykins Issued: 1985-1991 Rarity: C
DB167	Mother and Baby Bunnykins Issued: 1997 Still current Rarity: F		DB35	Music Box – Astro Bunnykins 'Rocket Man' Issued: 1985-1989 Rarity: C
DB155	Mother's Day Bunnykins Issued: 1995 Still current Rarity: F			

DB36	Music Box – Happy Birthday Bunnykins Issued: 1985-1991 Rarity: C	DB77	Paperboy Bunnykins Issued: 1989-1993 Rarity: C
DB37	Music Box – Jogging Bunnykins Issued: 1987-1989 Rarity: C	DB151	Partners in Collecting Issued: 1995 only Rarity: C
DB38	Music Box – Mr Bunnybeat 'Strumming' Issued: 1987-1989 Rarity: C	DB212	Pilgrim Bunnykins Issued: 1999 Special Edition of 2,500 Rarity: F
DB39	Music Box – Mrs Bunnykins 'At The Easter Parade' Issued: 1987-1991 Rarity: C	DB191	Piper Bunnykins Issued: 1999 Now sold out Special Edition of 3,000 Rarity: D
DB53	Music Box – Carol Singer Issued: 1986-1990 Rarity: C	DB64	Policeman Bunnykins Issued: 1988-2000 Rarity: E
DB197	Mystic Bunnykins Issued: July to December 1999 Rarity: D	DB71	Polly Bunnykins Issued: 1988-1993 Rarity: D
DB158	New Baby Bunnykins Issued: 1995-1999 Rarity: E	DB76	Postman Bunnykins Issued: 1989-1993 Rarity: D
DB74	Nurse Bunnykins Issued: 1989 Still current Rarity: (Red Cross): D Rarity: (Green Cross): E	DB147	Rainy Day Bunnykins Issued: 1994-1997 Rarity: E
		D6025	Reggie Bunnykins Issued: 1939 Rarity: A
DB217	Old Balloon Seller Bunnykins Issued: 2000 Special Edition of 2,000 Rarity: F	DB165	Ringmaster Bunnykins Issued: 1996 Now sold out Special Edition of 1,500 Rarity: C
DB28	Olympic Bunnykins - Australian Issued: 1984 only Rarity: C	DB11	Rise and Shine Issued: 1973-1988 Rarity: D
DB28	Olympic Bunnykins Issued: 1984-1988 Rarity: D	DB124	Rock and Roll Bunnykins Issued: 1991 Now sold out Limited Edition of 1,000 Rarity: B
DB160	Out for a Duck Bunnykins Issued: 1995 Now sold out Special Edition of 1,250 Rarity: C	DB205	Runner Bunnykins Issued: 1999 Limited Edition of 2,500 Rarity: F

DB166	Sailor Bunnykins Issued: 1997 only Rarity: D		DB215	Sightseer Bunnykins Issued: 2000 only Rarity: C
DB17	Santa Bunnykins 'Happy Christmas' Issued: 1981-1996 Rarity: E		DB15	Sleepytime Issued: 1975-1993 Rarity: D
DB62	Santa Bunnykins 'Christmas Ornament' Issued: 1987 only Limited Edition of 1,551 Rarity: C		DB123	Soccer Player Bunnykins Issued: 1991 Now sold out Special Edition of 250 Rarity: B
DB192	Santa's Helper Issued: 1999 Special Edition of 2,500 Rarity: F		DB209	Soccer Player Bunnykins *(Second Version)* Issued: 1999 Special Edition of 2,500 Rarity: B
DB186	Saxophone Player Bunnykins Issued: 1998 Now sold out Special Edition of 2,500 Rarity: C		DB198	Statue of Liberty Bunnykins Issued: 1999 Special Edition of 3,000 Rarity: E
DB66	Schoolboy Bunnykins Issued: 1988-1991 Rarity: C		DB9	Storytime Issued: 1972-1997 Rarity: E
DB57	Schooldays Bunnykins Issued: 1987-1994 Rarity: C		DB59	Storytime Issued: 1987 only Rarity: B
DB60	Schoolmaster Bunnykins Issued: 1987-1996 Rarity: E		D6056	Sugar Bowl Issued: 1939-1945 Rarity: A
DB180	Scotsman Bunnykins Issued: 1998 Now sold out Special Edition of 2,500 Rarity: C		D6040	Sugar Sifter Issued: 1939-1945 Rarity: A
DB177	Seaside Bunnykins Issued: 1998 only Rarity: D		DB213	Sundial Bunnykins Issued: 2000 only Rarity: E
DB136	Sergeant Mountie Bunnykins Issued: 1993 Now sold out Special Edition of 250 Rarity: B		DB70	Susan Bunnykins Issued: 1988-1993 Rarity: C
			DB83	Susan Bunnykins as Queen of the May Issued: 1990-1992 Rarity: C

DB130	Sweetheart Bunnykins Issued: 1992-1997 Rarity: E		DB162	Trick or Treat Bunnykins Issued: 1995 Now sold out Special Edition of 1,500 Rarity: A
DB174	Sweetheart Bunnykins Issued: 1997 only Special Edition of 2,500 Rarity: D		DB210	Trumpet Player Bunnykins Issued: 2000 Limited Edition of 2,500 Rarity: F
DB206	Swimmer Bunnykins Issued: 1999 Limited Edition of 2,500 Rarity: F		DB50	Uncle Sam Bunnykins Issued: 1986 Current (USA only) Rarity: E
DB195	Sydney Bunnykins Issued: 1999 Now sold out Special Edition of 2,500 Rarity: C		DB175	Uncle Sam Bunnykins Issued: 1997 Now sold out Special Edition of 1,500 Rarity: D
DB12	Tally Ho! Issued: 1973-1988 Rarity: C		D6996	USA President Teapot Issued: 1995 Now sold out Special Edition of 2,500 Rarity: D
DB78	Tally Ho! Issued: 1988 only Rarity: C		DB172	Welsh Lady Bunnykins Issued: 1997 Now sold out Special Edition of 2,500 Rarity: C
D6010	Teapot Issued: 1939-1945 Rarity: A			
DB72	Tom Bunnykins Issued: 1988-1993 Rarity: C		DB150	Wicket Keeper Bunnykins Issued: 1995 Now sold out Special Edition of 1,000 Rarity: C
DB29	Touchdown Bunnykins Issued: 1985-1988 Rarity: C Rarity: (Boston Colours 1985 only): A		DB69	William Bunnykins Issued: 1988-1993 Rarity: C
DB96-100	Touchdown Bunnykins Issued: 1990 Now sold out Special Edition of 200 sets Five different colourways Rarity: B		DB168	Wizard Bunnykins Issued: 1997 Now sold out Special Edition of 2,000 Rarity: C
DB190	Tourist Bunnykins Issued: 1999 only Rarity: D		DB137	60th Anniversary Bunnykins Issued: 1994 only Rarity: C

BUNNYKINS BACKSTAMPS

THIS selection of backstamps illustrates the variety of marks to be found on Bunnykins figures. The company name has been modified several times in the last twenty years and this has been reflected in the Bunnykins marks, which incorporate either "Doulton & Co. Limited", "Royal Doulton Tableware Limited", "Royal Doulton UK" or "Royal Doulton". The backstamp is not usually altered once a figure has gone into production and so the old style company names can still be found on figures made today. Bunnykins backstamps are therefore not very helpful for dating except to indicate that a model could not have been made before a certain date, for example figures marked "Royal Doulton UK" could not have been introduced before 1985. The Copyright date is usually the year before the figure is introduced although some Bunnykins models are copyrighted and launched in the same year. In recent years the proliferation of exclusive models for special events has necessitated extra information on the backstamps and this is particularly important when the edition is limited. As space is at a premium on the Bunnykins backstamps it is rare to find the designer or modeller acknowledged, as with other Royal Doulton products, and so this book is particularly helpful for attributing designs.

Backstamp with the copyright notice for "Royal Doulton Tableware Limited" used on new models introduced between 1972 and 1984.

This inscription 'Golden Jubilee Celebration 1984' was added to all Bunnykins figures produced that year.

Unusual backstamp featuring a copyright notice for "Doulton & Co. Limited" and two registration numbers to protect the design. Recorded on DB11 of 1974.

Backstamp including the new style company name "Royal Doulton UK" in the copyright notice. Used on models introduced in 1985 and 1986.

85

Backstamp omitting the 'UK' part of the company name in the copyright notice. Used on all new models introduced since 1987.

There are several varieties of backstamp wording for figures sold at the special events tours in the USA.

Special backstamp featuring the Collectors Club mark and the modeller's name. Devised especially for *Collector Bunnykins* DB54.

There are several varieties of backstamp wording for figures sold by U.S.A. retailers.

Backstamp incorporating the symbol for the Australian Bicentenary Celebrations of 1988. Found only on *Australian Bunnykins* DB58.

Backstamp found only on the *Drummer Bunnykins* DB89 from the Collectors Band. It is the first Bunnykins 'Special' edition where the numbers have been limited.

This logo indicates that the figure was made exclusively for the US retailer D.H. Holmes.

Backstamp found on special editions commissioned by UK International Ceramics Ltd.

86

Backstamp found on special editions commissioned by UK International Ceramics Ltd for Doulton Fairs in London.

Special backstamp used for the Canadian *Harry the Herald Bunnykins* DB115.

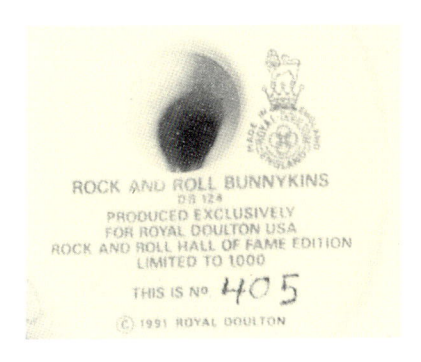

The first numbered backstamp used on *Rock and Roll Bunnykins* DB124.

Backstamp found on the *Aussie Surfer Bunnykins* DB133 produced exclusively for Royal Doulton Australia.

Backstamp found on *Sergeant Mountie Bunnykins* DB136 commemorating 120 years of the Canadian Mounted Police.

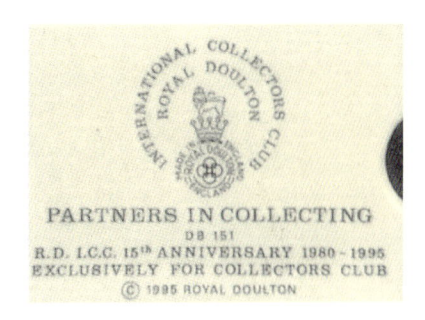

Backstamp for *Partners in Collecting Bunnykins* DB151.

87

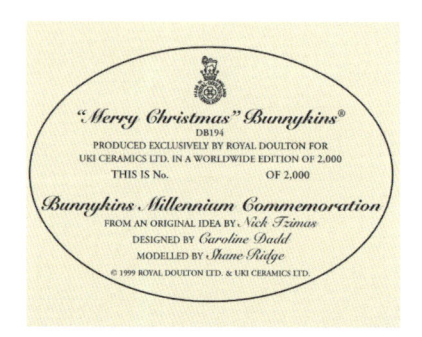

Special gold backstamp for the *Merry Christmas Bunnykins Tableau* DB194.

Special backstamp used for the limited edition *Businessman Bunnykins* DB203.

Backstamp used for the *Morris Dancer Bunnykins* DB204, the first figure to be used exclusively for Royal Doulton events.

Backstamp for *Sundial Bunnykins* DB213, the Bunnykins of the Year 2000.

Backstamp found on numbered limited edition Bunnykins commissioned from Royal Doulton by UK International Ceramics Ltd.

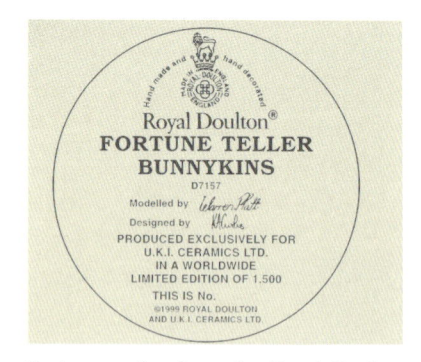

Backstamp found on the Royal Doulton Bunnykins Toby Jugs commissioned by UK International Ceramics Ltd.

> Royal Doulton introduced year ciphers for their collectables range in 1998 and these have appeared on Bunnykins backstamps. The cipher for 1998 was an umbrella; 1999 was a top hat and 2000 was a fob watch.

IN THE MARKET-PLACE
NICK TZIMAS

WHERE TO BUY

Current Bunnykins figures are available from specialist china and gift shops in many parts of the world. Details of stockists and other product information can be obtained from one of Royal Doulton's Distribution and Sales Companies.

Royal Doulton
Sales Division
Minton House
London Road
Stoke-on Trent ST4 7QD
England

Royal Doulton Canada Ltd
850 Progress Avenue
Scarborough
Ontario M1H 3C4
Canada

Royal Doulton USA INC.
700 Cottontail Lane
Somerset
NJ 08873
USA

Royal Doulton Australia Pty Ltd
17-23 Merriwa Street
Gordon
NSW 2072
Australia

Details of **UK International Ceramics** Limited Edition Bunnykins can be obtained by writing to:

Zoë Gilligan, Product Manager, UKI Ceramics Ltd
10 Wilford Bridge Spur, Melton, Woodbridge, Suffolk, England IP12 1RJ.
Tel: 01394 386662. Fax: 01394 386742.

Details of **Pascoe & Co.** Special Edition Bunnykins can be obtained from:
Pascoe & Co., 932 Ponce de Leon, Coral Cables, Fl. 33134, USA.
Tel: (305)445 3229. Fax: (305)445 3305.

Discontinued Bunnykins figures can be purchased from antique shops, markets and fairs as well as some auction houses. There are specialist dealers who attend the venues and events overleaf but it is also worth browsing at general shops and stalls as well as country auctions.

UK

Christies South Kensington
85 Old Brompton Road
London SW7 3LD
Tel: 0207 581 7611

New Caledonian Market
Bermondsey Square
London SE1
Friday mornings only
(Nearest tube London Bridge)

Portobello Road Market
London W11
Saturdays only
(Nearest tube Notting Hill Gate)

Alfie's Antique Market
13-25 Church Street
London NW8
Tuesday-Saturday
(Nearest tube Edgware Road)

Camden Passage Market
off Upper Street
London N1
Wednesdays and Saturdays only
(Nearest tube Angel)

Louis Taylor Auction House
10 Town Road
Hanley
Stoke-on-Trent ST1 2QG
Tel: 01782 214111

Phillips
101 New Bond Street
London W1Y 0AS
Tel: 0207 629 6602

Potteries Specialist Auctions
271 Waterloo Road
Cobridge
Stoke-on-Trent ST3 3HR
Tel: 01782 286622

Peter Wilson Auction House
Victoria Gallery
Market Street
Nantwich
Cheshire CW5 5DG
Tel: 01270 623878

The UK Doulton & Beswick Fair for Collectors
Dorking Halls
Reigate Road
Dorking
Surrey   *(October)*
Enquiries: 01394 386663

Stafford International Doulton Fair
Stafford County Showground
Stafford   *(May or June)*
Enquiries: 0114 2750333

Doulton & Beswick Collectors Fair
The National Motorcycle Museum
Birmingham   *(March and August)*
Enquiries: 0208 3033316

Alexandra Palace Collectors Fairs
Wood Green
London N22 4AM

Yesterdays Doulton Collectors Events
Various areas in England
(November)
Enquiries: 0208 500 3505

USA

Florida Doulton Convention
Fort Lauderdale
Florida   *(January)*
Enquiries: (305) 445 3229

Doulton Collectors Weekends
Enquiries: (305) 445 3229

Doulton Show
John S. Knight Convention Centre
Mill Street
Akron   *(August)*
Enquiries: (800) 344 9299

Information about general shows and markets can be found in the local press and specialist publications such as *The Antique Trader Weekly*.

The following china retailers also stock Bunnykins figures:

Curio Cabinet
679 High Street
Worthington
Ohio 43085
Tel: (614) 885 1986

Charles Dombeck
9720 Ridge Walk Court
Davie
FL 33328
Tel: (954) 452 9174

Colonial House Antiques
182 Front Street
Berea
Ohio 44017
Tel: (440) 826 4169

Seaway China Company
135 Broadway
Marine City
MI 48069-1607
Tel: (810) 765 9000

Pascoe & Co
932 Ponce de Leon Blvd
Coral Gables, FL 33134
Tel: (305) 445 3229

CANADA

Canadian Art and Collectibles Show
Kitchener Memorial Auditorium
400 East Avenue, Kitchener
Ontario   *(May)*
Enquiries: (519) 369 6950

Canadian Collectors Weekends
Enquiries: (604) 930 9599

Information about general fairs and markets can be found in the local press and specialist publications such as *Antique Showcase*.

The following china retailers also stock Bunnykins figures:

Laura Campbell
Site of The Green
RR # 1 Dundas
Ontario L9H 5E1
Tel: (905) 627 1304

George Bagnall
89 Trans Canada Highway
Charlottetown
P.E.I. C1E 1E8
Tel: (902) 368 1212

William Cross Antiques & Collectibles
8657 Terrace Drive, Delta, BC
Tel: (604) 930 9599

AUSTRALIA, NEW ZEALAND AND SOUTH AFRICA

Various general antique fairs and markets are held throughout these countries and information can be found in the local press and specialist publications such as *Carter's Australian Antique Trader*.

The following china retailers also stock Bunnykins figures:

Thorndon Antiques
PO Box 12-076
Wellington
New Zealand
Tel: (04) 473 0173

Wendy Tuck
28 Fairway Street
Bald Hills
Queensland 4036
Australia
Tel/Fax: (07) 3261 1581

Ken Wicks
Bayside Antiques
123 Herald Street
Cheltenham 3192
Australia
Tel: (03) 9555 7011
Fax: (03) 9553 4373

The Toby Jug
St. John's Road
Sea Point, Cape Town 8001
South Africa
Tel/Fax: (021) 434 8210

PLACES TO VISIT

Take a tour of the Beswick factory to see Bunnykins figures being made:

John Beswick
Gold Street, Longton, Stoke-on-Trent ST3 2JP
For opening times and tour information telephone (01782) 292292

CLUBS, MAGAZINES AND NEWSLETTERS

The Royal Doulton International Collectors Club publishes **Gallery**, a quarterly magazine which gives information about new Bunnykins introductions and articles on historical pieces. The Club also commissions collectable products exclusively for members and occasionally Bunnykins figures are offered. For details of membership, contact the nearest Royal Doulton Distribution and Sales company — addresses on page 89.

Collecting Doulton is a subscription magazine about Doulton and Beswick wares past and present and it regularly includes features about Bunnykins. For further information write to: P.O. Box 310, Richmond, Surrey TW9 1FS.

Collectors are welcome to subscribe to the following Bunnykins Newsletters written by dedicated collectors:

'Rabbiting On'
Mrs Leah Selig
2 Harper Street
Merrylands N.S.W. 2160
Tel/Fax: (02) 9637 2410

Cottontales Newsletter
Claire Green
6 Beckett Way
Lewes
East Sussex BN7 2EB

Bunnykins News
Chris Wren
7 Spout Copse
Sheffield S6 6FB
Tel: 0114 2340199

FURTHER READING

Royal Doulton Bunnykins Collectors Book   ISBN 0 903 685 32 9
By Louise Irvine. Richard Dennis Publications, 1993.
This revised edition of the 1984 book includes all the Bunnykins nurseryware patterns and shapes. There are also interesting chapters on character merchandise and bunny-shaped ware.

The Charlton Standard Catalogue   ISBN 0 88968 210 0
of Royal Doulton Bunnykins
By Jean Dale and Louise Irvine, 1999.

INDEX

	Page
Ace Bunnykins	25
Aerobic Bunnykins	25
Airman Bunnykins	44
Angel Bunnykins	43
Artist Bunnykins	22
Astro Bunnykins 'Rocket Man'	23
Aussie Explorer Teapot	48
Aussie Surfer Bunnykins	36
Australian Bunnykins	26
Australian Colourway	23
Ballerina Bunnykins	41
Banjo Player Bunnykins	41, 46
Basketball Player Bunnykins	45
Bathtime Bunnykins	37
Batsman Bunnykins	37
Be Prepared Bunnykins	26
Bedtime Bunnykins	26, 27, 29, 32
Beefeater Bunnykins	39
Billie Bunnykins 'Cooling Off'	21
Billie and Buntie Bunnykins 'Sleigh Ride'	21, 29
Billy Bunnykins	12
Bogey Bunnykins	24
Bowler Bunnykins	37
Boy Skater Bunnykins	38, 42
Bride Bunnykins	32
Bridesmaid Bunnykins	40
Britannia Bunnykins	46
Brownie Bunnykins	27
Bunnybank	70
Bunnykins Collectors Band	30, 32, 33
Bunnykins Games	45
Bunnykins Oompah Band	24, 33
Bunnykins Royal Family	25, 31, 33
Buntie Bunnykins 'Helping Mother'	21
Businessman Bunnykins	44
Busy Needles Bunnykins	22
Carol Singer Bunnykins	32
Cavalier Bunnykins	41
Cheerleader Bunnykins	36
Christmas Surprise Bunnykins	37
Clarinet Player Bunnykins	42, 46
Clown Bunnykins	35
Collector Bunnykins	26
Cook Bunnykins	30

	Page
Cowboy Bunnykins	44
Cream Jug	vi
Cymbals Bunnykins	24, 30, 32
Daisie Bunnykins 'Spring Time'	21
Detective Bunnykins	43
Doctor Bunnykins	41
Dollie Bunnykins 'Playtime'	21, 29
Double Bass Player Bunnykins	42, 46
Downhill Bunnykins	24
Drum-Major Bunnykins	24, 30, 32
Drummer Bunnykins	24, 30, 32, 33
Easter Greetings Bunnykins	37
Egg Cup	vi
England Athlete Bunnykins	45
Family Photograph Bunnykins	21, 28
Farmer Bunnykins	12
Father Bunnykins	38
Father, Mother & Victoria Bunnykins	28
Fireman Bunnykins	29, 41
Fisherman Bunnykins	30, 40
Footballer Bunnykins	34
Fortune Teller Bunnykins	46
Fortune Teller Bunnykins Toby Jug	10
Freddie Bunnykins	12
Freefall Bunnykins	25
Gardener Bunnykins	38
Geisha Girl Teapot	48
Girl Skater Bunnykins	38
Goalkeeper Bunnykins	34
Goodnight Bunnykins	38
Grandpa's Story Bunnykins	22
Groom Bunnykins	32
Guardsman Bunnykins	35
Gymnast Bunnykins	45
Halloween Bunnykins	36
Happy Birthday Bunnykins	23
Harry Bunnykins	28
Harry the Herald Bunnykins	25, 31, 33
Home Run Bunnykins	25
Ice Cream Bunnykins	29
Indian Bunnykins	44
Irishman Bunnykins	41

	Page
Jazz Band Bunnykins	46
Jester Bunnykins	39
Jockey Bunnykins	40
Jogging Bunnykins	23
John Bull Bunnykins	36
Joker Bunnykins	40
Judge Bunnykins	42
Juggler Bunnykins	39
King John Bunnykins	25, 31, 33
Knockout Bunnykins	24
Lawyer Bunnykins	45
Lollipopman Bunnykins	27
London City Gent Teapot	48
Magician Bunnykins	35, 38
Mary Bunnykins	12
Master Potter Bunnykins	35
Merry Christmas Bunnykins	43
Milkman Bunnykins	35
Minstrel Bunnykins	44
Morris Dancer Bunnykins	44
Mother Bunnykins	12, 42
Mother and Baby Bunnykins	39
Mother's Day Bunnykins	38
Mountie Bunnykins	36
Mr. Bunnybeat 'Strumming' Bunnykins	22
Mr. Bunnykins 'At the Easter Parade'	23, 26
Mr. Bunnykins 'Autumn Days'	21
Mrs. Bunnykins 'At the Easter Parade'	23, 26
Mrs. Bunnykins 'Clean Sweep'	21
Music Boxes	47
Mystic Bunnykins	43
New Baby Bunnykins	38
Nurse Bunnykins	28
Old Balloon Seller Bunnykins	46
Olympic Bunnykins	23
Out for a Duck Bunnykins	39
Paperboy Bunnykins	29
Partners in Collecting Bunnykins	37
Pilgrim Bunnykins	44
Piper Bunnykins	42
Policeman Bunnykins	27
Polly Bunnykins	28
Postman Bunnykins	29
Prince Frederick Bunnykins	25, 31
Princess Beatrice Bunnykins	25, 31

	Page
Queen Sophie Bunnykins	25, 31, 33
Rainy Day Bunnykins	37
Ringmaster Bunnykins	39
Rise and Shine Bunnykins	22
Rock and Roll Bunnykins	35
Runner Bunnykins	45
Sailor Bunnykins	39
Santa Bunnykins 'Happy Christmas'	23, 27
Santa's Helper Bunnykins	43
Saxophone Player Bunnykins	42, 46
Schoolboy Bunnykins	27
Schooldays Bunnykins	26
Schoolmaster Bunnykins	27
Scotsman Bunnykins	41
Seaside Bunnykins	41
Sergeant Mountie Bunnykins	36
Sightseer Bunnykins	45
Sleepytime Bunnykins	22
Soccer Player Bunnykins	34, 45
Sousaphone Bunnykins	24, 30, 32
Statue of Liberty Bunnykins	43
Storytime Bunnykins	22, 27
Sugar Bowl	vi
Sugar Sifter	vi
Sundial Bunnykins	45
Susan Bunnykins	28
Susan Bunnykins as 'Queen of the May'	30
Sweetheart Bunnykins	35, 40
Swimmer Bunnykins	45
Sydney Bunnykins	43
Tally Ho! Bunnykins	22, 29
Teapot	vi
Tom Bunnykins	28
Touchdown Bunnykins	24, 31
Tourist Bunnykins	42
Trick or Treat Bunnykins	39
Trumpeter Bunnykins	24, 30, 32
Trumpet Player Bunnykins	44, 46
Uncle Sam Bunnykins	26, 40
USA President Teapot	48
Welsh Lady Bunnykins	40
Wicket Keeper Bunnykins	37
William Bunnykins	28
Wizard Bunnykins	40
60th Anniversary Bunnykins	36

COLLECTORS NOTES

COLLECTORS NOTES

COLLECTORS NOTES

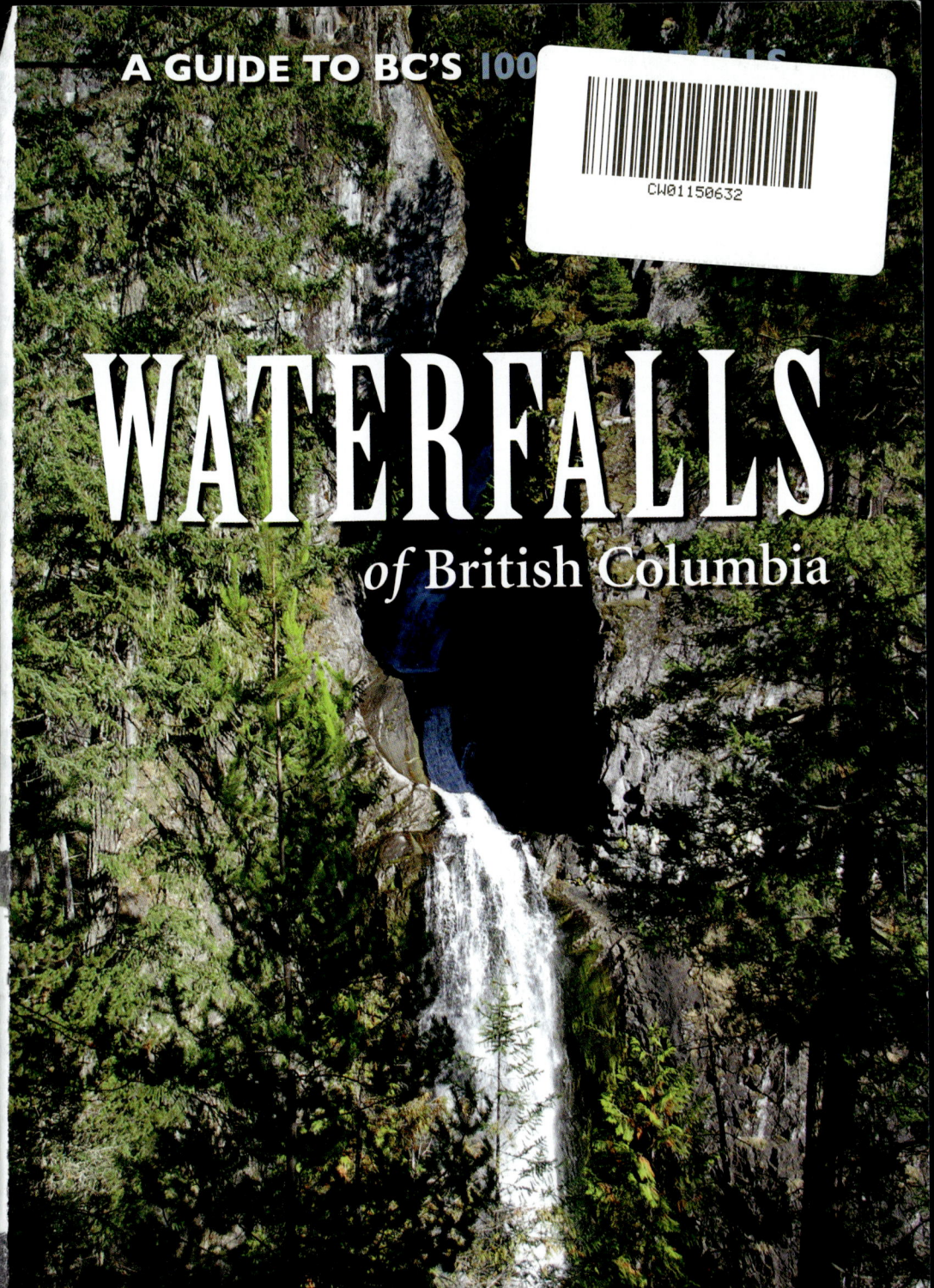

A GUIDE TO BC'S 100

WATERFALLS
of British Columbia

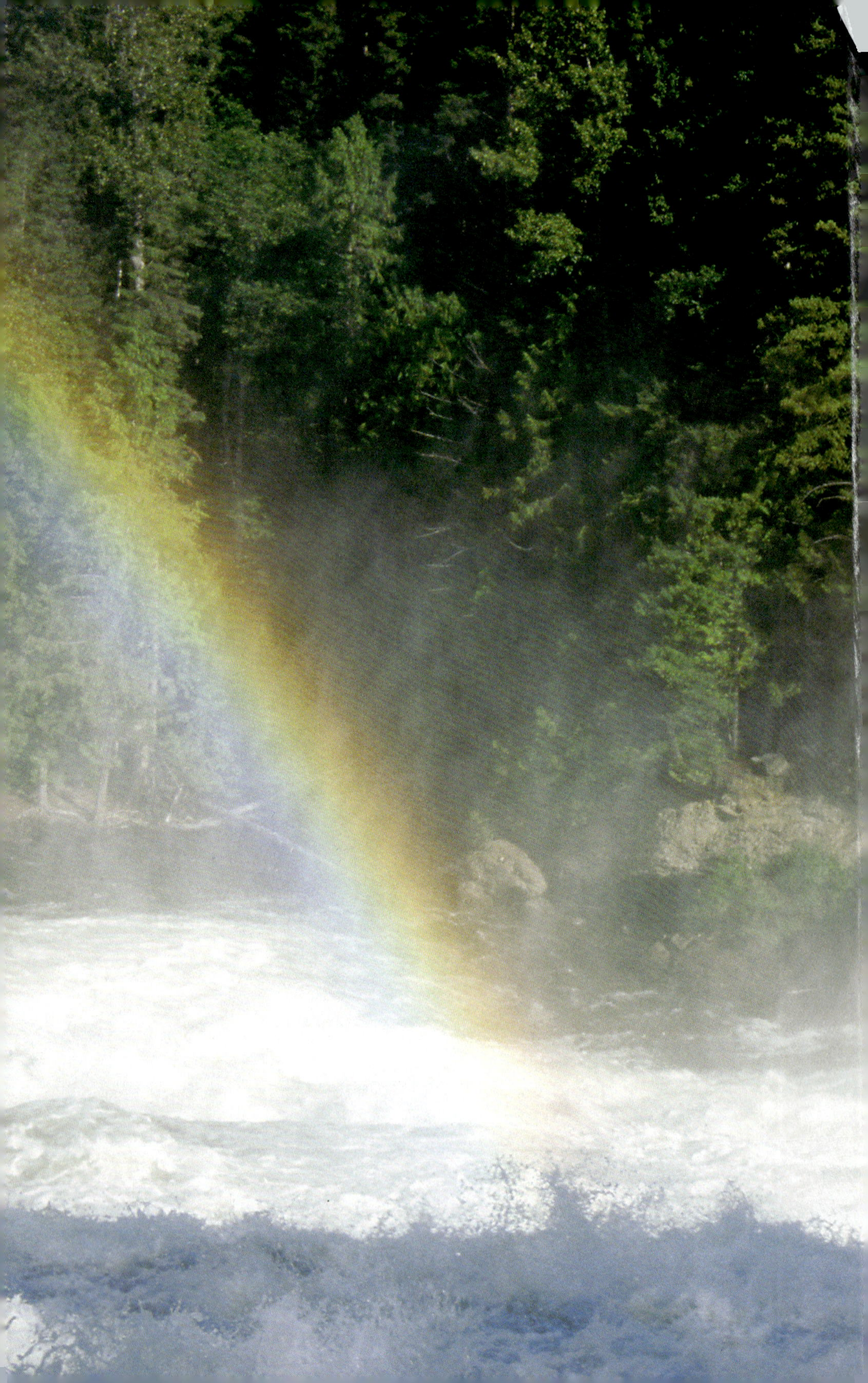

A GUIDE TO BC'S 100 BEST FALLS

WATERFALLS
of British Columbia

Tony Greenfield

HARBOUR PUBLISHING

This book is dedicated to four great ladies in my life:
Wife, Kathryn Angermeyer
Mother, Doris Greenfield
Daughter, Marnie Greenfield
And Diva, the Weimaraner

Copyright © 2009 Tony Greenfield

1 2 3 4 5 — 13 12 11 10 09

All rights reserved. No part of this publication may be reproduced, stored in a retrieval system or transmitted, in any form or by any means, without prior permission of the publisher or, in the case of photocopying or other reprographic copying, a licence from Access Copyright, www.accesscopyright.ca, 1-800-893-5777, info@accesscopyright.ca.

Harbour Publishing Co. Ltd. P.O. Box 219, Madeira Park, BC, V0N 2H0
www.harbourpublishing.com

All photographs by the author unless otherwise stated
Additional photo captions: Cover, Helmcken Falls; Page 1, High Creek Falls;
　pages 2–3, Dawson Falls; back cover, author at Morkill Falls by Rand Rudland
Edited by Margaret Tessman
Maps created by John Lightfoot, Lightfoot Art & Design Inc.
Text design and layout by Martin Nichols, Lionheart Graphics
Cover design by Anna Comfort
Index by Erin Schopfer
Printed in Canada
Printed on paper containing 10% post consumer waste
　using soy-based inks.

Harbour Publishing acknowledges financial support from the Government of Canada through the Book Publishing Industry Development Program and the Canada Council for the Arts, and from the Province of British Columbia through the BC Arts Council and the Book Publishing Tax Credit.

Library and Archives Canada Cataloguing in Publication

Greenfield, Tony, 1947–

　Waterfalls of British Columbia : a guide to BC's 100 best falls / Tony Greenfield.

　Includes index.
　ISBN 978-1-55017-462-5

　1. Waterfalls—British Columbia—Guidebooks. 2. British Columbia—Guidebooks. I. Title.
　GB1430.B75G74 2009　　917.1104'5　　C2009-900844-0

Caution: *Every effort has been made to ensure the reader's awareness of accessibility, hazards and level of expertise involved in reaching the destinations in this book, as well as to ensure the accuracy of maps and directions, but your own safety is ultimately up to you. Due to the possibility of changes to trails and roads, differences of interpretation or factual error, readers are advised to carry up-to-date maps, especially when travelling into the back country. The author and publisher take no responsibility for loss or injury incurred by anyone using this book.*

CONTENTS

Introduction 6

Preface 7

Waterfall Appreciation 8

British Columbia Waterfalls 10

Types of Waterfalls 13

Waterfall Safety: Beautiful but Deadly 15

Rating Systems 18

The 100 Best Waterfalls of BC:

Vancouver Island 20

Coast Range 37

Southern Interior 73

Southeast 85

Yoho—Kootenay National Parks 110

Wells Gray Provincial Park and Area 133

Central 162

Northwest 186

Tumbler Ridge 197

Alaska Highway 222

Glossary 229

Waterfall Checklist 231

Selected Bibliography 235

Acknowledgements 236

Index 237

Introduction

As a boy growing up on the BC Coast I was fascinated by falling water, all the way from a foot or two in a creek I was fishing to the towering wonders of Jervis Inlet and Desolation Sound. As a student I worked at Princess Louisa Inlet, at the head of Jervis Inlet, and we used to swim where a 100-foot cascade hit the water.

There are, of course, many beautiful falls in British Columbia–one of my favourites is Helmcken Falls near Clearwater on the Yellowhead–and this marvelous book takes you to 100 of them.

This book is very timely indeed because the waterfalls of British Columbia are threatened as never before. The provincial government of Gordon Campbell has initiated a policy of encouraging Independent Power Producers (IPPs) to construct "small hydro" projects on the province's secondary rivers and streams. These projects tend to be located in the same places as falls and rapids because they require a steep descent of water to drive their turbines. At the top of the descent 80–90 percent of the mean annual discharge is diverted into tunnels or pipes and channeled through the generating facility before being returned to the stream beds at lower elevations as far as 18 kilometres downstream. Several of the magnificent falls described in this book and many more across the province face having their flow reduced to a trickle and their unique spray-zone ecosystems destroyed.

Originally small hydro was promoted as a green energy solution but with 130 licences granted at the time of writing and over 585 applications going forward in all regions, and more applications appearing daily, the combined environmental impact on some of the province's most scenic and sensitive places is anything but small. Add the disruption caused by heavy construction, road building, siltation of fish habitat, unsightly structures and hundreds of kilometres of new transmission corridors and it is an environmental disaster of major proportions. It is all the more tragic in that BC has many greener options for meeting its energy needs, including upgrades to existing generating facilities and improved conservation.

This is not only a fine book, a beautiful book, it is pictorial evidence of what we are losing day by day and is an inspiration to all those trying to stop the destruction of that which makes our province so special.

Rafe Mair, writer and prize-winning broadcaster, is official spokesman for Save Our Rivers Society (www.saveourrivers.ca).

Preface

I grew up on the edge of the Fenlands in eastern England, one of the flattest places in the world. In the nearby Lincolnshire Wolds is a place I remember vividly from my childhood called Partney Mill, where a small stream produces the magic of falling water. The second waterfall I remember was on a visit to the Falls of Lenny in the Trossachs, Scotland, where my family bought a souvenir photograph in a cheap frame that graced our mantelpiece for the rest of my childhood. Soon after arriving in Canada I was introduced to Chapman Falls on the Sunshine Coast of British Columbia, and so began the start of a beautiful relationship. Chapman Falls is still one of my favourite places: it combines complex geomorphology, big trees, four separate waterfalls and the ever-changing flow of the river and the falling water. Twenty-seven years later, in a revelation, I had the idea of writing a book about the waterfalls of British Columbia. It seemed like an original concept, but a few minutes on the Internet quickly dispelled that notion. For example, *Among the Waterfalls of the World* by Edward C. Rashleigh was published in London in 1935. In 1989 Gregory Plumb published his seminal *A Waterfall Lover's Guide to the Pacific Northwest*, an access guide that covers the states of Washington, Oregon and Idaho.

When I first committed to this project in 1996, I blithely imagined that despite the enormous size of BC it would be a simple matter of making a list of the waterfalls and then methodically visiting them one by one. My thinking turned out to be erroneous for a variety of reasons. No list of BC waterfalls existed. Making a list was fraught with all manner of difficulties and years later I was still discovering significant new waterfalls, by chance, and in a variety of ways. The project morphed from an encyclopedic review of all BC waterfalls into the present project.

With a project called "The 100 Best," you have to visit 300 waterfalls to actually assess which are the best. This project has consequently been 12 years in gestation and it has been a wonderful trip. From my first acquaintance with a BC waterfall at Chapman Creek in May 1969, through sporadic encounters in the 1970s and 1980s at Shannon, Brandywine and Chatterbox falls, to the intensive research of recent years, it is hard to imagine a more appealing use of time than researching BC's great waterfall heritage. I have visited the four corners of our incredible province, from Vancouver Island and the Coast Range to the Rocky Mountains, the boreal wilderness of Tumbler Ridge and along the Alaska Highway to the extreme northwestern corner at Atlin. So many highlights come to mind, but I especially remember my visits to Keyhole Falls, the foot of Helmcken Falls, the Petain Waterfalls and the Monkman Cascades. These are the incandescent memories of a lifetime.

This adventure has, of course, not been entirely without its frustrations. Many times I set off seeking a waterfall with incomplete, wrong or misleading information, which led me to places and situations I would rather have avoided. I visited a number of features named as waterfalls on maps or in books or brochures, only to find a misuse of the term, or perhaps wishful thinking. One hot, muggy, mosquito-infested afternoon west of Fort St. James, I hiked into the putative Pinchi Falls and after scaring off two separate black bears and getting thoroughly soaked by a thunderstorm, I discovered that Pinchi Falls is nothing but a low-grade chute. Another time I drove 1,000 kilometres from Vancouver to Nimpo Lake with the intention of flying into Hunlen Falls, only to be told that a forest fire was burning in the area and that no flying was possible.

Hopefully my carefully written directions will expedite your outings and help avoid the many ambiguous, misleading, incomplete or non-existent directions that I sometimes tried to follow. Be aware though that access can change over time, particularly to destinations outside of parks.

Enjoy your adventures.
Tony Greenfield
Halfmoon Bay, BC
December 2008

Waterfall Appreciation

Of all geographic features, waterfalls may exert the strongest attraction to humans. We are attracted to waterfalls like iron filings to a magnet, like moths to a flame. We are seduced into visiting them, secure in the knowledge that exciting visual treats await us. They have been a constant source of wonder, awe, inspiration, romance and introspection for poets, lovers, travellers, explorers and the general public. The waterfall symbolizes the central sacrament of the nature experience. If the Great Outdoors is the cathedral in which we worship, then the waterfall is the altar we bow down before. What is it about falling water that strikes a chord with us?

Waterfalls are not only beautiful in and of themselves, but they exist in wondrous natural settings of mountains and fjords, lakes, rivers and streams, surrounded by endless varieties of trees, flowers, moss, ferns, birds, mammals and insects.

Waterfalls are famous. Some of the most visited destinations in the world are waterfalls—Niagara in North America, Iguazu in South America and Victoria Falls in Africa.

Waterfalls encapsulate the randomness of the natural world. Their structure is the result of the random geologic events of the eons, while at the same time they obey the inexorable laws of physics and chemistry. They change with the seasons, the weather and the time of day, as snowmelt, rain and drought, and the ambiance of sunrise, midday and sunset interact. Waterfalls have many moods, from the frozen icefall of a snowy winter, to the high water of the spring freshet or the winter deluge, to the low flow tranquility of summer and fall.

Waterfalls bring an element of sentient life to the physical landscape, like blood flowing through veins. The living presence of a chimera of falling water flowing over lifeless rock seems to symbolize the fundamental evolution from the inorganic to life itself.

Waterfalls occur in infinite variety, from the monumental, with thundering volumes plunging into dark abysses, to tranquil little gems hidden away on forest trails. No two waterfalls are the same. Some are attended by millions of visitors and may be surrounded by unbridled crass commercialism (we think of Niagara); others exist in remote wilderness settings, little known or visited. Fortunately, most BC waterfalls are of the latter persuasion.

Waterfalls are uniquely inspirational forces of nature that focus our attention like a mantra and generate introspection and metaphysical wonderment. They are an allegory of timelessness and the eternal as personified by Tennyson:

> "For men may come and men may go,
> But I go on forever."

Waterfalls serve to concentrate our attention on the workings of nature and the somewhat abstract notions of geology and geomorphology. We can look at a waterfall and see dynamic geomorphologic processes at work and the visible geology of millions of years. Mountains tumble to the sea before our eyes.

If waterfalls are a central icon of the nature experience it has not always ensured their immunity from development. Many waterfalls around the world have been tapped in whole or part for their hydro-electric potential, with Niagara Falls, the most famous waterfall in the world, being the prime example. In Canada the Churchill Falls hydro development in Newfoundland which came on stream in 1971 stilled the once mighty Churchill Falls, one of Canada's natural wonders. In the United States I visited the great Shoshone Falls, "the Niagara of the West", on the Snake River in Idaho, only to find it completely dry, its waters diverted for irrigation.

In BC numerous waterfalls have been modified partly or completely for power generation, including Clowhom Falls, Stave Falls, Bonnington Falls and Seymour Falls. In the 1970's BC's premier waterfall, Helmcken Falls, was threatened with a power development until the province's fledgling environmental movement intervened.

As this book is written a new threat to BC's waterfalls has emerged, with the province's encouragement of Independent Power Producer (IPP) projects. Under this program the integrity of as many as 11 of the waterfalls in this book are threatened with developments of unknown impact. Diversion of part of a water-

Waterfalls of British Columbia

> ## Famous Waterfalls of the World
>
> The Big Three waterfalls of the world are Iguazu, Victoria and Niagara.
>
> *North America*
> **Niagara Falls** Canada/USA, world's most famous waterfall
> **Yosemite Falls** California, USA, highest North America, 740m
>
> *South America*
> **Angel Falls** Venezuela, world's highest, 979m
> **Iguazu Falls** Argentina/Brazil, world's greatest annual discharge
> **Kaieteur Falls** Guyana, one of world's most powerful
>
> *Africa*
> **Victoria Falls** Zambia/Zimbabwe, world's biggest waterfall
> **Tugela Falls** South Africa, world's second highest, 947m
>
> *Europe*
> **Dettifoss** Iceland, Europe's most powerful falls
> **Mardelsfossen** Norway, one of highest falls in Europe
>
> *Asia*
> **Khone Falls** Laos/Cambodia, Mekong River, very high discharge

fall's discharge may be tolerable (Niagara?) but there are wider implications if formerly pristine natural areas are cluttered with visual eyesores, the most prominent of which are transmission lines. BC is still one of the wildest regions of the world and it would be regrettable indeed if this irreplaceable patrimony was impaired by environmental vandalism at a time when civilization encroaches more and more on the planet's diminishing wilderness.

For BC's waterfalls eternal vigilance is the operative word.

British Columbia Waterfalls

British Columbia is nearly 1,000,000 square km (620,000 sq mi) in area, bigger than Washington, Oregon and California combined, and four times the area of the United Kingdom. It covers an incredible range of biogeoclimatic zones, from hypermaritime rainforest to desert, from boreal and sub-arctic forest to the glaciers of 5,000 m (16,000 ft) mountains. The province is also one of the steepest, highest, most glaciated and wettest/snowiest jurisdictions in the world. If this sounds like the perfect scenario for a cornucopia of waterfalls, it does not disappoint.

The waterfall heritage of any region is a matrix of its geology, geomorphology, climate and weather. Within the vastness of British Columbia these individual factors interact in a multitude of ways to produce a magnificent variety of waterfalls.

Waterfalls of British Columbia

Weather influences BC's falls. Shannon Falls is extremely variable, depending on precipitation.
Brytta / iStockphoto

British Columbia is the product of the geological collision and subsequent massive crumpling of the Pacific and North American tectonic plates, which has created the successive cordilleras from Vancouver Island and the Coast Range to the Rocky Mountains. These orogenic forces were imposed upon a variable geology of limestone and sandstone sediments, metamorphic rocks and more localized pockets of igneous activity.

Superimposed on the surface geology of the province are the geomorphologic effects of glaciation that generate dramatic and predictable landscape elements such as overdeepened main valleys with tributary hanging valleys. This process produced hundreds of waterfalls around the northern hemisphere, including many of the most famous ones. At the conclusion of the Ice Age, the vast volumes of water released from the mountain icefields carved notably huge canyons now occupied by smaller "misfit" streams. An unseen process still at work today is the isostatic rebound as the land recovers from the depression created when it was weighed down by the astronomical weight of hundreds of metres of ice.

British Columbia has four regions where significant waterfalls are clustered: Vancouver Island and the Coast Range Mountains, the Rocky Mountains, Wells Gray Provincial Park and the Tumbler Ridge area in the foothills of the northern Rockies. Most of the province is mountainous, but vast areas in the Chilcotin, the Fraser–Nechako plateau and the northeast of the province have little in the way of variable relief and are poorly represented with waterfalls.

Climatically, British Columbia is ideally suited for waterfalls. The successive cordilleras are the dumping grounds for the moisture-laden weather systems that sweep in from the Pacific Ocean. In winter the moisture falls as snow, which is then released to feed the rivers, streams and waterfalls until the start of the rainy season in October. This runoff is important for BC waterfalls as it fuels perennial falls rather than ephemeral ones. In this book I describe a single ephemeral waterfall,

Fintry Falls in the Okanagan Valley. To the south of BC throughout the American West many waterfalls are ephemeral, being dry by mid- to late summer.

Weather has an enormous influence on BC's waterfalls as the mountains capture incoming Pacific weather systems that can produce spectacular amounts of precipitation in short periods of time. In November 2006 a "pineapple express," the remnants of typhoon Cimaron, was pushed all the way from the vicinity of the Philippines by a powerful jet stream. After picking up moisture for thousands of kilometres across the open ocean it zeroed in on the Howe Sound area and dumped 18 in (457 mm) of rain in four days on the Squamish Valley. At times like these the volume of water in Shannon Falls is truly mind-boggling. Conversely, in early November 2002 after a long dry summer and the driest October on record, Shannon Falls was virtually dry.

Types of Waterfalls

"If it looks like a waterfall, sounds like a waterfall and acts like a waterfall–then it's a waterfall." There is no exact definition of a waterfall.

Rivers and streams flow over every level of gradient, from 90 to 0 degrees. Plunge falls, where the water flows 90 degrees over a vertical face, are the most obvious type of waterfall and the best known–think of Niagara Falls, the most famous waterfall in the world. Apart from plunge falls, water flows down every degree of gradient and of necessity it must maintain some contact with the bedrock. Steeper gradients with flowing water are called cascades, but as the angle diminishes to the level of a rapids we cease to label them waterfalls, even though they may still be very exciting places.

The volume of water in a waterfall is highly variable due to spring snowmelt, winter monsoons or 100-year rainfall events. At the opposite end of the scale there are ephemeral falls, which only flow intermittently due to drought (or human interference). Many falls also become icefalls in the winter months.

Some authors who have written about waterfalls have devised their own system to classify them. However, there are essentially only two types of waterfalls, plunges and cascades, though in reality many waterfalls are complex and contain elements of both types.

Waterfalls are heavily influenced by the geology over which they flow. Characteristically, igneous rocks such as basalt (Wells Gray area) and sedimentary rocks such as sandstone (Tumbler Ridge) or limestone produce plunge waterfalls, while metamorphic rock (typically the Coast Range) produces irregular cascades. However, geology is often superceded by geomorphologic effects such as hanging valleys (Coast Range, Yoho Valley).

Three main waterfall descriptives are used in this book, the plunge, the cascade and the punchbowl, with several specific modifications to these types.

1. Plunge waterfalls: The stream free falls over a ledge and descends vertically without contacting the rock face. Plunge falls occur where a resistant stratum forms a caprock overlaying more easily eroded strata, or where glacial action has created a hanging valley. Helmcken Falls is a classic plunge waterfall.

> Block plunge: The falls are wide, usually the full width of the stream (Brandywine and Moul falls). Frequently the falls are wider than they are high (Dawson Falls).
>
> Ribbon: The falls descend in a narrow, ribbon-like plunge, often from a great height (Helmcken and Spahats falls).

2. Cascade waterfalls: At a cascade, the stream flows down a non-vertical wall. The degree of interaction with the wall depends upon factors such as the angle of the rock (which may vary from near vertical to near horizontal) and the presence of impediments to the even flow of the water such as twists and turns, constrictions, steps, arches and boulders. Many plunge falls have cascading sections at their base, where the stream flows over jumbles of collapsed caprock (Sikanni Chief and Bergeron falls). Cascades are typically found where metamorphic rocks predominate, so many Coast Range waterfalls (Della and Shannon falls) are cascades because of the prevalence of granitic rock types.

> Horsetail: The falls are almost vertical, but maintain some contact with the bedrock (Bridal Veil Falls). The name refers to their supposed similarity to the tail of a horse.
>
> Fan: The width of the falls increases downward, in the shape of a fan.
>
> Both plunges and cascades may also be tiered or segmented.
>
> Tiered: The stream falls over a succession of ledges with short, level stretches between (the Monkman Cascades, Sukunka Falls and Emperor Falls/Falls of the Pool/White Falls).
>
> Segmented: The falls are divided into separate streams by rock outcrops (Majerus and Pine falls). Falls can be further characterized as triple segmented (Matthew Falls).

3. Punchbowl waterfalls: The dictionary defines a punchbowl as a "round, deep hollow (in hills)," and the term has been applied to waterfalls where the stream makes a low plunge from one pool to another through a constriction of the channel, giving a characteristic hourglass appearance (The Mushbowl).

Selected Waterfalls of Canada

Athabasca Falls	Athabasca River, Alberta
Panther Falls	Nigel Creek, Alberta
Nistowiak Falls	Rapid River, Saskatchewan
Pisew Falls	Grass River, Manitoba
Niagara Falls	Niagara River, Ontario
Kakabeka Falls	Kaministiquia River, Ontario
Montmorency Falls	Montmorency River, Quebec
Chaudiere Falls	Chaudiere River, Quebec
Churchill Falls *(now diverted)*	Newfoundland
Pissing Mare Falls	Gros Morne NP, Newfoundland
Grand Falls	St. John River, New Brunswick
Barrow Falls	Melville Peninsula, Nunavut
Wilberforce Falls	Hood River, Nunavut
Louise Falls	Hay River, NWT
Virginia Falls	Nahanni River, NWT
Million Dollar Falls	Takhanne River, Yukon

Waterfall Safety: Beautiful but Deadly

Every year around the world, of the millions of people who are attracted to waterfalls, hundreds will die. Safety around waterfalls should be a constant consideration. The dangers cannot be expressed any more lucidly than the following sign at Chatterbox Falls: "Do not go near the top of the falls. The surrounding flat rocks are moss covered and slippery. 12 people have lost their lives by not observing this warning." The "12" is now crossed out and replaced by "13."

At Osprey Falls in Wells Gray Provincial Park, 18 people have gone over the falls, and not in barrels. In the United States the Great Falls of the Potomac claims more than six lives every year.

The topography around waterfalls is generally steep, the ground wet and the rocks slippery and loose. Frequently the main attraction is hidden or obscured by the geography or vegetation. Waterfall seekers are under a constant imperative to

The vantage points for many falls, including Chatterbox Falls, can be slippery and unstable—use extreme caution.

achieve the best possible views of the quarry, which can lead us to venture into dangerous places. Many waterfalls, especially in parks, have safety fences or viewing platforms, but many others do not. It is particularly crucial to supervise children, as they may not be aware of the hazards.

When we are engaged in photography of waterfalls we tend to push the safety limit to achieve a better shot, while at the same time our attention is distracted from safety concerns. A warning sign at Marble Canyon in Kootenay National Park tells of two people who have inadvertently stepped back into the canyon while framing their photographs.

Beware also of standing on the edge of cliffs with a backpack on. The pack can affect your balance, and I have even seen someone turn and almost nudge the person next to them over the edge with their pack.

Almost every destination in this book is potentially dangerous if you push the limits of common sense. Many of the waterfalls have dangerous, unguarded edges where a lack of concentration, a slip or a trip might result in catastrophe. Two of the province's greatest waterfalls, Hunlen and the South Rim of Helmcken, have terrifying unguarded edges with guaranteed catastrophic results should you inadvertently go over the precipice. At the present time I am aware of fatal incidents at the following waterfalls: Elk, Chatterbox, High, Nairn, Cariboo and Marble Canyon.

Bears: Close Encounters of the Ursine Kind

Any trip into the outdoors in BC entails a long list of potential hazards, all with a very low chance of actually happening. Bear encounters are one of the threats that frequently loom large in people's minds. Bears are everywhere in BC, both black and grizzly.

During the course of researching this book the only grizzly I encountered on a trail was sighted in an avalanche chute on the hike to Helmet Falls in Kootenay National Park. Other grizzlies were observed while driving logging roads en route to various waterfalls. Black bears are abundant in BC and likely to be encountered almost anywhere. The good news is that they generally spook easily and are likely to bolt when they detect you. Surprising a bear is never the preferred option so making noise on the trail is encouraged. If you detect a black bear on or close to your trail, making noise will usually be sufficient for it to vacate the area. In such a situation there is always safety in numbers, so you should reconsider the wisdom of hiking alone before setting out. If you do encounter a black bear on a trail, backing up slowly is recommended. Do not turn and run as this may trigger a pursuit reflex in the bear. Climbing a tree might work to avoid a grizzly attack (they are not tree climbers), but never try this with a black bear.

Doing what you can to avoid bear confrontations should be your best practice, but it is wise to be prepared for all eventualities. I strongly recommend carrying bear spray on the trail. Bear spray does work and it can help to fortify your confidence about possible encounters. Make sure you know how to maximize the effectiveness of this option by practising, by knowing its limitations and by ensuring your spray is currently viable.

If avoidance techniques fail and you are faced with a charging bear, it is always best to have done your homework before setting out–reading a manual in the face of a charging grizzly is not recommended. Much literature is available on this topic in books and pamphlets, as well as on DVD and the Internet. Pamphlets on bear safety are widely available at provincial government agent and tourist information offices. In brief, it is recommended to play dead with a grizzly bear by dropping to the ground, face down, knees up and hands over neck with elbows spread to make it more difficult for the bear to roll you over. With black bears, fighting back by any conceivable method is preferred.

Logging Roads and Traffic: Hold the Timbits

The most dangerous part of your waterfall visit is the potential for meeting logging road traffic, which far surpasses the likelihood of falling into the falls or meeting up with wild animals. Many of the locations in this book do not require travelling on logging roads, but I have noted those that do, especially if the road was being used for active logging when I visited. The decision to use a road for logging can change from day to day. Consequently, it is imperative to comply with any signage as you enter a logging road. These instructions may specify only using the road between certain hours, on certain days such as weekends or request that you follow a logging truck up the road. In these situations do not try to wing it–it is not worth the danger to yourself and others of meeting an off-road logging truck on a blind corner, a steep hill or a single lane section of road with no shoulder.

Where entry is allowed, drive with headlights on at all times, even in places where there is no active logging. Comply with all requests, drive slowly or at the stated speed limit, keep to your side of the road and play it safe on blind corners. If you do see a logging truck approach, pull over as far to the side of the road as possible and park until the truck passes. Beware of the blinding dust storms that can accompany logging trucks in very dry conditions. If you stop for any reason on a logging road pull off into a wide spot.

Phoning the Ministry of Forests office or the local logging company in advance may save you trouble and increase your safety. It is also generally safe to follow behind a logging truck, whether it is loaded or not.

The bottom line for driving on logging roads is Be Prepared. Be prepared for traffic approaching around every corner, and remember that it may not only be loggers (who generally know how to drive on logging roads and will make every effort to avoid accidents) but other recreationists, hunters, fishermen, mushroom pickers and assorted weekend drivers. Also watch for ATVs, motorbikes, mountain bikes and wildlife.

I do not recommend that you follow the advice of one author who suggested, tongue in cheek I hope, that you should carry a box of Timbits in case you "blow it" with a logging truck driver. You might find you and your vehicle irretrievably squashed and last rites more appropriate than Timbits.

Waterfall Rating System

Each waterfall in the book is given a rating from 3 to 5. The system is completely subjective and incorporates a variety of elements which may include height, width, discharge, fame, unique attributes and scenic qualities of the environs of the waterfall.

▲▲▲▲▲ A rating of 5 indicates a waterfall of the highest magnitude within British Columbia, based on one or more of the attributes listed above. In many cases a rating of 5 indicates that the waterfall is a continentally significant feature.

▲▲▲▲△ Ratings of 3 and 4 indicate the waterfall is one of the 100 best within British Columbia, but of a lesser magnitude than a 5.

▲▲△△△ Ratings of 1 and 2, not used in this book, would indicate smaller or less significant waterfalls.

Access Rating System

All the waterfalls are accorded an access rating of **Easy**, **Moderate**, **Difficult** or **Very Difficult**. These are subjective terms.

Easy indicates that almost any mobile person can visit the falls without any prior planning. Frequently the falls are at roadside, or accessed by short, level trails.

Moderate indicates that a degree of effort, usually a moderately strenuous hike is involved, or that logging road travel is required.

Difficult indicates that there are logistical problems involved in visiting the falls and that planning is required. It may also indicate that a strenuous hike is needed to view the falls.

Very Difficult indicates there may be complex or expensive logistical issues involved in visiting the falls. Also, strenuous or very strenuous hiking and/or overnight camping may be required.

The 100 Best Waterfalls of BC

Kayaker Kelsey Thompson shoots down Chapman Falls near Sechelt, BC. Emily Lussin photo

VANCOUVER ISLAND

Vancouver Island is 450 km (280 mi) long, approximately 100 km (60 mi) wide and almost completely mountainous, rising to a height of 2,195 m (7,200 ft) at Mt. Golden Hinde in Strathcona Provincial Park. The island is geologically diverse, with extensive areas of metamorphosed granitic rock and localized sedimentary areas of sandstone and limestone. The west coast of Vancouver Island boasts a hypermaritime climate: Henderson Lake near Ucluelet set the Canadian record for the highest annual recorded precipitation with 9,479 mm (370 in) in 1997 and averages 6,655 mm (260 in) of precipitation annually. The southeastern coast has a Mediterranean-type climate that features mild, wet winters and warm, dry summers.

FALLS 1-7

The narrow breadth of the island predicates small watersheds with relatively low discharges. The waterfalls are mainly cascades or low, tiered plunges typical of granitic geology. Elk Falls on the Campbell River is the island's greatest waterfall by volume. Della Falls in Strathcona Park is accorded the title of Canada's Highest Waterfall by virtue of its 440 m (1,444 ft) cascade. Many small, hidden waterfalls dot the island's hundreds of rivers and creeks.

1 ELK FALLS

Rating:	▲▲▲▲△
Type:	Plunge
Location:	5 km (3 mi) W of Campbell River
Access:	Easy. Short hike
Status:	Elk Falls Provincial Park
When to go:	Year-round

Directions: At the junction of Hwys 19 and 28 at the north end of Campbell River turn west on Hwy 28, the Gold River Highway, and drive 5 km (3 mi), ignoring the other entrances to Elk Falls Provincial Park on the left and right. Turn right onto the Brewster Lake and Loveland Lake Road, which is also posted as Elk Falls Provincial Park picnic area. Cross the bridge over the penstocks from the dam and immediately bear right onto a park road that leads to the parking lot. From here a circular trail leads to the official viewpoint of Elk Falls and continues on past Deer and Moose Falls back to the parking lot.

Facilities: Elk Falls Provincial Park can be accessed by a number of entrances: the Quinsam River campground has campsites, fishing, hiking trails, water and firewood; 4 km (2.5 mi) to the west, the Elk Falls picnic area has picnic tables, toilets, hiking trails and swimming.

Highlights: The Campbell River flows from John Hart Lake through Elk Falls canyon. The John Hart Dam and associated penstocks allow much of the water to be diverted from the canyon and the three waterfalls, but even so, Elk Falls is still mightily impressive, as the river plunges 27 m (89 ft) over the precipitous brink.

The Campbell River is the second largest drainage on Vancouver Island. Today, the river is dammed in three places and the hydro facility produces 11 percent of Vancouver Island's electricity.

The circular trail cuts through a magnificent stand of gigantic Douglas firs and western red cedars, one of the finest lowland old-growth forests in BC. The short trail to Elk Falls drops down the riverbank to the rim of the falls, but the viewing

Elk Falls. Olivier Robert photo

platform allows only an oblique view because of the difficult geography. Here the primeval river butted heads with an immovable object and the result is a deep abyss with a high wall of rock that forces the river to make a 90-degree turn to the left. Elk Falls is a pure plunge waterfall, dropping dramatically into a narrow, black canyon with deep, dark, forbidding pools. The trail also gives access to the wide expanse of rock above the falls, which is the old riverbed. You can approach the rim of the falls here; extreme caution is advised.

Beyond Elk Falls the trail continues upstream beside the river to Deer Falls, a minor falls between two wide, placid pools, Dolphin and Sturgeon. A little further along is the access to the wide pool below Moose Falls, which consists of two separate 3 m (10 ft) cascades. The trail then continues up the hill and back to the parking lot. The whole circuit can be completed in about 30 minutes, but allow longer to absorb this beautiful trail and its waterfalls.

From the parking lot an unofficial trail leads about 300 m (330 yd) along the east rim of the canyon. After a steep, loose scramble down an incline, you will arrive at an unprotected viewpoint on a rock bluff directly across the canyon from Elk Falls. This spot allows magnificent, full frontal views of the falls, but extreme caution is advised.

The BC Hydro John Hart generating station is located between the Quinsam campground and the Elk Falls picnic area. It is worth visiting here and walking all or part of the Canyon View Trail, including the bridge across the canyon high above the limpid river. The whole Canyon View circuit can be hiked in about an hour.

Snapshot: I visited once on a misty November afternoon when the huge trees visible down the canyon were wreathed in fog. As I stood at the brink of the falls the black pools of water and the gleaming black wall of the canyon had an ominous air about them.

This is a magical place to visit, even just to appreciate the monumental trees.

2 MYRA FALLS

Rating:	▲▲▲△△
Type:	Tiered plunges
Location:	84 km (52 mi) W of Campbell River, 37 km (23 mi) W of Buttle Narrows
Access:	Easy. Blacktop highway to short trail
Status:	Strathcona-Westmin Provincial Park
When to go:	Year-round

Directions: At the junction of Hwys 19 and 28 at the north end of Campbell River drive west on Hwy 28, the Gold River Highway, for 47 km (29 mi). At Buttle

23

Myra Falls, Mike Biro (TMPH) photo

Narrows the highway to Gold River crosses the lake. Bear left and follow the south shore of the lake for 37 km (23 mi). A BC Parks sign for the Myra Falls Trail marks the short access road to the falls. From the parking lot a 500 m (550 yd) gravelled trail, about a five-minute hike, leads to upper and lower viewpoints.

Facilities: Trails, outhouse, interpretive signage.

Highlights: Distant views of the falls can be seen from the highway across the head of Buttle Lake. BC Parks interpretative signage explains that local earthquakes caused breaks in the Earth's crust that vertically displaced sections of rock and created the conditions for the convoluted 70 m (230 ft) total drop. The falls consist of a series of plunges separated by wide, jade-green pools. The whole complex can be explored by entering the bed of the creek from the lower viewpoint and clambering both upstream and downstream over the ledges. The creek bed is a wide platform of bedrock, cleanly scoured by the river, but huge logs stranded within the falls give some indication of the mayhem during high water flows.

The upper trail leads to a viewpoint at the foot of the first series of falls. Here Myra Creek plunges through a narrow gap and falls 10 m (33 ft) into a bowl and a further 2 m (6.5 ft) into a plunge pool. The water then emerges onto a rock shelf before plunging again into a cleft jammed with log debris.

A Guide to BC's Best 100 Falls

Snapshot: Myra Falls is a microcosm of the geomorphologic forces at work in the Coast Mountains. The geology comprises metamorphic granite and limestone permeated by igneous intrusions. The forces of nature on display here include: faulting caused by earthquakes; chemical weathering of the limestone; and fluvial erosion by the action of the creek.

3 ENGLISHMAN FALLS

Rating:	▲▲▲△△
Type:	Tiered plunges
Location:	47 km (29 mi) NW of Nanaimo, 52 km (32 mi) E of Port Alberni
Access:	Easy. 45-minute loop trail
Status:	Englishman River Falls Provincial Park
When to go:	Year-round

Directions: From Nanaimo drive north on Hwy 19 to Hwy 4, the Port Alberni highway. About 4 km (2.5 mi) west of the interchange turn south onto the signed road to the village of Errington and Englishman River Falls Provincial Park. Proceed 9 km (5.5 mi) to the park. The main waterfall is 150 m (165 yd) beyond the parking lot.

Facilities: Full provincial park facilities with trails, campsites, water, picnic tables, toilets, a gazebo and a children's adventure playground.

Highlights: Englishman Falls consists of an upper and a lower falls about 400 m (440 yd) apart along a picturesque canyon. The upper falls has a feature that is unique among BC waterfalls: the 40 m (130 ft) wide Englishman River plunges over the brink and disappears into a deep slot canyon that sits at 90 degrees to the approaching river. A footbridge carries the trail high above the slot canyon and makes it possible

Englishman Falls

VANCOUVER ISLAND

25

to peer down into the deep recesses where the river has been captured by a fault line in the rock. Beneath the bridge the slot is only about a metre wide at the top and of an unknown depth. All manner of debris is carried into the canyon's maw: stumps, chunks and logs are lodged in the crevice while some logs are suspended high and dry far above the normal tide line of the river, indicating periodic very high water flows.

On the other side of the bridge the river spews out into the canyon with a minor 3 m (10 ft) falls before it plunges over the 4 m (13 ft) lower falls. The plunge pool below the lower falls is deep and clear, ideal for swimming in summer and for viewing spawning salmon in the fall.

According to legend the river takes its name from a long ago incident when local First Nations people found the skeleton of a white man along the river near the falls.

Snapshot: The structure of this falls is similar to that of Elk Falls at Campbell River, as the river is forced through a right-angled turn by the uncooperative geology.

The old-growth Douglas fir forest of Englishman River Falls Provincial Park had a wonderful green ambiance when I visited on a sunny December afternoon. Especially notable was the lush growth of mosses glistening on the canyon walls and the trunks of the maple trees after recent rainfall.

4 LITTLE QUALICUM FALLS

Rating:	▲▲▲△△
Type:	Tiered plunges
Location:	Hwy 4 between Parksville or Qualicum Beach and Port Alberni
Access:	Easy. 30-minute loop trail
Status:	Little Qualicum Falls Provincial Park
When to go:	Year-round

Directions: Look for the park signs 19 km (12 mi) west of Parksville or 27 km (17 mi) east of Port Alberni on Hwy 4. From the parking lot and picnic area a trail to the left leads to the upper falls by an easy, level, five-minute hike. To the right the lower falls can be hiked in about five minutes via a trail with a series of steps. The loop trail that links the upper and lower falls via two bridges is recommended. It can be hiked in about thirty minutes.

Facilities: Full range of park facilities including campground, picnic tables and gazebo, water, flush toilets (wheelchair accessible), adventure playground and hiking trails.

Little Qualicum Falls, upper falls

Highlights: The upper falls are the main attraction and consist of three distinct drops: a 5 m (16 ft) cascade and plunge pool; a 7 m (23 ft) plunge and pool; and a canyon section followed by another 2 m (6.5 ft) drop. The trail crosses the river by a bridge above the upper falls and follows it down to the lower falls where there are a further three drops, but none as spectacular as those upstream.

The Little Qualicum River periodically experiences very high water flows as evidenced at the upper falls by the tide line of debris stranded on the wall of the plunge pool 7 m (23 ft) above the low flow level.

The circular trail crosses the river by a bridge above the upper falls, follows it down to the lower falls and back to the picnic area and parking lot. Above the lower falls bridge there is a confused 3 m (10 ft) cascade, and below the bridge are more minor falls, pools, canyons and a dry channel that is plugged with a log-jam.

Snapshot: The convoluted course of the Little Qualicum River is typical of many Vancouver Island and Coast Range rivers as it tumbles over a series of waterfalls within a sinuous canyon. On hot summer days the volatile oils from the old-growth Douglas firs and cedars impart a wonderful fragrance to the air in the park.

5 STAMP FALLS

Rating:	▲▲▲△△
Type:	Tiered plunges
Location:	14 km (9 mi) NW of Port Alberni
Access:	Easy. Short trail, less than 5 minutes
Status:	Stamp Falls Provincial Park
When to go:	Year-round

Directions: From Port Alberni take Hwy 4, the Pacific Rim Highway, heading west toward Tofino. After turning right at the traffic light at the foot of the main street, bear right again after 250 m (275 yd) onto Beaver Creek Road and proceed for 12 km (7.5 mi). Once in the park follow the main park road to the very end.

Stamp Falls. R. Michael van Dam photo

Facilities: Toilets, riverside picnic tables, tent/vehicle camping, water, firewood, hiking trails.

Highlights: The trail begins amid some huge Douglas firs alongside the river. It is about 500 m (550 yd) from the parking lot to the falls. Stamp Falls is one of the most adulterated waterfalls in BC. The natural falls have been much altered in the worthy cause of fisheries enhancement. Amid all the water and cascades are concrete abutments, tunnels, platforms, pipes and grilles. It sounds bad, but the waterfall and the convoluted geography of the canyon manage to incorporate the foreign elements into a new whole. The falls are a series of ledges with no great drops, but the volume of water more than compensates. The river both above and below the falls is about 40 m (130 ft) wide, but in the canyon below the falls it is constricted down to 2 m (6.5 ft) in places. I recommend that you walk the trail for another 200 m (220 yd) beyond the main falls to view the canyon.

Beginning in August nearly half a million sockeye, coho and chinook salmon pass through the ladder that allows them to reach the natural spawning beds upstream and the Robertson Creek hatchery. The sockeye run from late June to early September, coho from August to December and chinook from September to mid-November, with October being the best month to observe the fish circling in the jade green pool before attempting the falls or the fish ladder. Signage along the trail describes the significance of the Stamp River as a fish corridor to the spawning grounds on the upper Stamp and Great Central Lake. Be aware that bears may be in the area when the fish are running.

The Stamp River and falls are named for the pioneer settler who established the first sawmill in Port Alberni.

Snapshot: The elemental colours of a foaming white waterfall, a black-walled canyon with bright green mosses and a blue sky are memorable. In the fall, the decaying maple leaves combine with the faint aroma of decomposing salmon to bespeak of the great cycle of life and death playing out here.

Each time that I have visited Stamp Falls, an American dipper has been present on the concrete abutment in the middle of the falls.

American Dipper.
Rand Rudland photo

6 DELLA FALLS

Rating:	▲▲▲▲▲
Type:	Segmented and tiered plunges and cascades
Location:	65 km W of Port Alberni
Access:	Very difficult. Water access only to trailhead, 16 km (10 mi) trail one way
Status:	Strathcona Provincial Park
When to go:	Late June to early October

Directions: From Port Alberni take Hwy 4 west toward Tofino for 13 km (8 mi). Turn right onto Great Central Lake Road and proceed 8 km (5 mi) to the Ark Resort. Here you can either launch your own boat, rent one from the resort or charter the water taxi ($125 per person return in 2008, two-person minimum, about 45 minutes) for the trip up the lake. The resort can be contacted at 250-723-2657, or via the website: www.arkresort.com.

The trailhead is 34 km (21 mi) west of the Ark Resort, near the head of Great Central Lake. A return trip (one way hiking time is five-plus hours) is possible as a long day-hike for strong hikers. However, it is recommended to camp overnight in the vicinity of the falls and to hike the Love Lake trail on the second day. The trail allows stunning views of the entirety of Della Falls.

There is a possible route to Della Lake and the top of the falls that involves bushwhacking and scrambling over the dangerous bluffs to the south, or left-hand side of the falls. Only experienced climbers should attempt this option.

The 16 km (10 mi) trail from the lakehead to the foot of the falls abuts Drinkwater Creek the entire way. The easy-to-follow route is not challenging and the elevation gain is largely imperceptible. Good drinking water is available everywhere along the trail.

Hiking Trails 3: Northern Vancouver Island Including Strathcona Park, published by the Vancouver Island Trails Information Society, is an excellent resource for this trail and many others in the area. The Ark Resort website has trail directions, information and a trail report where hikers can read and post the latest trail conditions covering such things as snow, mud, flooded and overgrown trails, blowdown, landslides and bear activity.

This is a high snowfall area in the heartland of Strathcona Provincial Park and snow may be present on the upper sections of the trail through June. At times of high water discharge early in the season, whether from snowmelt and/or rainfall, the trail may be impassable beyond the second Drinkwater Creek crossing at km 12.5 (mi 7.75). The trail from the foot of the falls to Love Lake gains rapid elevation, 830 m (2,700 ft) in 4 km (2.5 mi), and snow is a problem on this trail into July.

A Guide to BC's Best 100 Falls

VANCOUVER ISLAND

Della Falls

Avalanches are a possible hazard early in the year. To see Della Falls at its best, the discharge is greatest in June and early July and remains substantial into August. In the late summer and fall the flow may decline to a trickle.

Facilities: The Ark Resort has a full complement of facilities including cabins, campsites, parking, boat launch and a store for supplies. The trailhead at the head of Great Central Lake and the Main or Sawmill campsite near the foot of the falls both have good sites with tables (lake only), outhouses and bear cache. There are other campsites en route, with no facilities.

Highlights: At 440 m (1,443 feet) Della Falls is the highest waterfall in Canada and one of the highest recognized waterfalls in the world. It cascades over a lip from Della Lake, an alpine tarn over 1 km (.6 mi) long at an elevation of 1,080 m (3,500 ft), surrounded by the summits of Nine Peaks (1,842 m/6,040 ft) and Big Interior Mountain (1,862 m/6,100 ft), which are at the heart of Strathcona Park. The Della Falls trail leads directly to the foot of the falls, but to observe their magnificent entirety it is necessary to ascend the Love Lake trail and view the falls from across the Drinkwater Valley.

Tallest Waterfalls of BC

Waterfall	Height
Della Falls	440 m / 1443 ft
Harmony Falls	427 m / 1400 ft
Takakkaw Falls	384 m / 1260 ft
Petain Waterfalls	375 m / 1230 ft
Helmet Falls	352 m / 1155 ft
Shannon Falls	335 m / 1100 ft
Odegaard Falls	280 m / 918 ft
Hunlen Falls	260 m / 853 ft
Twin Falls #3	183 m / 600 ft
Nicoamen Falls	152 m / 500 ft
Helmcken Falls	141 m / 463 ft
Bridal Veil Falls	122 m / 400 ft
Bergeron Falls	100 m / 326 ft

Della Falls and the trail up Drinkwater Creek are intimately connected with Joe Drinkwater, a prospector and trapper who discovered the falls in 1899 and staked claims in the area shortly thereafter. The valley now bears his name, and it was Joe who chivalrously named the highest falls in Canada for his wife (though it was many decades later that the primacy of Della Falls became widely known and accepted). He also founded the Ark Resort.

The first 7 km (4 mi) of the trail from Great Central Lake to the Margaret Creek bridge follows an old railroad logging grade through a young Douglas fir forest. Watch here for the saprophytic and deathly looking flower clumps of Indian pipe. The Margaret Creek bridge, an excellent location for your first rest, has a minor waterfall and a beautiful emerald pool where dragonflies and swallowtail and Lorquin's admiral butterflies can be seen. The bridge also has views westward up the Drinkwater Valley to the high snowcaps at the heart of Strathcona Park.

The trail continues through old-growth forest and the Douglas fir gives way to western hemlock and balsam as elevation is gained and precipitation increases. At km 11 (mi 7) the bridge across Drinkwater Creek is another mandatory resting place. The bluffy constriction beneath the bridge creates a 5 m (16 ft) waterfall that can be observed from above, or by clambering down the bluffs on the north side. If you backtrack 50 m (50 yd) along the trail from the bridge it is possible to climb down through the trees to observe a significant waterfall that plunges and cascades through the rugged Drinkwater Canyon, with another falls visible further down the valley. Look upstream from the bridge some 5 km (3 mi) distant for the first views of the upper cascade of Della Falls. Drinkwater Creek is a classic Coast Range stream with sparkling waters running and tumbling through canyons, around cabin-sized boulders and along gravel bars.

Beyond this bridge the trail crosses a series of talus slides and avalanche chutes to the second Drinkwater crossing on a narrow metal span at km 12.5 (mi 7.75). The trail now runs along the north side of the scenic creek and as you cross a bridge over a side drainage look up and observe for the first time the entirety of Della Falls. Shortly after to the left is the long, narrow torrent of Beauty Falls, which drops from Beauty Lake to Drinkwater Creek. At km 15 (9 mi) is the Main or Sawmill campsite, just beyond is the third Drinkwater Creek bridge and the trail crosses brushy avalanche chutes to the foot of the falls at km 16 (10 mi).

The Love Lake trail is posted just before the Main campsite. The trail switchbacks steeply through huge hemlock, balsam and eventually yellow cedar old-growth timber. Beneath the trees watch for pinesap and twinflowers, and in the openings good displays of tiger lilies (late July), valerian and lupine. Typical bird species that can be heard rather than seen include sooty grouse, grey jay, red-breasted nuthatch, brown creeper, winter wren, hermit thrush and dark-eyed junco.

At about the 1,200 m (3,900 ft) level the trail emerges from the trees to a bluffy area with magnificent views across the Drinkwater Valley to the aptly named Nine Peaks and Big Interior Mountain. Della Creek flows from its lake amid a barren, rocky bowl and falls over the brink to become Della Falls, the highest waterfall in Canada and one of the highest in the world. The falls are a convoluted affair with the main volume of water pursuing a cascade–plunge–cascade–plunge–cascade sequence down the cliff, as a separate stream on the left-hand side follows an independent route downwards. Further off to the left Beauty Falls is one long, continuous cascade that appears to fall an even greater height than Della Falls.

After absorbing the view from here, it is only 15 minutes further to the alpine beauty of Love Lake surrounded by mounts Rosseau (1,962 m/6,437 ft), and Septimus (1,960 m/6,430 ft).

Snapshot: Early in my research on the waterfalls of BC I learned that Della Falls was the highest waterfall in Canada, and it became my Holy Grail in the pantheon of waterfall experiences. It is not an easy destination, and is protected from the masses by difficult access in the form of a long lake and an overnight hike. Finally, on July 26, 2003 on an incandescent midsummer morning, I stood before Della Falls, took in the unique persona of the highest waterfall in Canada and savoured the fulfillment of a personal milestone.

7 TSUSIAT FALLS

Rating:	▲▲▲▲△
Type:	Tiered plunge
Location:	West Coast Trail
Access:	Difficult. Overnight hike from Bamfield, multi-day hike from Port Renfrew
Status:	Pacific Rim National Park Reserve
When to go:	Spring, summer, fall

Directions: Tsusiat Falls is 25 km (15 mi) south along the West Coast Trail from Bamfield. This section of the trail is the least strenuous. The falls can be reached in one long day's hike, which makes it possible to camp overnight at the falls and return to Bamfield the following day. The entire trail from Bamfield to Port Renfrew, 77 km (48 mi) in total, usually takes between five and seven days to complete and can be accessed from either end. If you are contemplating hiking

A Guide to BC's Best 100 Falls

Tsusiat Falls. Justin Coughlin photo

the trail or visiting the falls visit the Parks Canada website, www.pc.gc.ca, to learn about the numerous regulations including reservations, permits and fees. The trail is open May 1 to September 30 and is busiest during July and August. The falls are at their best earlier rather than later as the discharge is much reduced as summer progresses. However, rainfall at any time can replenish the flow in Tsusiat Creek.

Facilities: Full facilities with campsites and telephones are available at either end of the trail. Once on the trail you are in a wilderness environment and self-sufficiency is required. At Tsusiat Falls camping is on the beach. There is an outhouse.

Highlights: Tsusiat Falls is 15 m (50 ft) high with an uncommon stepped plunge form. Another unique aspect of the falls is its location: Tsusiat drops out of the rainforest directly into a pool on a sandy beach on the edge of the Pacific Ocean. The falls is an integral part of the greater experience of hiking the West Coast Trail, which can be the trip of a lifetime.

The trail was constructed as a life-saving trail for shipwrecked mariners. This stretch of coast is known as the graveyard of the Pacific: 240 ships have foundered here. The word *tsusiat* means waterfall in the Didaht dialect.

Snapshot: Thousands of people hike the West Coast Trail each year and all leave with memories, most with photographs and many with blisters. For some it is a muddy, tiring expedition they will not repeat, while for others it is an inspirational rite of passage. Whatever initiates feel about their experience, it is safe to say that most remember Tsusiat Falls as the highlight of their trip. It is a special place along the long, hard trail. Some recall bathing in the pool at the foot of the falls, others showering in the waterfall itself; some remember a gorgeous sunset, others shared trail yarns with visitors from around the world. Some even wax lyrical about the outhouse.

For men may come and men may go,
but I go on forever.

Alfred, Lord Tennyson, "The Brook"

COAST RANGE

The region is dominated by the Coast Range mountains, formed mostly of metamorphosed granite and rising to a height of 4,016 m (13,177 ft) at Mt. Waddington. Coastal BC is a virtual textbook on Quaternary glaciation, a period when enormous ice depths accumulated in the valleys of the Coast Range. The retreat of the glaciers in the last 12,000 years and the subsequent rise in sea level created a submergent coastline, and the flooded glacial valleys are now long, sinuous fjords, the most prominent feature of the region. These fjords stretch from Harrison Lake in the east, through Howe Sound, to the famous quartet of Jervis, Toba, Bute and Knight inlets, and then to Kingcome Inlet and beyond.

During the glacial period the rivers of ice deeply eroded the existing valleys and left many hanging valleys that are custom-built for waterfalls. The hanging valley phenomenon is best exemplified at Shannon Falls, near Squamish, or at Harmony Falls in Jervis Inlet, where the stream drops directly into the ocean. Keyhole Falls on the upper Lillooet River is the region's greatest waterfall, with a high discharge through a unique keyhole canyon, the child of both volcanic and fluvial forces. Chatterbox Falls is perhaps the region's most famous waterfall, by virtue of its impossibly enchanting location at the head of Princess Louisa Inlet.

Within the mostly metamorphic rocks of the Coast Range are scattered islands of lava, but in general, recent volcanism is poorly represented. Where basaltic lava is present it typically produces plunge waterfalls in deeply eroded canyons, such as at Brandywine and Keyhole falls.

The Coast Range attracts very high winter precipitation that is stored in the mountain snowsheds and icefields and is released gradually to maintain high discharges into mid- and late summer. In the fall and winter, extreme rainfall events can produce periodic flood-level discharges at many Coast Range waterfalls. Many minor waterfalls occur on the thousands of creeks that drain the Coast Range mountains.

8 TWIN FALLS #1 (TEAQUAHAN RIVER)

Rating:	▲▲▲△△
Type:	Plunge
Location:	In the Teaquahan River valley at the head of Bute Inlet
Access:	Very difficult. Wheeled or float plane or boat 7 km (4 mi) hike one way
Status:	Provincial forest
When to go:	Spring, summer, fall

Waterfalls of British Columbia

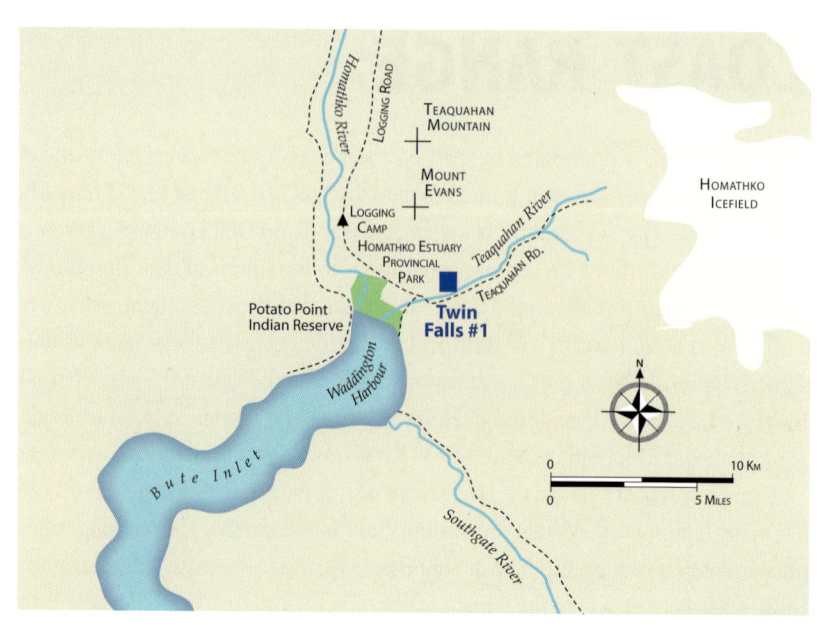

TWIN FALLS

Directions: From Homathko Camp the Teaquahan Road runs eastward for 3.5 km (2 mi) until it crosses the Teaquahan River. Immediately after the bridge at a T-junction, bear left onto a road that is growing in with brush. The road, despite being heavily waterbarred and encroached by brush, is still passable with a four-wheel drive vehicle. The viewing spot for Twin Falls is 3.5 km (2 mi) along this road.

If you hike into the falls, it is mandatory to be aware of the possibility of a bear encounter, as both black and grizzly bears frequent the area. All of the normal precautions for hiking in bear country should be rigorously followed.

It is also possible to be driven to the falls by arrangement with Bute Inlet Adventure Tours (buteinletadventures.com, 1-877-551-2628).

Facilities: Bute Inlet Adventure Tours operate tours into the head of Bute Inlet and the Homathko River and have cabins in the area. There are no facilities at the falls. Camping is inadvisable due to the prevalence of both black and grizzly bears.

Highlights: An unnamed mountain torrent tumbles off the ramparts of Teaquahan Mountain (2,533 m/8,300 ft) and Mount Evans and is fed by the Teaquahan Glacier. As the stream spills over a sheer precipice into the Teaquahan River it divides into two separate plunges of equal volume about 70 m (230 ft) high. Maximum discharge is during the spring snowmelt and following heavy rains but flow is maintained through the summer by the glacier. During the summer the twin plunges descend in lacy pulses that race each other to the bottom.

A Guide to BC's Best 100 Falls

COAST RANGE

Twin Falls #1

Snapshot: The head of Bute Inlet and the Homathko River are at the epicentre of the Coast Range Mountains, with the highest peak in the Coast Range, Mt. Waddington, rising to 4,016 m (13,181 ft) off to the northwest and the Homathko Icefield to the northeast. The scenery in the vicinity is of epic proportions with high, precipitous mountains, icefields, glaciers and wild wilderness rivers.

Waterfalls of British Columbia

Twin Falls is a true wilderness falls, extremely remote, difficult to access and little known and visited. Consequently, it is with a real sense of achievement that you stand before its twin plunges.

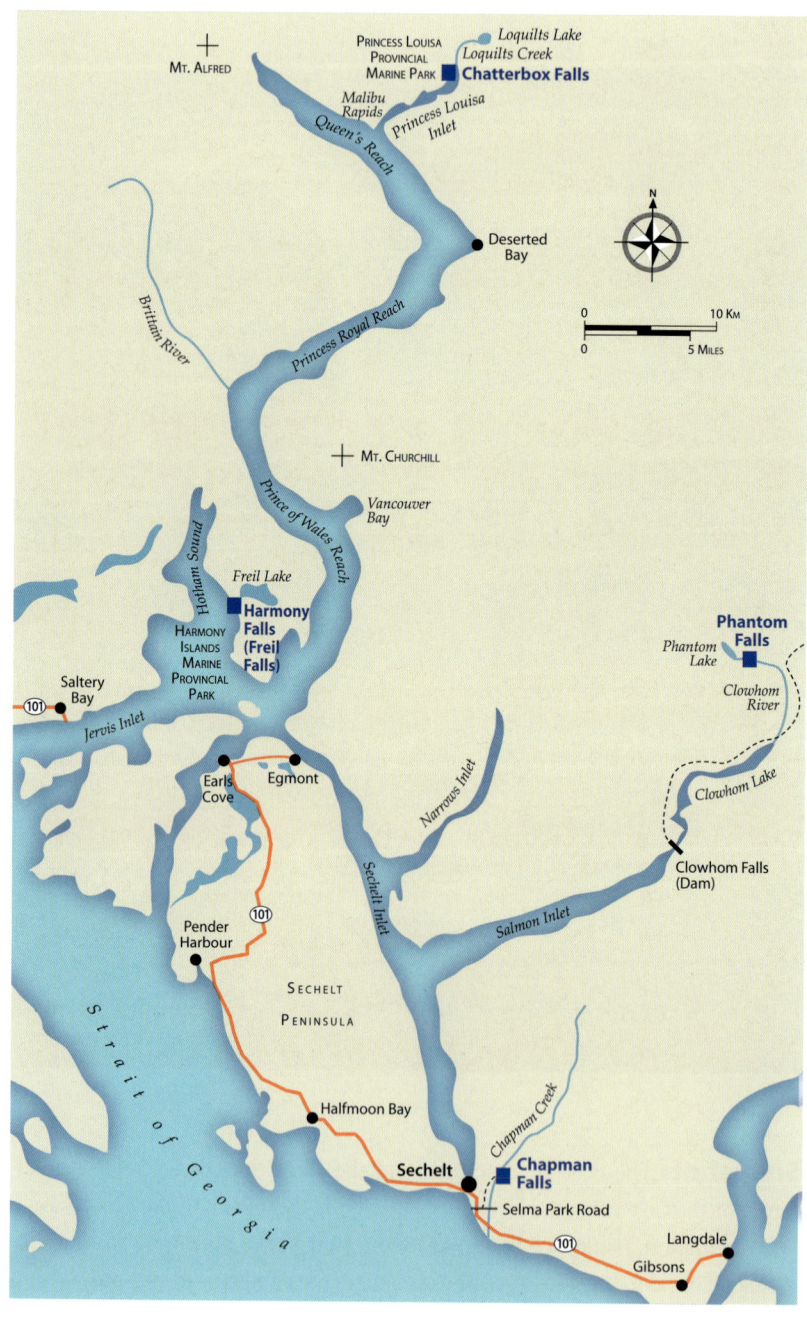

FALLS 9–12

9 CHATTERBOX FALLS

Rating: ▲▲▲▲▲
Type: Plunge
Location: At the head of Princess Louisa Inlet, an arm of Jervis Inlet
Access: Difficult. Water or air access only
Status: Princess Louisa Provincial Marine Park
When to go: Year-round

Directions: Daily scheduled excursions operate from Egmont in the summer. Charter boats can be hired in Pender Harbour and Egmont (Sunshine Coast Tours, 1-800-870-9055, High Tide Tours, 604-883-9220 and Malaspina Water Taxi, 604-989-2628).

By private boat or kayak follow Jervis Inlet to Princess Louisa Inlet. Extreme caution is advised for all vessels navigating Malibu Rapids as the tidal rip can reach 10 knots. Prior knowledge of slack tide is recommended. The nearest put-in is at Egmont, 65 km (40 mi) distant. Kayakers should note a strong prevailing outflow wind on many summer afternoons in Jervis Inlet.

Scheduled or charter float plane service to the wharf at Princess Louisa Inlet is available from Sechelt or directly from Vancouver.

Chatterbox Falls

Facilities: Wharf, campsites, toilets, firepits, picnic tables, fresh water, gazebo, hiking trail.

Highlights: Princess Louisa Inlet and Chatterbox Falls have a variety of seasonal moods. Summertime is high tourist season when the inlet displays its splendour to visitors from around the world and the wharf at Princess Louisa Inlet Marine Park is crowded with expensive boats. The inlet is a particular favourite of the Seattle boating community. On flawless, blue-skied, mid-summer days, time stands still inside Malibu Rapids as the vertical walls, their narrow entrance guarded by the rapids, create an otherworldly ambiance within the inlet. If there is a Shangri-La on the west coast of Canada, then Princess Louisa Inlet is it.

Water flow is at the maximum in the springtime, as the snow melts from the surrounding high mountains and as many as 60 minor waterfalls dribble down the monolithic granite walls of the fjord. Solitude is possible at this time before the summer rush. In the fall peace returns to the inlet as the maples turn golden and fresh snow skiffs the peaks again. Winter has two faces. On days of grey, wet, frontal weather the clouds languish against the walls of the fjord, perspective blurs, and the rock faces stream with the countless silver threads of ephemeral waterfalls. Winter high-pressure systems bring cold, clear weather, and the inlet becomes a winter wonderland. After a few days of freezing weather the head of the inlet may be covered with ice, and then close approach to the falls is impossible.

Any discussion of Chatterbox Falls is inextricably linked to its setting at the head of Princess Louisa Inlet, widely recognized as one of the most scenic places on the planet. The Shishalh (Sechelt First Nation) thought of the inlet as "a sacred place, appreciated more for its spiritual character than any particular resource value," and many current visitors would agree with that assessment. The Shishalh named the inlet *suivoolot*, meaning sunny and warm.

At the head of the inlet is its crowning glory, the spectacular, 30 m (100 ft) Chatterbox Falls. Chatterbox Falls might even be the most famous waterfall in BC in terms of name recognition. It is neither the biggest, nor the most spectacular, nor the most visited, but it has a fame that equals or surpasses other contenders such as Della, Helmcken or Takakkaw. Its own attributes are relatively modest, but a calculating god saw fit to place it at the head of the most magical fjord in the world.

Chatterbox Falls is located on Loquilts Creek, which flows from an alpine area to the east. A hiking trail follows the creek to Loquilts Lake and beyond to high snowfields and peaks. This trail is also the route for a multi-day traverse over the ridge to the Elaho River and the Squamish area. The name Chatterbox Falls was bestowed by James "Mac" Macdonald, who lived by the falls from 1927 until 1972 and who is forever associated with Princess Louisa Inlet. It was an inspired choice, based on Mac's observation that "there was an ever-changing rhythm in the falling water… the falls were always talking or chattering so that's why I gave them the name."

Despite the grandeur of the location the falls are no stranger to tragedy and the warning sign posted by BC Parks should be heeded: "Danger: Do not go near the top of the falls. The surrounding flat rocks are moss covered and slippery. Thirteen people have lost their lives by not observing this warning."

For further reading on Princess Louisa Inlet and Chatterbox Falls see *Beyond Understanding*, by William H. Schweizer.

Snapshot: One pristine April day in 1980 a crew of tree planters on a day off from a planting project near Malibu Rapids were relaxing by the falls. Suddenly a powerful speedboat came up the inlet and a person with a sheaf of papers jumped ashore. To the astonishment of everyone present they were informed that it was Census Day in Canada. After much filling in of forms, the population of Princess Louisa Inlet was enumerated at twelve in 1980.

Numerous people have tried to describe the beauty of Princess Louisa Inlet, but the most eloquent attempt was that of Erle Stanley Gardner (of Perry Mason fame). Gardner wrote, "There is no use describing that Inlet. Perhaps an atheist could view it and remain an atheist, but I doubt it." Other people refer to it as the Eighth Wonder of the World.

10 HARMONY FALLS (FREIL FALLS)

Rating:	▲▲▲▲△
Type:	Tiered plunges and cascades
Location:	Hotham Sound, an arm of lower Jervis Inlet
Access:	Difficult. Water access only
Status:	Provincial Forest
When to go:	Year-round

Directions: The falls are clearly visible at a distance of about 8 km (5 mi), looking north into Hotham Sound from the Earls Cove–Saltery Bay BC Ferries route between the lower Sunshine Coast and the Powell River area. The foot of the falls can be reached by private boat, charter boat or kayak from put-ins at Egmont (closest at 12 km/7.5 mi), Pender Harbour, Earls Cove or Saltery Bay.

Facilities: None. The nearby Harmony Islands Provincial Marine Park has protected anchorage for mariners.

Highlights: Harmony (Freil) Falls has a total drop of 427 m (1,400 ft) and a longest single drop of 259 m (850 ft) as it descends directly out of Freil Lake into the salt water of Hotham Sound. The large lake is not visible from the water; it drains the peninsula of land between Hotham Sound and the Prince of Wales Reach of Jervis Inlet.

In the 1980s a commercial proposal was made to load fresh water directly from Harmony Falls into bulk-water vessels for export to California. The proposal ran into a host of regulatory and environmental concerns and was shelved. The main environmental concern was the introduction of foreign water and its associated organisms from the ballast tanks of the vessels into Jervis Inlet.

Waterfalls of British Columbia

Harmony Falls

    The falls are visible at all times of the year from the Earls Cove–Saltery Bay ferry and especially after torrential winter rains when the water volume increases radically. Discharge is also high during the springtime snowmelt. During the summer the water volume decreases until the first fall rains, but the summer months are an idyllic time to visit Hotham Sound and its great waterfall.

A Guide to BC's Best 100 Falls

Snapshot: I have seen Harmony Falls innumerable times in all seasons. Its many moods range from the refined strand of silver set amid gloriously dense greens and blues on pristine summer mornings, to the wild, unrestrained outpourings after December monsoons when the mountains and waters of Jervis Inlet vaguely define themselves in a hundred shades of grey.

At the eleventh hour of the eleventh day of the eleventh month of 1998 I was aboard the Earls Cove–Saltery Bay ferry when the captain announced that the ferry would be coming to a halt for two minutes in remembrance of the armistice. For those two minutes we stopped in the middle of Jervis Inlet with Harmony Falls in full view, and as I contemplated the unending flow of the water over the falls, the eternal sacrifice of those who gave their lives in the great wars of the last century came into sharp context.

I once had the opportunity to hover alongside the main plunge of Harmony Falls in a helicopter for a truly spectacular perspective of this high waterfall.

11 PHANTOM FALLS

Rating:	▲▲▲▲△
Type:	Plunge/cascade
Location:	On the Clowhom River, NE of Sechelt
Access:	Very difficult. Boat or float plane, plus long hike or cycle
Status:	Provincial forest
When to go:	Summer. High water in late spring or early summer

Directions: The head of Salmon Inlet is accessible by personal boat or kayak, a distance of 32 km (20 mi) from Sechelt. Scheduled or charter float plane service or charter water taxi service is also available from Sechelt. From the head of the inlet, the waterfall is a further 31 km (19 mi) up the Clowhom River via a mainline logging road that closely approaches the falls. This distance must be hiked or cycled, or it might be possible to hitch a ride with the logging company. The waterfall is clearly visible from the road, but to reach the falls it is necessary to bushwhack upstream alongside the river. The approach to the foot of the falls is via the north side of the river as impregnable sheer cliffs protect the south side. Close approach to the base of the falls is difficult until the deep snowpack in the back end of the Clowhom Valley has melted, which is likely to be late June in most years.

Facilities: None

Highlights: At the head of Salmon Inlet and clearly visible from the water is the late, lamented Clowhom Falls. The Clowhom River was dammed in 1950 and the

Phantom Falls. John Humphries photo

dam now impounds the 10 km (6 mi) long Clowhom Lake. Today barely a trickle of water normally flows in the spot that once was one of BC's greatest falls. At times of high water in the lake, usually during the spring freshet or winter monsoons, the floodgates are periodically opened and Clowhom Falls is temporarily restored to its former wild and unrestrained glory as a long, river-wide cascade.

The Clowhom Valley has beautiful scenery, though much modified by logging. Especially memorable are the views of the south aspect of the Tantalus Range that rises to 2,605 m (8,547 ft) and towers above the river valley.

A Guide to BC's Best 100 Falls

Phantom Falls are so named because the Clowhom River above the falls drains the magnificent subalpine Phantom Lake. The falls are set amid spectacular Coast Range scenery of green forests and high snowfields. The river spills through a notch and tumbles down a high headwall via a cascade that leads to the main 100 m (330 ft) plunge. At the foot of the falls a plunge pool is followed by a lower cascade.

Clowhom Falls

Snapshot: One pristine blue October day I was flying into Vancouver International Airport from northern BC, enjoying the magnificent vistas of the Coast Range stretching to far horizons. However, a temperature inversion and resultant fog pervaded the Strait of Georgia and the airport, so we were put into a holding pattern over the Sunshine Coast. Our plane did a couple of circuits from Howe Sound to Jervis Inlet and back and I scanned the view trying to identify rivers, mountains and other features. I located Clowhom Lake and the prominent white slash of Phantom Falls highlighted against the green forest with its source, Phantom Lake, just off to the west, a unique panoramic view of this remote waterfall.

12 CHAPMAN FALLS

Rating:	▲▲▲▲△
Type:	Tiered plunges and cascades
Location:	Near Sechelt, on the Sunshine Coast
Access:	Moderate. Short, rough road, 2 km (1 mi) of level trail
Status:	Provincial forest and Sunshine Coast Regional District watershed
When to go:	Year-round

Directions: From the traffic light at Wharf Road and Hwy 101 in Sechelt follow Hwy 101 south for 1.9 km (1.2 mi) and turn left up the hill at Selma Park Road. After 400 m (440 yd) take the first left turn onto a rough, gravel road and proceed about 600 m (660 yd) to the power line. Pass under the power line, bear left and skirt a reservoir for 200 m (220 yd). Park here at the gate and walk in about 2 km (1 mi) to the first view of the falls.

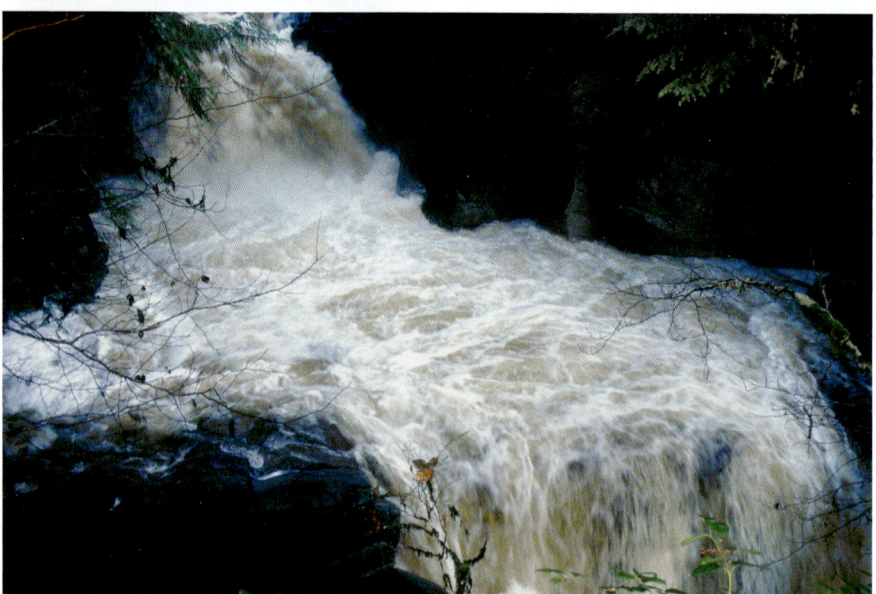

Chapman Falls, tier 1 (top) and tier 2–3 (above)

Facilities: None

Highlights: This highly complex waterfall has four tiers, comprising a cascade, two plunges and another cascade. A beautiful miniature canyon, shallow, golden pools and deep, dark plunge pools coexist within a steep-sided valley encircled by old-growth trees. The big Douglas firs and western red cedars have stood undisturbed on the steep slopes here for centuries, but windfall is beginning to take a toll. The Chapman Falls area is not pristine; the site was previously the main water intake for the Sunshine Coast, and is blessed with some water pipes and concrete work.

As you approach the falls, the first sight is of the lowest of the four drops, a cascade. Just past this viewpoint the trail crosses the first of two curving trestles that carry a large diameter water pipe. Across the trestles and 50 m (50 yd) on, the trail leads to a viewpoint beside the creek at the topmost of the four falls. At this spot Chapman Creek emerges from a miniature canyon 30 m (100 ft) long and 2–3 m (6.5–10 ft) wide, with walls 3–4 m (10–13 ft) high. It is possible, with a little scrambling, to explore alongside this sunless canyon, where the creek flows deep, dark and languid before it enters the series of falls. At the top of the first falls is a shallow pool, wonderfully golden in the sunshine.

The uppermost falls is a 5 m (16 ft) cascade that flows down the bedrock and divides around a residual rock before entering a pool. The smooth granite bedrock is impregnated with dark igneous dykes. The second falls is a 3 m (10 ft) block plunge that enters a very deep, black, plunge pool surrounded by high canyon walls. A ledge of smooth granite with rounded, sculpted runnels where the water swish-swashes perennially contains the pool. At low water the creek exits this pool on the left side, but at high water the whole ledge is engulfed. More igneous intrusions here create patterns in the light-coloured granite.

As it leaves the pool, the creek pours over the precipice in a 10 m (33 ft) plunge into a scoured, narrow canyon before the final 7 m (23 ft) cascade, which is the falls first observed as you approach on the trail. On your return to this spot you can look back and observe parts of the four components of this convoluted waterfall.

The separate parts of Chapman Falls can all be closely approached by short side trails, but caution is advised as there are steep, slippery sections and dangerous edges.

Snapshot: Chapman Falls is my personal local waterfall and beauty spot. I first made its acquaintance in May 1969, soon after I arrived in BC and Canada, and it became an instant icon for all that is beautiful and wild about British Columbia. On that day in 1969 I actually took a dip in the freezing waters of the spring snow-melt, and in retrospect it was something of a baptism, or a rebirth. Since that day I have visited countless times in all seasons and weathers and the thrill remains undiminished.

Chapman Falls has been a constant in my life for 40 years now and is central to all that I hold dear about BC. It is the essence of BC and the inspiration behind this book.

Waterfalls of British Columbia

FALLS 13–21

13 SHANNON FALLS

Rating:	▲▲▲▲▲
Type:	Cascade
Location:	Hwy 99, 2 km (1 mi) S of Squamish, 58 km (36 mi) N of Vancouver, 39.5 km (24.5 mi) N of Horseshoe Bay
Access:	Easy. 350 m (380 yd) trail to foot of falls
Status:	Shannon Falls Provincial Park
When to go:	Year-round

Directions: Take Hwy 99, the Sea to Sky Highway, from Vancouver to Squamish. Shannon Falls Provincial Park is beside the highway 2 km (1 mi) south of Squamish.

Shannon Falls

Facilities: Parking (including oversized vehicles), picnic tables and group picnic facilities, restrooms, water fountain, concession shop, lawns, trails with logging artifacts and interpretive signage. The facilities and the base of the falls are wheelchair accessible. There is a restaurant and commercial campsite directly across the highway.

Highlights: The short trail and stairway lead to a viewing platform in a spectacular location at the foot of the falls. From here you peer up into the sky and see most, but not all, of Shannon Falls as it cascades down the sheer cliff face. At 335 m (1,100 ft), Shannon Falls is the sixth highest waterfall in BC. Shannon Creek tumbles in a wild torrent down a monolithic granite wall of the famous Stawamus Chief, formed as a batholith 93 million years ago when magma solidified beneath the earth's surface and metamorphosed into the present granitic rock. Subsequent denudation of the overlying rock has left The Chief sitting imperiously 650 m (2,130 ft) above present-day Squamish, a lure for rock climbers from around the world and a destination for 50,000 hikers a year. Shannon Creek collects water from Mt. Habrich and Sky Pilot before plunging down the precipice of its hanging valley. The valley was formed when a Pleistocene river of ice up to 2,000 m (6,500 ft) deep flowed out of the Squamish Valley 15,000 to 25,000 years ago and sculpted the present dramatic scenery. Howe Sound is one of the most southerly fjords in the northern hemisphere.

The trail to the foot of the falls is through a second-growth forest of cedar, hemlock, alder and broad-leafed maple. Watch also for Douglas maple in the understory, a brushy species with tiny, maple-shaped leaves that turn colourful in late October. Vestiges of the giant old-growth forest remain in the cedar stumps with the telltale springboard notches that show where old-time loggers worked with their crosscut saws some 90 years ago. An American dipper frequents the creek below the falls, winter wrens sing from the forest floor and look for evidence of red-breasted sapsuckers in the lines of holes drilled into the bark of the hemlocks. Interpretive signage along the trail informs of the tailed frog, the only North American amphibian that inhabits cold, fast-flowing streams. The frogs are silent, nocturnal and retiring, so a sighting is unlikely.

Maximum flows occur during winter monsoons and during spring runoff (peak in May), when the snow is melting in the upper reaches of Shannon Creek. The volume of water is greatly reduced by late summer. The park is an extremely popular roadside attraction with almost half a million annual visits, most through the summer months. In the winter you could have the whole park to yourself.

Shannon Falls was once known as Fairy Falls, but the creek and falls were renamed after William Shannon, a Squamish pioneer who operated the largest hop farm in the valley, near Brackendale. Squamish hops were reputed to be among the best in the world, and much of the crop was exported to the United Kingdom. The connection with the brewing industry was maintained into the 1970s when the Shannon Falls site was acquired by the Carling O'Keefe company, which used the water in brewing their Heidelberg brand beer. In 1982 Carling donated the land to BC Parks.

A Squohomish (Squamish) Indian legend tells of a two-headed sea serpent, Say-noth-kai, who lived in Howe Sound, travelled on both land and water and created the spillway of the falls by slithering and twisting up through the rock.

Snapshot: I have visited Shannon Falls many times in all seasons and weathers to experience its many moods. I have stood alone at the foot of the falls on a grey, dripping, November afternoon after three days of torrential rain and seen the cascade transformed into an out of control maelstrom of cold, white foam with blasts of icy air full of vaporized water assaulting the observation deck. This violent, watery holocaust is a stark contrast to the scene on idyllic August afternoons when T-shirted tourists gather to admire the gentle sliver of silver water descending from the azure sky. On June evenings a visit to the falls will be accompanied by the spine-tingling songs of Swainson's and varied thrushes, two of the finest songsters of the coastal forest. In early November 2002, after a long, dry summer and the driest October on record, so little water flowed down the wall that the mighty Shannon Falls was almost stilled.

In 1792 when Capt. George Vancouver first explored the coast of British Columbia he set up camp just west of Shannon Falls, and despite the enormous changes along the Sea to Sky Highway, Shannon Falls has remained essentially unchanged since then. From a geological point of view, this notable landform was created over a short period of time during the Ice Age, only a few thousand years ago.

Directly across the highway from Shannon Falls, The Roadhouse restaurant affords patrons what is unequivocally "the best view of a waterfall while dining" to be found anywhere in BC. Ask for a window table to enjoy the spectacular view.

14 HIGH CREEK FALLS

Rating:	▲▲▲▲△
Type:	Tiered plunge
Location:	37 km (23 mi) N of Squamish
Access:	Moderate. Logging road and steep hike
Status:	Provincial forest
When to go:	Spring, summer, fall

Directions: From the traffic light at the intersection of Hwy 99 and downtown Squamish drive north for 10 km (6 mi) and turn left (west) onto Squamish

High Creek Falls upper plunge. Tim Gage photo

Valley Road, across from the turnoff to Alice Lake Provincial Park. Keep left at the Y-junction after 3.7 km (2.3 mi) and proceed to the end of the blacktop, 32.7 km (20.3 mi) from your start point. After 1.3 km (0.8 mi) the Ashlu bridge is to the left, but stay right on the main line to a BC Hydro powerhouse at 3.6 km (2.2 mi). Park in the wide spot immediately before the High Falls Creek bridge, 0.8 km (0.5 mi) beyond here.

Walk across the bridge and locate the trailhead on an old road to the right. Look for a small sign indicating the High Falls Trail and some flagging tape. The hike/scramble to the lower viewpoint takes about 35 minutes. This route is not for everyone; the trail ascends a series of bluffs, some so steep that you must scramble with the aid of fixed ropes to pull yourself up. Dogs may have trouble finding a route. Pay close attention, as the trail and viewpoints are perilously close to a fatal abyss if you misstep. A fatality occurred here in 1994. This hike is not suitable for children. It is possible to make a longer circular route by taking a trail from above the third viewpoint that leads to the High Falls logging road.

Facilities: None

Highlights: High Falls Creek powers down a sensationally rugged canyon that is a contender for "most rugged" in a province full of them. The creek descends from the upper slopes of 2,130 m (6,990 ft) Tricouni Peak, with the lower slopes of Cloudburst Mountain forming its precipitous southern wall. The canyon walls in the vicinity of the falls are 200 m (660 ft) vertical cliffs.

The main plunge is about 100 m (330 ft) high, but the impossible geography precludes any views of the entire waterfall. The lowest of the three viewpoints provides the best, but still incomplete, views of this difficult-to-observe behemoth. This first viewpoint is just a few metres off the trail, and by hanging on to a conveniently located rock you can peer over the edge into the dizzying depths of the chasm. The middle viewpoint is about 50 m (55 yd) off the trail and affords a vantage at the mid-point of the main plunge. From here you can also observe the upper plunge as it falls into the pool above the main drop. The upper viewpoint allows a full view of the upper falls, notable for a car-sized rock that is wedged between the canyon walls, forcing the creek to flow under and around it.

Just beyond the third viewpoint a short side trail to the left leads to a treeless bluff with panoramic views of the Squamish River Valley and the peaks of the Tantalus Range. The final destination is the bluffs above the upper falls, from where the backside of the big rock can be seen.

Snapshot: High Creek Falls is spectacular, but the total package of this hike, including the extreme nature of the canyon and the exquisite views of classic Coast Range scenery, make this a memorable outing. I visited on a warm, sunny, blue day in late November and after absorbing the noise, motion and intensity of the falls and the canyon we adjourned to the sunny bluff above the third viewpoint. We surveyed the magnificent scenery of the braided Squamish River flanked by its cottonwood-clothed floodplain and the ice-gouged walls of the valley that rise to the snowy heights of mounts Tantalus (2,605 m/8,547 ft), Alpha, Zenith, Ossa and Pelion.

From this viewpoint you can also see three waterfalls on Sigurd (Crooked Falls), Madden and Mawby creeks as they tumble down their hanging valleys. On the day I visited we watched as a kettle of 10 bald eagles rode on a thermal, the vanguard of the world-famous gathering of thousands of bald eagles in the Squamish Valley.

15 BRANDYWINE FALLS

Rating:	▲▲▲▲▲
Type:	Plunge
Location:	Beside Hwy 99, 47 km (30 mi) N of Squamish, 13 km (8 mi) S of Whistler
Access:	Easy. 400 m (440 yd), five-minute walk on level trail
Status:	Brandywine Falls Provincial Park
When to go:	Year-round

Directions: Brandywine Falls Provincial Park is on the east side of the Sea to Sky Highway, 47 km (30 mi) north of Squamish. The park is well-posted in the

Waterfalls of British Columbia

summer, but the park signs are removed in the winter. In winter look for a wide parking area on the east side of the road 200 m (220 yd) after crossing the railroad tracks. The trail from the parking lot to the falls observation deck is 400 m (440 yd) long and about a five-minute walk.

Brandywine Falls

It is possible to visit the base of Brandywine Falls. From the railway crossing on Hwy 99 just south of the park, locate a small creek 200 m (220 yd) further to the south. Follow the creek downslope toward Brandywine Canyon. This side creek has eroded a gap in the sheer canyon wall, which allows access to Brandywine Creek. Use caution when walking here on the loose, unstable talus blocks. When you reach the creek, use the log-jam to cross to the other side and then walk upstream. After about 200 m (220 yd), climb the low bank and find the trail that leads toward the falls. Allow about one hour to reach the base of the falls. This route may be more difficult, or impossible, during high water and is not recommended in the winter and spring.

Facilities: Provincial park campground, picnic tables, pit toilets, trails. The campground is open from mid-May to mid-October.

Highlights: This is unquestionably one of BC's most beautiful waterfalls, as Brandywine Creek flows with great equanimity over a high precipice. The magnificent falls, 70 m (230 ft) high, is a classic of the plunge form, supremely elegant in its simplicity and perfectly formed with "nary a hair out of place."

There are competing stories about the naming of the falls. One version has it that in 1910 two railway surveyors, Jack Nelson and Bob Mollison, wagered for a bottle of brandy who could estimate most accurately the height of the falls. They measured the height with a chain and Mollison won the bottle, but Nelson named the falls Brandywine. The word brandy is actually the shortened form of brandywine.

Another version has it that around 1890 two old-timers, Charles Chandler and George Mitchell, were on their way to a trapline for the winter. They stopped at the falls to brew some tea and also partook of a bottle of brandy and a bottle of wine, with the result that they passed out at the falls for an entire day.

The hike to the falls is through a Douglas fir and lodgepole pine forest alongside Brandywine Creek. Just before the observation deck the trail crosses the BC Rail tracks and you may have to wait while the boxcars roll leisurely by (and in the process catch the piney fragrance of BC forest products heading to distant export markets).

The observation deck is perched spectacularly on the edge of a 100 m (330 ft) high precipice that allows superb views of the falls and the great plunge pool. The escarpment of columnar basalt was formed when molten lava collided with ice. Basalt typically produces classically beautiful waterfalls with high sheer drops and deeply eroded plunge pools. Brandywine Falls is the epitome of the type.

For waterfall aficionados the trip to the foot of the falls is well worth the effort, as the experience, and the photographic opportunities, are so different from the conventional view from the observation deck. As with all high waterfalls that drop into a confined canyon, the experience of being close to the falling maelstrom can be overwhelming. These are cold, wet, noisy, hostile environments, far removed from the picturesque photo ops from distant viewpoints. Water volume is highest during early summer snowmelt or after winter rains. Choosing a time to visit the falls involves this question: do you enjoy the camera-toting summer crowds or winter solitude in the sometimes-snowy rainforest? Both are recommended.

In the 1970s Brandywine Falls starred in one of the first major movies filmed in BC, *The Trap,* in which Oliver Reed was attacked by a black bear at the brink of the falls.

Snapshot: The three major waterfalls beside the Sea to Sky Highway are a study in contrasts. Shannon Falls is a wild, unrestrained plummet down a high, chaotic cliff. Nairn Falls to the north is a convoluted rampage through a constricted canyon, while Brandywine Falls has the classical, refined elegance of a fine wine or brandy.

On a trip to the foot of the falls I offered my hiking companion a bottle of wine plus a bottle of brandy if he would circumnavigate behind the falling water. He declined.

16 ALEXANDER FALLS

Rating:	▲▲▲▲△
Type:	Plunge/cascade
Location:	55 km (34 mi) N of Squamish,
	12 km (7.5 mi) S of Whistler
Access:	Easy. Rough-surfaced logging road
Status:	BC Forest Service Recreation Site
When to go:	Spring, summer, fall

Facilities: A bench is strategically located for relaxed viewing of the falls. There is an outhouse, table and barbeque pit at the parking lot.

Directions: 12 km (7.5 mi) south of Whistler, or 4 km (2.5 mi) north of Brandywine Falls Provincial Park turn west off Hwy 99 onto the Callaghan Forest Service Road, and proceed 8.4 km (5.2 mi) on the main line to the second spur road to the left. There is a small, blue trail marker at the junction. Drive in 200 m (220 yd) to the BC Forest Service Recreation Site. The fenced viewpoint is adjacent to the parking at the end of the road. Be alert for possible logging traffic on the main road. Any vehicle can drive the road, while slowly circumventing the potholes. Given that the Callaghan Valley is a major site for the 2010 Winter Olympic Games, the valley and the access are destined for significant upgrades in the near future.

A Guide to BC's Best 100 Falls

Alexander Falls

Highlights: This is a complex waterfall that changes appearance depending on the volume of water flow. The Callaghan Forest Service Road may be snowbound until June 1 in some years. Maximum flow is in late spring and early summer as the snow melts, or again in the fall and early winter after the rains begin. Flow is reduced through the summer, but this remains an attractive waterfall.

The 43 m (140 ft) high falls consists of six separate steps framed by the crumbling basalt of the headwall. The dominant attribute of the upper steps is the plunge, while the lower steps are cascades. The central plunge from the third step actually falls past the fourth and fifth steps, while both wings of the falls are cascading.

The waterfall is on Madeley Creek, just above its confluence with Callaghan Creek. The Callaghan Valley supports an old-growth forest of yellow cedar, balsam and hemlock and the air is full of the distinctive aromatic scent of yellow cedar. There is a magnificent view of the iconic Black Tusk in Garibaldi Provincial Park, as you drive out of the valley back toward the highway.

Snapshot: On a mid-August visit Vaux's swifts were flying over the falls, and delectable mountain blueberries and black huckleberries were available in abundance around the parking lot.

17 SOO FALLS

Rating:	▲▲▲▲△△
Type:	Plunge and cascade
Location:	On the Soo River, N of Whistler
Access:	Moderate. Good 2WD logging road, short hike through timber
Status:	Provincial forest
When to go:	Spring, summer, fall

Directions: At 16.2 km (10 mi) north of Whistler Junction, turn west (left) onto the Soo River–Sixteen Mile Creek Branch Forest Service Road. This road may be active with logging traffic, so drive with headlights on and exercise caution. After 3.4 km (2 mi) along the south side of the Soo River with the impressive Soo Bluffs looming overhead, take the spur to the right that leads to a bridge across the river. There is a BC Hydro weir just above the bridge. From the bridge drive exactly 12 km (7.5 mi) to a logging road gate and park in a wide pullout on the left of the road.

Soo Falls

The observant traveller will have noted an obscure sign nailed to a tree in the old-growth forest just before the gate that reads "Soo Falls Scenic Reserve." To reach the falls hike for about five minutes from the pullout through the timber in the direction of the river, and eventually the roar of the falls will indicate your destination. The easiest route from the parking lot delivers you to the top of the falls, where you can sit on a rock and look down at the two drops. From here there is a spectacular view downstream to the snowcaps of Mount Currie (2,595 m/8,500 ft) and Hibachi Ridge, on the opposite side of Hwy 99.

Facilities: None

Highlights: This is a major but little known and little visited BC waterfall. The wide, whitewater Soo River squeezes through a 2 m (6.5 ft) cleft into a short roiling canyon, powers over an 8 m (26 ft) plunge into a turbulent pool, splits around a rock and falls in a wild 10 m (33 ft) cascade with multiple tall roostertails. A whitewater plunge pool becomes a leisurely, jade green stretch of the river. As with many other waterfalls, a couple of beached logs high above the river are evidence of periodic very high water here.

For good viewpoints of the middle and lower sections of the falls it is necessary to bushwhack. The middle viewpoint is particularly difficult, but access is possible to a craggy outcrop in the spray zone. The brush here is covered with dried glacial "flour" from the river. There are good spots to view the lower falls from the flat riverbank. When I visited late on a July day an intense rainbow was visible over the lower pool and an American dipper and a great blue heron were fishing.

Snapshot: Soo Falls is rarely visited, as evidenced by the lack of any trail from the road to the falls, and it is a welcome contrast to the other busy waterfall destinations of the Sea to Sky Highway. The fragrance of the undisturbed hemlock and balsam old-growth forest and the wilderness ambiance of the spot is complete and haunting.

18 NAIRN FALLS

Rating:	▲▲▲▲△
Type:	Tiered plunge
Location:	Beside Hwy 99, 32 km (20 mi) N of Whistler, 3 km (2 mi) S of Pemberton
Access:	Moderate. 1.5 km (1 mi) dirt trail, a 20-minute walk
Status:	Nairn Falls Provincial Park
When to go:	Year-round

Waterfalls of British Columbia

Nairn Falls

Directions: Nairn Falls Provincial Park is 34 km (21 mi) north of Whistler on the east side of Hwy 99. The easy trail from the parking lot to the falls runs alongside the Green River.

Facilities: Parking, toilets, tent/vehicle and group campsites, picnic tables, interpretive signage.

Highlights: The trail to the falls parallels the rushing waters of the Green River as it cuts through a jagged gorge that was the ancestral route of the Lil'wat Nation and of the early European settlers who crossed the river here on the way to Mt. Currie. Along the trail the canopy of lofty Douglas fir veterans and western red cedars supply shade on hot summer afternoons, and their boughs frame spectacular views of Mt. Currie (2,595 m/8,500 ft), which dominates this corner of the world. The understory shrub level species are indicative of the transitional forest between the wet coastal type and the dry interior, with many of the dry indicator species present including paper birch, Douglas maple and box, with stonecrop on the hot, bare, arid rocks at the falls.

The falls are a complex creation as the Green River twists and threads its way through a sinuous 50 m (165 ft) keyhole canyon, probably originally following fractures in the granite. There are two separate drops, each about 10 m (30 ft) high, joined by a boiling cauldron of white water that narrows to only 2 m (6.5 ft) at one point. The total drop at the falls is about 60 m (200 ft). A rock bridge and numerous large potholes stud the canyon, some now high and dry above the river. Logs and debris are abandoned high above the water in crevices and ledges, evidence of the tumult here when the river is in flood. Nairn Falls is a textbook example of powerful fluvial forces at work.

On the canyon walls bonsai fir, cedar and pine struggle to maintain existence in a hostile environment, but splotches of purple penstemon and golden arnica appear in June. The park is also home to the secretive rubber boa snake. In June and July listen for the enthusiastic song of the common but drab warbling vireo.

Nairn Falls, like many other BC waterfalls, has seen its share of tragedies over the years. In the late 1980s alone a kayaker missed the pullout, there was a suicide

COAST RANGE

A Guide to BC's Best 100 Falls

and a woman from California accidentally fell in. Protective fencing is now in place for the benefit of the many visitors to the viewing areas.

Snapshot: On a hot August afternoon the trail was filled with a piney woods fragrance and it was delightful to drop off the trail and sit on a rock beside the cool, jade-coloured waters of the Green River. At the falls, the river seethed and imploded skyward while dragonflies played in the mist.

19 LIZZIE FALLS

Rating:	▲▲▲▲△
Type:	Cascade
Location:	E side of Lillooet Lake, E of Pemberton
Access:	Difficult. Rough 2WD or 4WD, walk or 4WD to viewpoint
Status:	Provincial forest
When to go:	Spring, summer, fall

Directions: From Pemberton Junction drive 6.7 km (4 mi) on Hwy 99 (the Duffey Lake Road) to Mount Currie. Continue on Hwy 99 toward Lillooet for 10 km (6 mi). Watch for Lillooet Lake Road on the right, now signed as the In-Shuck-Ch Forest Service Road. Proceed south alongside Lillooet Lake for 16 km (10 mi) to the Lizzie Creek FSR, just past the Lizzie Creek Recreation Site. The road beyond here is rough two-wheel drive with cross ditches. At 8.2 km (5 mi) look for a junction with an arrow pointing left to Lizzie Lake Recreation Site. Take this turn and almost immediately you will encounter a spur road to the right that is initially steep, rocky and growing in with slide alder. Either park here and walk in for 600 m (660 yd or six minutes), or engage four-wheel drive. The first 200 m (220 yd) of this road is the worst for both road conditions and slide alder. If you are concerned about brush scratches on your vehicle do not enter this road. The access may already be undriveable as the alder continues to encroach.

Lizzie Falls

63

Facilities: None. Lizzie Creek Recreation Site on Lillooet Lake and Lizzie Lake Recreation Site beyond the falls are both close by.

Highlights: The falls are on a branch of Lizzie Creek that drains Lizzie Lake. The creek plummets over a precipice in a spectacular, wide cascade about 66 m (220 feet) high, with a vertical crag looming beside it. The falls themselves are framed by old-growth timber, though surrounded by a regenerating clear-cut.

Snapshot: I tracked this waterfall from an X on a map in the Backroad Mapbook series. I had no idea whether to expect a major waterfall or merely a blip in the creek, so I was elated to find this spectacular beauty.

20 PLACE FALLS

Rating:	▲▲▲▲▲
Type:	High cascade/plunge
Location:	Near D'Arcy, NE of Pemberton
Access:	Moderate. Steep, rough, 30-minute hike to viewpoint
Status:	Provincial forest
When to go:	Spring, summer, fall

Directions: From Pemberton Junction drive 27.9 km (17.3 mi) on the D'Arcy Road (21.4 km/13.3 mi beyond Mount Currie) to a railway crossing. Immediately beyond the crossing look up to see the white slash of Place Falls high on the green mountainside to the right. Proceed a further 600 m (660 yd) to Anson Place on the right, and 20 m (22 yd) along Anson bear left onto the dirt track for 50 m (55 yd). Park at the rail tracks.

Cross the tracks, climb over the gate and follow the trail through the woods to the power line right-of-way. Walk to the right along the power line for a short distance and find where the trail enters the woods again. This path quickly leads to the east bank of Place Creek and a steep ascent alongside the creek on a rough trail that may be very slippery when wet.

Total hiking time is less than 30 minutes to the main viewpoint. Beyond here the trail continues alongside the falls giving access to its upper parts. Caution is advised. There are more exciting waterfall features above the main falls and the trail continues steeply to the snout of the Place Glacier at about 2,000 m (6,500 ft).

Facilities: None

Highlights: Place Falls can be viewed from the highway immediately after crossing the railway tracks and appears as a broad white cascade on the mountainside.

A Guide to BC's Best 100 Falls

However, hiking to this fabulous waterfall is strongly recommended. The trail beneath old-growth, transition zone Douglas fir delivers you to a precipice around the middle of the falls, bombarded with spray drifting from the plunge pool. Care should be exercised here, as the trail is wet and slippery.

This waterfall is a monster: a high, wide wall of water that cascades in its upper parts and plunges at the foot. It has an estimated total height of 70 m (230 ft) and is suggestive of Shannon Falls in the way it falls from on high out of a forested slope. The upper cascading section can be closely inspected and there are good views across the falls to a jagged pile of mountain peaks.

Beyond the top of the main falls Place Creek plunges, cascades and generally boils down a narrow, rugged canyon within 30 m (100 ft) walls. In total, the creek drops about 1,500 m (5,000 ft) in 3 km (2 mi) from the snout of the Place Glacier.

Place Falls

Snapshot: Even viewing this waterfall from the highway I had no idea of its powerful grandeur until I actually stood in the spray zone. I visited late in the day during a July heat wave and the meltwater from the Place Glacier was producing a very high discharge. I found myself involuntarily mouthing the word "Wow," genuinely shocked that such an enormous waterfall was previously unknown to me. It is a worthy equal of the three well-known waterfalls beside the Sea to Sky Highway–Shannon, Brandywine and Nairn–and should take its place (pun intended) among its better-known brethren.

The cool, drenching spray on the trail was a real bonus after a scorching hot day in the Pemberton Valley and the steep ascent up the trail.

21 KEYHOLE FALLS

Rating:	▲▲▲▲▲
Type:	Plunge
Location:	Upper reaches of the Lillooet River, NW of Pemberton
Access:	Difficult. 50 km (30 mi) of 2WD gravel logging road
Status:	Provincial forest
When to go:	Spring, summer, fall

Directions: From downtown Pemberton drive north on the Pemberton Valley Road for 23.5 km (14.6 mi). Turn right onto the Lillooet River FSR. After a few kilometres the Hurley Road splits off to the right and the Lillooet River Road continues along the east side of the river. The Meager Creek FSR, on the left at km 39 (mi 24), will take you to Meager Creek Hot Springs. Stay on the main line for another 11 km (7 mi) past here; at one point you will ford a shallow creek that flows across the road. At km 50 (mi 30) from the Pemberton Valley Road and FSR junction the road crosses the deep, narrow canyon of the river. Park here and walk in on the left side of the canyon on an indistinct trail. The trail goes in for about 200 m (220 yd) and leads to the headwall above the brink of the falls.

Facilities: None. Camping is available at Meager Creek Hot Springs Recreation Site at km 39 (mi 24) on the access road.

Highlights: Reaching Keyhole Falls from Vancouver involves driving through 200 km (125 mi) of magnificent Coast Range scenery. In many ways the scenery just gets better and better as the Sea to Sky Highway leads to the glorious Pemberton Valley and follows the Lillooet River as it runs upstream to its headwaters in the Pemberton Icefield. Perhaps the excellence of the drive is meant to compensate for the lack of views once you arrive, for it is impossible to actually view this waterfall from above.

A Guide to BC's Best 100 Falls

Keyhole Falls

Keyhole Falls is a rare and unique landform: it is one of BC's greatest waterfalls and a continentally significant feature. Although it is only 200 km (125 mi) from Vancouver, Keyhole Falls is largely unknown and rarely visited. Photographs of it are rare; I have only ever seen one published photograph taken from the base, and two shots taken from a helicopter.

The falls resulted from an eruption of Mount Meager about 2,350 years ago. In the aftermath of the eruption the Lillooet River was blocked with breccia to a height of about 100 m (330 ft) and impounded an upstream lake. The temporary dam was soon broken, which resulted in a catastrophic outburst flood that swept 15 m (50 ft) boulders as far as 3.5 km (2 mi) downstream. The flood was neither long nor large enough to complete the erosion of the entire breccia deposit and the remnant remains, about 500 m (1,600 ft) long with a gorge 30–40 m (100–130 ft) deep and 10 m (30 ft) wide. In places the long, sinuous canyon is only 2–4 m (6.5–13 ft) wide at the top, narrow enough to jump across (definitely not recommended). The Lillooet River is an extremely abrasive stream, loaded with silt and glacial flour accumulated in its headwaters within the Pemberton Icecap. Keyhole Falls is a very recent and temporary stage in the river's attempt to re-establish equilibrium here. As the river emerges from its keyhole canyon it plunges about 30 m (100 ft) to the plunge pool, with the dark incision of the 40 m (130 ft) slot above it.

Base of Keyhole Falls

Access: Difficult. For actual views of the falls it is necessary to follow a faint trail within the canyon below the falls. This requires crossing a number of steep, sliding slopes and involves an element of danger.

Directions: Just before the km 44 sign on the access road, and 200 m (220 yd) beyond the ford crossing of an unnamed creek, a spur road to the left leads into the campsite above the Pebble Creek hot springs. It is possible to bushwhack past the hot springs upstream toward the falls. A better route is to enter the forest about 400 m (440 yd) past the campsite spur and locate a faint trail that leads down into the canyon in the vicinity of where the sheer canyon wall ends. It takes about 90 minutes to hike in to the base of the falls.

The approach to the falls within the canyon is guarded by a series of steep talus slides, some of fine sandy material, and others of loose, round, rolling, tennis-ball sized talus debris. There is an element of danger here and extreme caution is urged. The best route is to stay along the foot of the canyon wall as closely as possible; this option will avoid the dense thickets of slide alder downslope. One hazard on this hike is the presence of stinging nettles, so long pants are mandatory, and a pair of gloves will also prevent discomfort.

By staying high along the bottom of the canyon wall you will reach a good vantage point close to the falls, but some may want to venture down to the river to experience the full enormity of the falls and the canyon. Close approach to the plunge pool guarantees a soaking in the spray zone.

A Guide to BC's Best 100 Falls

Highlights: The hike up the canyon is redolent of the access to the base of BC's greatest waterfall, Helmcken, with the same high, sheer, encompassing basalt walls. On our first successful outing, my hiking partner and I, not knowing the best route to follow, found ourselves bushwhacking through steep, almost impossible slide alder thickets. Suddenly we emerged to a full view of the waterfall plunging from its keyhole, dwarfed by the enormity of the canyon and its amphitheatre.

Snapshot: My first visit to Keyhole Falls, when I returned empty-handed, was a frustrating experience, but I did learn that an expedition up the canyon was necessary to observe the falls. Perhaps the most satisfying moment in the entire saga of writing this book was when I finally attained the base of Keyhole Falls. The improbable uniqueness and rarity of this great landform in its awe-inspiring setting of Promethean proportions was compounded by the knowledge that so few people had previously witnessed it. It was a pure "eureka" moment, suggestive of the feelings expressed by Samuel Prescott Fay when he stood before Kinuseo Falls (see Kinuseo Falls).

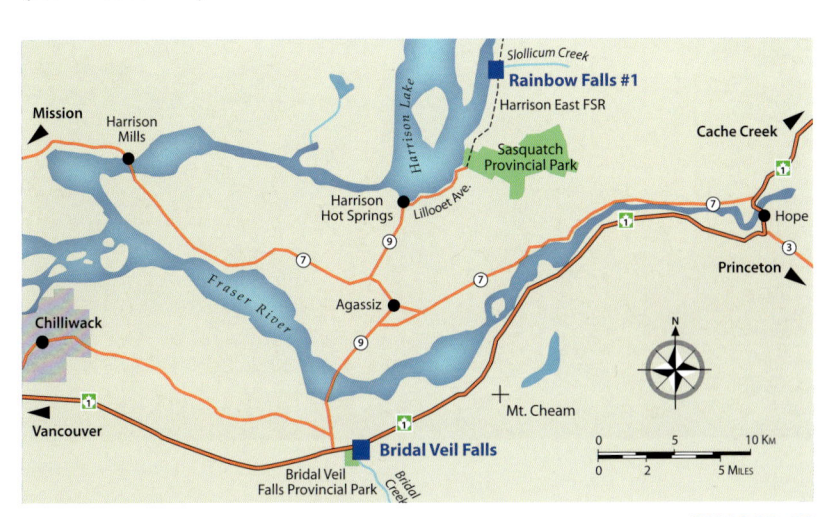

FALLS 22–23

22 BRIDAL VEIL FALLS

Rating:	▲▲▲▲△
Type:	Cascade
Location:	16 km (10 mi) E of Chilliwack, 36 km (22 mi) W of Hope
Access:	Easy. Beside Hwy 1
Status:	Bridal Veil Falls Provincial Park
When to go:	Year-round

Waterfalls of British Columbia

Bridal Veil Falls. Christopher Porter photo

Directions: From Chilliwack drive 16 km (10 mi) east on Hwy 1 and take exit 135 for Bridal Falls. If you are travelling west from Hope take exit 138. Follow the signs for 1 km (.6 mi) to Bridal Veil Falls Provincial Park. The hike to the foot of the falls takes about 10 minutes on an easy trail.

Facilities: A day-use park with picnic tables, water and handicapped accessible toilets. A major commercial development adjacent to the park offers roadside attractions for children, as well as a restaurant, store and gas station.

Highlights: This is a busy park, and deservedly so. You have your choice of trails through the advanced second-growth forest of Douglas fir, cedar, hemlock and giant broadleaf maples, with an understory of ferns, devil's club and elderberry. The trails are particularly attractive in the summer when they are dappled with sunlight and coolness.

Bridal Creek descends from the slopes of Mt. Cheam (2,107 m/6,900 ft), the towering mountain that dominates this part of the Fraser Valley.

Bridal Veil Falls, as its name suggests, is a classic, lacy waterfall that creates a veil-like effect as it cascades down the steeply inclined rock wall. It is very sedate during low water flows in August and September, but the mood changes after heavy rains or snowmelt. The total height of the falls is given as 122 m (400 ft), but this is not all visible from the foot. Water volume is greatest in the winter and spring. The trails are busy in summer, but largely deserted in the winter. When temperatures drop below freezing, an unstable wall of ice may form around the falls and this creates a potential hazard from falling ice. In the winter of 1997–98 a debris blockage above the falls impeded the flow of water. When it finally gave way the resulting catastrophic torrent wiped out the observation platform.

A now-gone interpretive sign told of the more than 250 species of mosses and liverworts that flourish in the cool dampness of the microclimate around the falls. The incredible variety is enhanced by the different rock types, as each species prefers its own particular substrate. Some of the species are unique in North America and one species is recorded only here and in Scotland.

The present park occupies the same site as the ancient village of Popkum, which is a First Nations word for the puffball mushroom, an abundant species in the area. In the early years of the 20th century, Bridal Falls was used to generate electricity for the nearby Bridal Falls Chalet.

Snapshot: On a scorching hot day in August the trails were a blessed oasis of cool and shade. At the observation platform the breeze and a light mist from the falling water felt as if they came straight from heaven itself.

23 RAINBOW FALLS #1 (HARRISON LAKE)

Rating:	▲▲▲▲△
Type:	Tiered plunge
Location:	E side of Harrison Lake, 14 km (9 mi) N of Harrison Hot Springs
Access:	Moderate. 7.4 km (4.5 mi) of blacktop, 6.6 km (4 mi) of gravel logging road
Status:	Provincial forest
When to go:	Year-round

Rainbow Falls #1

Directions: From downtown Harrison Hot Springs proceed east along Lillooet Avenue to the east shore of Harrison Lake, and continue 6 km (3.7 mi) to Sasquatch Provincial Park. Just before the park turn right, and then bear left onto the gravel Harrison East Forest Service Road that heads up the hill. The falls are beside the road after 6.6 km (4 mi). Choose a sunny day to visit if you want to see a rainbow.

Facilities: None

Highlights: Slollicum Creek flows down the steep ridge on the east side of Harrison Lake from Slollicum Lake. The creek emerges from a gully and tumbles 30 m (100 ft) in a slender, graceful plunge to a hidden pool. The water then flows over a second, lesser falls, down a steep gradient and finally over a third, minor ledge and out under the bridge to continue its course to Harrison Lake.

Rainbow Falls is an elegant plunge waterfall that strongly contrasts with the gnarly, rugged rock walls of its near vertical canyon, where trees cling to impossible rocky spots or lean wildly over the chasm.

Snapshot: As you drive north admiring the beautiful panoramic scenery from high above Harrison Lake you suddenly round a hairpin corner and are confronted point blank with the stunning spectacle of Rainbow Falls enshrined within its atrium setting. If a rainbow is present it can truly take your breath away.

SOUTHERN INTERIOR

The Southern Interior is not well endowed with waterfalls as much of the region is composed of intermontane plateaus with limited relief. The Southern Interior is relatively arid due to its location in the rain shadow of the Coast Range, and extensive areas approach desert conditions. Annual precipitation in Kamloops is 280 mm (11 in), and only 150 mm (6 in) at Ashcroft, the driest community in all of southern Canada. Despite the winter snowpack in the surrounding mountains the hot, arid summer climate quickly reduces many streams to ephemeral status. Fintry Falls is the only ephemeral waterfall in this book.

Evidence of volcanic activity is only sporadic, but has created the region's most imposing waterfall at Deadman Falls, north of Savona.

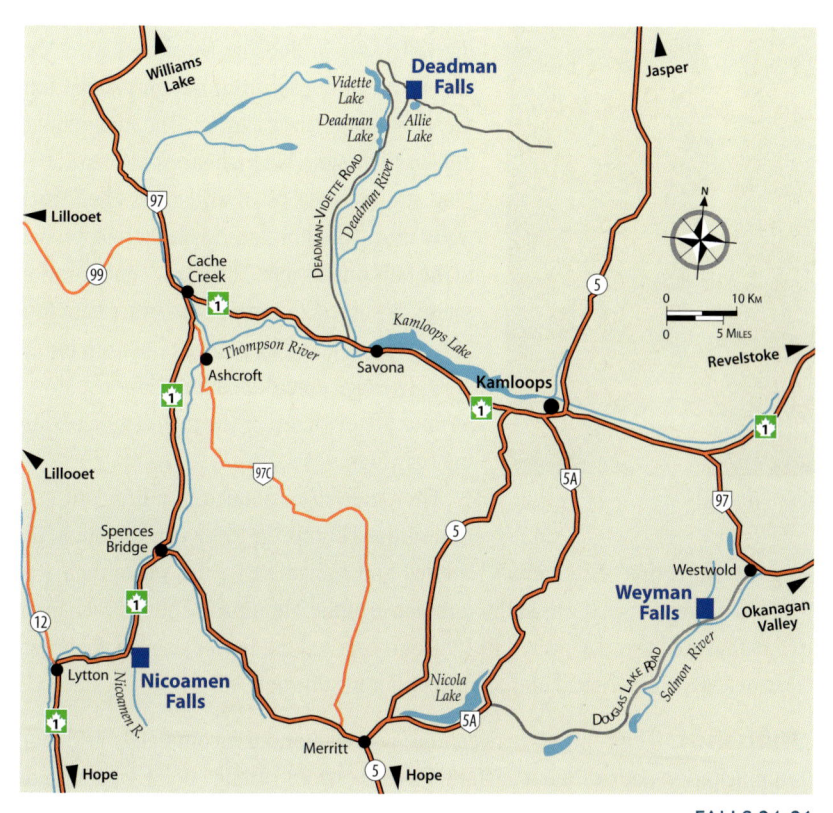

FALLS 24–26

24 NICOAMEN FALLS

Rating:	▲▲▲△△
Type:	Plunge
Location:	18 km (11 mi) N of Lytton Junction, 20 km (12.5 mi) S of Spences Bridge
Access:	Easy. Beside Hwy 1
Status:	Nicoamen First Nation reserve
When to go:	Maximum water volume during spring runoff

Directions: Beside Hwy 1, with access off the highway into a wide, gravel parking area. There are partial views of the falls from here with no further effort required.

Nicoamen Falls.
Marc-Andre Leclerc photo

Facilities: Parking only.

Highlights: This is one of the most intriguing waterfalls in BC. The Nicoamen River descends precipitously from a high plateau into the Thompson River canyon. The final plunge, only partly visible, is a high drop between 150 m (500 ft) castellations of arid rock. Sheer rock walls, crags and hoodoos make close approach to the falls impossible. The whole configuration seems designed to protect the inner sanctum of the waterfall and its plunge pool from public view. The logs abandoned far above usual waterlines are evidence of the mayhem here during very high flows.

The waterfall is situated in a dramatic section of the Thompson River canyon where the long freight trains of Canadian National and Canadian Pacific snake their way along the riverbanks. It was at the confluence of the Thompson and the Nicoamen rivers that gold was discovered in 1858 and sparked the Fraser Canyon gold rush. The area is extremely arid and often very hot in summer.

Snapshot: The contrast between the waterfall and the completely arid, barren precipices that confine it is stark. From a certain vantage point a hoodoo on the north side bears a stunning resemblance to the famous mountaintop statue of Christ the Redeemer in Rio de Janeiro. Or you might imagine the hunched profile of a peregrine falcon perched atop a crag.

25 DEADMAN FALLS

Rating:	▲▲▲▲△
Type:	Plunge
Location:	Remote area NW of Kamloops and NE of Cache Creek
Access:	Moderate. 57 km (35 mi) of good gravel road, 200 m (220 yd) walk-in
Status:	Provincial Forest
When to go:	Spring, summer, fall

Deadman Falls. Tylor Sherman photo

Directions: Take the Deadman–Vidette road 30 km (19 mi) east of Cache Creek on Hwy 1. If approaching from Kamloops drive west on Hwy 1 for 46 km (29 mi) to Savona. Immediately west of the town the highway crosses the Thompson River. Proceed 4.3 km (2.7 mi) to the Deadman River bridge and after a further 1.5 km (1 mi) bear right onto the Deadman–Vidette Road. Stay on this road for 57.2 km (35.5 mi). At km 52 (mi 32) a spur road to the left leads into Vidette Lake Resort at the head of Vidette Lake, and the main road climbs up a steep hill, leaving the valley of the Deadman River for the plateau. Exactly 5 km (3 mi) after the resort look for a spur road to the right. In 2006 there was a green and white marker nailed to a tree, and orange flagging tied around big firs either side of the access road. If you miss this turn and reach a buffalo ranch or Allie Lake you have gone too far.

The access road has deep, muddy puddles, so park at the first turnaround and walk in the 200 m (220 yd) to the falls viewpoint at the canyon edge. A trail along the canyon edge for 200–300 m (220–330 yd) allows other views of the falls and canyon.

Facilities: None. There are BC Forest Service recreation sites at both Vidette and Deadman lakes in the 10 km (6 mi) before the falls.

Highlights: The 57 km (35 mi) drive along the Deadman–Vidette Road is a relaxing, scenic route through dry forest and ranching country, with hoodoos beside the road and a series of attractive lakes. Along the Deadman Valley the forest is comprised of Douglas fir and ponderosa pine, but this gives way to open, grassy slopes and aspen groves as you climb onto the plateau just before the falls. Many bird species may be seen and heard, including common loon, turkey vulture, magpies, mountain bluebird and western meadowlark. Deadman is a classic Cariboo waterfall with a basalt headwall and a large, deeply eroded amphitheatre. The Deadman River has cut a narrow notch through the upper layer of basalt and its black waters are transformed into snow white as it falls in a high-volume ribbon plunge 65 m (210 ft) to the pool. After the plunge the river tumbles down a deep, rugged canyon to eventually join the Thompson River.

Caution is advised at the canyon edge, especially for children and dogs, as there are no fences or railings, and the potential for catastrophe is high.

The Deadman River and valley were named in 1817, after a French fur trader named Charette was murdered during an argument.

Snapshot: Deadman Falls' high plunge and large amphitheatre are redolent of Brandywine Falls. However, Brandywine is on the tourist trail and is visited by hundreds of people daily, while solitude is almost guaranteed at Deadman Falls due to its remote location far off the beaten track.

26 WEYMAN FALLS

Rating:	▲▲▲▲△△
Type:	Cascade
Location:	Douglas Lake Road, 88 km (55 mi) NE of Merritt, 20 km (12 mi) SW of Westwold
Access:	Moderate. Good gravel road and short, steep trail
Status:	Provincial forest
When to go:	Best during spring runoff

Directions: From Merritt take Hwy 5A to Nicola Lake and bear right onto the Douglas Lake Road at the log church, three-quarters of the way along Nicola Lake and 29 km (18 mi) from Merritt, or 68 km (42 mi) from Kamloops. Follow the Douglas Lake Road for 59 km (37 mi) to the Weyman Falls bridge, which is posted.

To access Weyman Falls from Hwy 97, the Okanagan Highway, proceed to the village of Westwold, 62 km (39 mi) north of Vernon, and turn south onto the Douglas Lake Road. The Weyman Creek bridge is exactly 20 km (12 mi) from the turnoff.

At the bridge, park in the pull-off on the northeast side of the creek and locate the very steep, loose trail. It is less than five minutes to the main viewpoint and the trail continues beyond here to the top of the falls.

Facilities: None

Highlights: The Douglas Lake Road makes a scenic tour through the rolling grasslands and lakes of one of the world's

Weyman Falls. Ryan Van Veen photo

largest ranches. Weyman Falls is a 30 m (100 ft) high cascade that falls into an enormous rocky plunge pool with a sheer headwall. The creek then turns through a right angle to circumvent a resistant wall that is the observation point for unobstructed views of the falls. The trail climbs past the lower vantage point to the top of the falls, opening up views of the fir-covered slopes of the Salmon River Valley.

Snapshot: Weyman Falls is secluded and seems to receive few visitors. The deep moss and cooling drafts in the spray zone are a welcome respite on a hot afternoon.

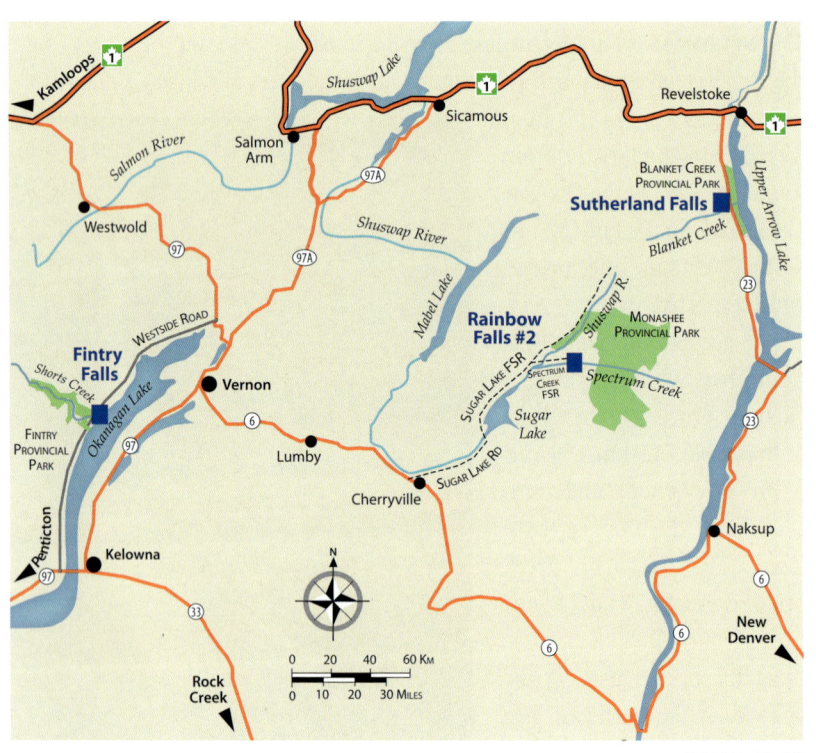

FALLS 27–29

27 FINTRY FALLS

Rating:	▲▲▲△△
Type:	Ephemeral cascade/plunge
Location:	W side of Okanagan Lake, 35 km (22 mi) N of Kelowna, 48 km (30 mi) SW of Vernon
Access:	Easy. Blacktop road, 400 steps to the upper viewpoint
Status:	Fintry Provincial Park
When to go:	Best during spring runoff

A Guide to BC's Best 100 Falls

Fintry Falls. Amanda Polson photo

Directions: From Kelowna drive 35 km (22 mi) via Westside Road on the west side of Okanagan Lake. From Vernon proceed north on Hwy 97 for 13 km (8 mi), turn left onto Westside Road and follow the signs 35 km (22 mi) south to Fintry Provincial Park.

Facilities: Fintry Provincial Park is a full-facility provincial park, and extremely popular through the summer.

Highlights: Shorts Creek flows down a steep, craggy canyon amid the Douglas fir and ponderosa pine and falls 35 m (115 ft) via a cascade and a plunge, with a pool halfway down the descent. When the creek is running high during spring runoff, typically in May, flying spray from the falls can soak viewers on the platforms. From the top of the falls there are views eastward to Okanagan Lake and over the delta of Shorts Creek. California bighorn sheep frequent the area.

Fintry Provincial Park and falls acquired their name through Capt. James C. Dun-Waters, the "Laird of Fintry," who in the early 1900s owned the land that later became the park. He named the property after his birthplace in Scotland. Over a 30-year period Dun-Waters developed a productive farm, orchards and estate by capturing the water from Shorts Creek for irrigation and the energy from Fintry Falls for electricity to power a sawmill.

Snapshot: Waterfalls are quite rare in the Okanagan Valley because of both the geology and the climate. Fintry Falls is the premier waterfall of the Okanagan Valley, but even so it is still an ephemeral falls (the only one in this book), and if you visit in midsummer or fall there may be no flowing water. There are actually very few ephemeral falls in BC because high-elevation snowfields feed most rivers and creeks, which maintains flow throughout the year.

On hot spring or early summer days the cool downdrafts from the falls are delightfully refreshing.

28 RAINBOW FALLS #2 (SPECTRUM CREEK)

Rating:	▲▲▲▲△
Type:	Plunge
Location:	Spectrum Creek, N of Sugar Lake
Status:	Disjunct portion of Monashee Provincial Park
Access:	Moderate. 30 km (19 mi) gravel logging road, five-minute hike on a medium-steep trail
When to go:	Spring, summer, fall

Directions: From Vernon head east on Hwy 6 through Lumby, and at the Cherryville General Store turn left (north) onto the Sugar Lake Road. The road surface becomes gravel after 13.3 km (8.25 mi) and at 16.3 km (10 mi) crosses the Shuswap River on a bridge at the south end of Sugar Lake. Proceed on the Sugar Lake Forest Service Road for 21.3 km (13.2 mi) before bearing right onto the Spectrum Creek FSR (also signed "13 km to Monashee Provincial Park"). After 4 km (2.5 mi) bear left up the hill at the sign indicating the falls, and 400 m (440 yd) later take the right fork for a further 300 m (330 yd) to the parking lot. The total distance from the Cherryville store is 42.3 km (26.3 mi).

Facilities: Outhouse, map of Monashee Provincial Park

Highlights: The trail to the foot of the falls passes through a typical Interior Wet Zone forest of cedar and hemlock with some large old-growth trees on the flood plain adjacent to the creek. At the shrub level are devil's club, thimbleberry and ferns, and wildflowers such as mitrewort, self-heal, Hooker's fairybell, fairycup and bunchberry. Arnica blooms in the spray zone. The trail leads to two viewing platforms at the edge of Spectrum Creek below the falls.

Rainbow Falls is a ragged, 17 m (56 ft) plunge, notable for a gigantic rock perched at the very brink of the falls that forces the stream to divide around it. Clouds of spray drift downstream at high water.

Rainbow Falls #2

The top of the falls can be accessed via a steep, rough trail. From here, Spectrum Creek can be seen racing chaotically through a steep canyon in a maelstrom, bouncing back and forth from one bank to the other, before the plunge over the falls. It is possible to descend to the foot of the falls and to peer behind the curtain of falling water. The confined space makes this a very noisy spot.

Snapshot: On one visit a dipper passed across the face of the falls, flirting with the torrent, and flew in behind the sheet of falling water into the seemingly hostile environment of cold, wet noise. Obviously this is my anthropocentric view of life behind a waterfall, but it must be perfectly normal to a dipper.

The big question at this waterfall: when is that perching rock finally going to fall?

29 SUTHERLAND FALLS

Rating:	▲▲▲▲△
Type:	Plunge
Location:	17 km (10.5 mi) S of Revelstoke on Hwy 23
Access:	Easy. 200 m (220 yd) hike on level trail
Status:	Blanket Creek Provincial Park
When to go:	Spring, summer, fall

Directions: From the junction of highways 1 and 23, 800 m (875 yd) west of the main junction at Revelstoke, proceed south on Hwy 23 for 17.2 km (10.7 mi). Turn left into Blanket Creek Provincial Park (posted). After 1.5 km (1 mi) bear left into the parking lot for the falls. A short, 200 m (220 yd) trail leads to the falls.

Facilities: Full-facility provincial park with campsites, picnic tables, adventure playground and swimming lagoon.

Sutherland Falls

Highlights: Sutherland Falls is a high discharge waterfall, as Blanket Creek delivers meltwater from the Monashee Mountains to the west into the Columbia River just north of Upper Arrow Lake. There is a tangible reverberation as Blanket Creek thunders 12 m (40 ft) over the precipice in a perfect block plunge into a sheer-walled pool. Around the plunge pool two bryophytes (a moss and a liverwort) were discovered 1,000 km (600 mi) south of any other known locality in North America. This phenomenon of bryophytes appearing in unexpected locations is also seen at Bridal Veil Falls.

Blanket Creek Provincial Park was formerly the Domke homestead, which was pioneered in the 1920s. Remnant trees from the original orchard are still alive and in the fall the fruit frequently attracts black bears to the site.

Snapshot: Sutherland Falls is the very essence of a plunge waterfall, beautiful in its simplicity and absolute in its power. Back at home, Internet research yielded an amazing image of a whitewater/waterfall kayaker freefalling down the face of Sutherland Falls.

30 CASCADE FALLS

Rating:	▲▲▲▲△
Type:	Cascade
Location:	2 km (1 mi) S of Christina Lake
Access:	Easy. Beside Hwy 395, 0.5 km (0.3 mi) from the junction with Hwy 3
Status:	Provincial Forest
When to go:	Spring and early summer

Directions: The trailhead is 0.5 km (0.3 mi) east of the junction of Hwy 3 and 395 at the bridge across the Kettle River. The trail south of the road leads up some steps and hugs the side of the gorge as the Kettle River surges through Cascade Canyon. The trail to the top of the falls is about 600 m (660 yd), with side trails to numerous viewpoints.

Facilities: None

Highlights: The Kettle River drains a large area between the Okanagan and the West Kootenay, en route to its confluence with the Columbia River in Washington state. During the spring freshet an enormous volume of meltwater from the mountains surrounding its watershed tumbles through the confines of Cascade Canyon. The main falls within the canyon are about 20 m (65 ft) high and the total drop about 30 m (100 ft). This produces a mind-boggling maelstrom of pulverized whitewater and spray as the river rages down the narrow, rugged canyon. After the

Waterfalls of British Columbia

Cascade Falls. Leon Turnbull / waterfallswest.com photo

freshet the canyon becomes more sedate as summer progresses and water volume decreases.

Snapshot: Cascade Canyon is the site of an unresolved effort to develop the site for hydroelectricity. A previous hydro development here in 1897 played an important role in the development of the world's electricity industry. It was at the Cascade site that the rivalry between Thomas Edison, who favoured direct current, and Nikola Tesla from Westinghouse, who promoted the new technology of alternating current, was resolved in favour of Tesla.

The contemporary proposal involves an 800 m (2,600 ft) tunnel that would run from a weir above Cascade Canyon and divert part of the river to a powerhouse on the opposite side of the highway.

May your trails be crooked, winding, lonesome, dangerous, leading to the most amazing view.

Edward Abbey, "A Prayer for the Traveler"

84

SOUTHEAST

This region consists of the Columbia Mountains in the west, the Rocky Mountain Trench and the southern Rocky Mountains. The Rocky Mountain Trench is a long rift valley through which the Columbia River flows southwards to the United States. Geologically, Southeastern BC consists of mainly sedimentary rocks, with sandstones well represented. Sandstone is prone to undercutting, which accounts for the numerous plunge waterfalls in the region, such as Marysville Falls near Kimberley and Morrissey Falls near Fernie. However, local geomorphologic complexities have resulted in a diverse range of waterfalls, including significant cascades. The premier waterfall of the region is Josephine Falls, a cascade on the Fording River. Lower Bugaboo Falls is located on the fall line of the Rocky Mountain Trench; other falls show evidence of igneous intrusions that created the local conditions necessary for a break in the stream profile. The Petain Waterfalls are located in an alpine area among some of the most spectacular scenery in the province.

FALLS 30–35

Beaver Falls. Leon Turnbull / waterfallswest.com photo

31 BEAVER FALLS

Rating:	▲▲▲▲△
Type:	Plunge
Location:	Between Trail and Fruitvale off Hwy 3B
Access:	Easy. 1.6 km (1 mi) hike, about 20 minutes
Status:	Provincial forest
When to go:	Spring, summer

Directions: From the Fruitvale Esso station head west on Hwy 3B toward Trail. After 2 km (1.25 mi) turn left onto Bluebird Road and cross the rail tracks 100 m (110 yd) further along. Park here and walk westward along the tracks until you reach a high trestle across Beaver Creek. Immediately before the trestle a rough trail to the right leads to various viewpoints of the falls. The best of these are accessed along the short, steep, loose and dangerous spurs that lead to the rim of the canyon from this main trail. Maximum caution is advised.

Facilities: None

Highlights: Beaver Creek meanders peacefully in a shallow valley until it enters a constriction and plunges about 18 m (60 ft) over the falls into an enormous, deep canyon. The waterfall discharges powerfully during the spring freshet, but the rate of flow slows through the summer, when the plunge pool at the foot of the falls becomes a popular swimming hole. Below the plunge pool Beaver Creek flows over another unseen falls. In July the waterfall is a beautifully complex series of three separate plunges with the outer sides of the falls plunging directly to the lower pool while the central stream first hits an intermediate level.

Snapshot: A persistent rumour has it that Bing Crosby, who grew up in nearby Spokane, Washington, used to hop freight trains to visit Beaver Falls to fish.

32 DEER CREEK FALLS

Rating:	▲▲▲▲△
Type:	Plunge and cascade
Location:	33 km (20.5 mi) NW of Castlegar
Access:	Moderate. 17 km (10.5 mi) of logging road, 1 km (.6 mi) trail
Status:	BC Forest Service Trail
When to go:	Spring, summer, fall

Directions: On the north side of the Columbia River in Castlegar turn onto Broadwater Road, which is signed to Robson and to Syringa Creek Provincial Park,

Waterfalls of British Columbia

Deer Creek Falls

and leads past the Keenleyside Dam. After 16.2 km (10 mi) bear right onto the Deer Park Forest Service Road. The Tulip Falls trailhead is on the right after 4 km (2.5 mi). At 29.4 km (18.25 mi) keep right on the Deer Creek FSR and then turn left onto a spur at 32.8 km (20.4 mi). Drive in 100 m (110 yd) and park. A 1 km (.6 mi) forested trail leads to the falls.

Facilities: There is an outhouse halfway along the trail, and a picnic table at a sunny vantage point from which to view the falls.

Highlights: In many ways a perfect little waterfall as it combines all the top elements: a 10 m (33 ft) plunge into a circular plunge pool, immediately followed by 10 m (33 ft) cascade, all within sheer, craggy canyon walls. The ambiance of this gem is spoiled by a small, recent clear-cut on the east bank and some related blowdown of a riparian leave strip that has deposited a rat's nest of fallen trees across the creek below the falls. It is possible to cross the creek on the fallen logs and to climb up the steep opposite bank and work your way toward the upper falls. A very steep chimney leads down to the plunge pool.

Snapshot: There were wonderful cooling draughts and pools at this waterfall on a blazing hot July day. While I was there a pair of belted kingfishers paid a fleeting visit. A possibly unique feature of the trail to the falls is its diversity of coniferous species. I counted an amazing nine species along the 1 km (.6 mi) trail, representative of the complex biogeoclimatic interactions that exist at this location. I identified wet zone species (Douglas fir, western hemlock, western red cedar, western white pine and Pacific yew), dry zone species (ponderosa and lodgepole pine) and elevational components (larch and Engelmann spruce). I know of no other location in BC where so many coniferous species co-exist. Foresters refer to this combination as the "Kootenay mix."

Many waterfalls in BC are called Rainbow Falls. This book also refers to three falls known as Deer Falls. Other than this one, there are the Deer Falls that are part of the Elk Falls complex, and Red Deer Falls.

33 FLETCHER FALLS

Rating:	▲▲▲▲△△
Type:	Cascade
Location:	Off Hwy 31, between Nelson and Kaslo
Access:	Easy. 500 m (550 yd) trail from Hwy 31
Status:	BC Forest Service Recreation Site
When to go:	Spring, summer, fall

Directions: From Nelson take Hwy 3A north toward Balfour, Ainsworth Hot Springs and Kaslo. At the Balfour ferry terminal Hwy 3A becomes Hwy 31, which turns north and follows the west side of Kootenay Lake to Kaslo. The Fletcher Falls Recreation Site is 12.5 km (7.75 mi) north of Ainsworth Hot Springs, immediately south of the Fletcher Creek bridge. Look for a small sign on the east side of the road that indicates "Fletcher Falls," or a driveway on the west side numbered 5031. If you reach Thompson Road on the left you have gone a few hundred metres too far. There is parking and a gate at the top of the trail that winds down to the falls and the beach. From the beach, the trail to the foot of the falls is a mere 50 m (165 ft) across the rustic bridge.

Fletcher Falls

If you approach Fletcher Falls from Kaslo to the north, the trailhead is 8 km (5 mi) south of Kaslo on Hwy 31.

Facilities: This is a day-use area with an outhouse and picnic tables.

Highlights: The cascade is about 15 m (50 ft) high in total, but it is not completely visible from the foot of the falls. The trail leads to the claustrophobic little plunge pool that has igneous dykes running through the sedimentary strata. The falls result from one of these resistant intrusions. On the opposite bank the wall towers overhead with a significant overhang. The headwall has a good display of blue harebells in summer and there are verdant moss gardens in the spray zone. Look for the rectangular drilled holes of pileated woodpeckers in the cedars beside the trail. There is a rough, steep, unofficial trail on the south side of the creek that allows a full view of the waterfall.

Snapshot: The drama of this falls is heightened by the confining nature of the high walls and it must be particularly impressive to share the space when Fletcher Creek is running high during the freshet. There was a huge western toad in the rocks of the spray zone when I visited.

34 WILSON CREEK FALLS

Rating:	▲▲▲▲▲
Type:	Block plunge
Location:	17 km (10.5 mi) N of New Denver
Access:	Moderate. 12 km (7.5 mi) of good logging road, 1 km (.6 mi), about 25 minutes hiking, on a steep, switchbacked trail
Status:	Goat Range Provincial Park
When to go:	Spring, summer, fall

Directions: From New Denver proceed north on Hwy 6 along the east shore of Slocan Lake and after 4.9 km (3 mi) turn right onto East Wilson Creek Road, 300 m (330 yd) before Rosebery Provincial Park. This road soon becomes the Wilson Creek Forest Service Road and caution is advised in case logging is in progress. Continue up the road for 16.3 km (10 mi), ignoring all roads to the right. At km 16.3 bear right up the hill and note a sign that indicates "Wilson Creek Falls Trail 1 km." At km 17 the trailhead is on the left with parking on the right. The trail is initially level, passing through a regenerating clear-cut, but soon enters the forest and switchbacks steeply down to the foot of the falls.

Wilson Creek Falls.
Leon Turnbull / waterfallswest.com photo

Facilities: Campsites, picnic tables, outhouses and water are available at Rosebery Provincial Park at the foot of the logging road access.

Highlights: The trail switchbacks steeply down into a deep valley, giving the impression of walking among the cedar and hemlock treetops. The waterfall is a spectacular block plunge listed at 63 m (205 ft), though this is not all visible from the viewpoints below the falls. From the telltale spray there appears to be another falls above the visible portion, but this is not accessible. The plunge pool has a gigantic vertical wall on the west side with a steep forested sidehill to the east. This is a stupendous waterfall, one of BC's biggest, with a great volume of water thundering into the plunge pool. The discharge is especially impressive at high water during the June snowmelt.

Wilson Creek drains southwest from the slopes of Cascade Mountain in the high country of Goat Range Provincial Park in the Selkirk Range.

Snapshot: Take the side trail to a rocky ledge beside the falls where the falling water is almost close enough to touch. This intimidating spot truly conveys the power of falling water and is reminiscent of similar locations at Twin Falls in Yoho National Park and Feather Falls in California.

35 MOYIE FALLS

Rating:	▲▲▲▲△
Type:	Plunge
Location:	18 km (11 mi) SW of Cranbrook
Access:	Moderate. 7 km (4 mi) on gravel road, 15-minute hike
Status:	Provincial forest
When to go:	Spring, summer, fall

Directions: From the main traffic lights in downtown Cranbrook, proceed 1.7 km (1 mi) west on Hwy 3 to the Tourist Information Centre. Drive a further 9.8 km (6 mi) and turn right onto Lumberton Road, which becomes the gravel Moyie River Forest Service Road. After 6.6 km (4 mi) take the left spur (with Negro Lake West Road to the right). After 300 m (320 yd), park at the gate, walk down the hill, cross the Moyie River on the wooden footbridge and then walk upstream for 500 m (550 yd) on the road alongside the river.

Facilities: None

Highlights: The river cascades into a 15 m (50 ft) deep notch eroded into the horizontal strata, and plunges a further 15 m (50 ft) to a massive plunge pool with

Moyie Falls

50 m (160 ft) walls. A resistant residual wall then constricts the river through a 2 m (6.5 ft) opening, and a second wall creates an almost exact replica of the first. A huge flat rock is conveniently located at the plunge pool, close to the falls, for intimate views of this awe-inspiring place.

A unique feature of Moyie Falls is that the headwall of the plunge pool is riddled with old mine shafts and tunnels created by generations of miners searching for the motherlode. When I visited in July 2000, a new tunnel was being punched into the rock from the back of the main plunge pool. One of the current miners gave me a tour and described the complete fascinating history of the mining here. He told me of a huge flood surge in November 1999 that moved even the largest of seemingly immoveable rocks.

Apparently the brave and foolhardy have been filmed jumping from the rim of the headwall into the plunge pool, which is an excellent swimming hole.

The name Moyie is an anglicized corruption of the French word *mouille*, meaning wet, which was given by early French trappers.

Snapshot: This really happened! I visited Moyie Falls on the evening of a scorching hot day in July. As I stood on the big rock at the mouth of the plunge pool, the ultimate male waterfall fantasy unfolded. A beautiful, blonde, buxom maiden in a brief bikini was swimming in the pool. This siren swam over toward me and made conversation, and indelibly I found myself looking down into her blue eyes. Her shoulders and breasts sparkled with watery diamonds and her sunny disposition was a joy to mankind. I had to pinch myself, expecting to wake from this archetypal fantasy that springs from Homer or Keats or *The Lord of the Rings*. I christened her Galadriel.

A Guide to BC's Best 100 Falls

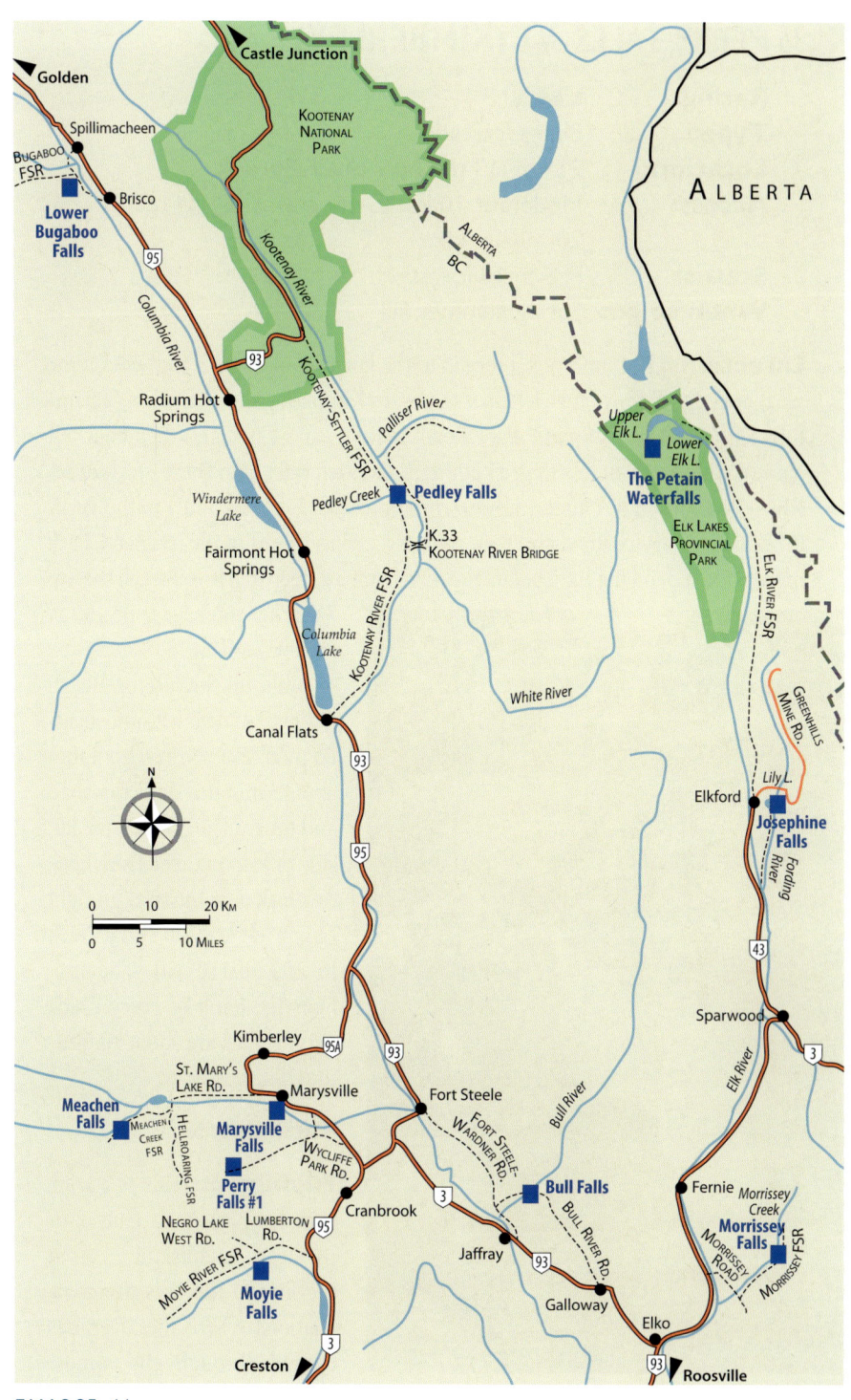

SOUTHEAST

FALLS 35–44

93

36 PERRY FALLS #1 (KIMBERLEY)

Rating:	▲▲▲▲△
Type:	Plunge/cascade
Location:	21 km (13 mi) NW of Cranbrook
Access:	Moderate. 10 km (6 mi) gravel logging road, 20-minute hike
Status:	Provincial forest
When to go:	Spring, summer, fall

Directions: In Cranbrook, proceed to the junction of Hwys 3 and 95A on the northern edge of town. Turn left on 95A toward Kimberley and after 4 km (2.5 mi) turn left (west) onto Wycliffe Park Road. Drive 6 km (4 mi) and then bear left onto Wycliffe Road for less than a kilometre and then right onto Perry Creek Road, which becomes gravel after 1 km (.6 mi). Proceed 5.5 km (3.5 mi) to the Perry Creek Forest Service Road and then right for 4.8 km (3 mi) to the trailhead. Park in the wide spot on the right before the road climbs a steep hill. If you reach the km 8 marker you have gone 150 m (165 yd) too far.

Walk up the hill for 100 m (110 yd) and go left onto a gated road. You will reach a cabin about 5 minutes along this road and the trail goes down the left side of Lisbon Creek from here. At a fork near the river go right (going left leads to Perry Creek in 100 m/110 yd). The trail hugs the bank of Perry Creek and the falls are about 10 minutes hike upstream.

Facilities: None

Highlights: This is a wild, complex place with truly Promethean architecture. From the foot of the falls the crenellations where the river has eroded through the almost vertically inclined strata tower

Perry Falls #1

70 m (230 ft) into the blue sky like a medieval castle. High up, Perry Falls divides, with one half slithering down a high sheer wall and the other descending in a deeply incised tube. Near the foot of the waterfall, part of the creek flows under a rock arch through which it is possible to clamber at lower discharges and emerge into a beautiful plunge pool. Below the arch Perry Creek plunges a final 6 m (20 ft) to a green pool. The best viewpoint to observe the entire waterfall is from a wall of resistant, vertically inclined rock that protrudes into the creek near the foot of the falls. This is the site of a relict waterfall, where the creek has punched its way to a final green pool.

The intrepid explorer will want to continue up to the top of the falls. Be warned that this is a steep, loose, potentially dangerous exercise with only limited rewards, as the precipitous and complex architecture mitigates against further good viewpoints. However, two thoughtfully provided ropes help you to pull yourself up the extremely steep, loose sections. Having navigated this hazard you may approach the edge of the chasm at your peril. At the top, sweating and thirsty, you can only look down at the gorgeous green and golden pools in the rugged canyon; there is no sightline to the actual falls.

Perry Creek is named for Frank Perry who prospected here in 1867–8. The base of the falls was called the Jewellery Box, indicating this was a profitable claim.

Snapshot: I visited Perry Falls during an East Kootenay heat wave. It is an idyllic spot on a hot summer day as the cool, jade-coloured pools at the foot of the falls complement the fragrance of the pine, fir and birch forest and the wind whispers through the green Kootenay hills.

I was very impressed with the stone arch near the foot of the falls and I clambered through this feature to the pool within. It was years later that I discovered the arch had actually been drilled by the old-timers, presumably in search of the motherlode.

While visiting Perry Falls you may see or hear a flock of grey, white and black birds calling raucously. These are Clark's nutcrackers, a member of the crow family.

37 MARYSVILLE FALLS

Rating:	▲▲▲▲△
Type:	Cascade
Location:	Near Marysville, a suburb of Kimberley
Access:	Easy. Short, level trail off the main street in Marysville
Status:	Municipal Park
When to go:	Year-round

Directions: Marysville is on Hwy 95A, 6.5 km (4 mi) southeast of Kimberley and 20 km (12 mi) northwest of Cranbrook. The parking lot for the falls is well posted beside the bridge on the north edge of town. Cross the road and follow the trail 250 m (270 yd) to the falls.

Marysville Falls

Facilities: Parking, viewing platform. The park and trail are adjacent to the main street of Marysville.

Highlights: Between the highway and the falls, Mark Creek flows in a minor canyon of horizontally stratified sandstone sediments. As the creek eroded downwards through the strata, it created a series of steps that give the impression that the creek bed is constructed from rectangular building blocks. Within this stepped format, however, the creek has eroded the various levels into rounded forms, potholes and pools.

These minor steps suddenly give way to the major leap of Marysville Falls, a 14 m (46 ft) cascade into a large plunge pool, with the vertical wall showing the many perfectly horizontal strata. On the right a flat, 3 m (10 ft) high bench creates a diving platform for the kids to jump or dive right into the foaming foot of the falls.

Below the falls there is an interesting canyon with minor falls, steps, ledges, pools and constrictions.

Snapshot: When I visited on a hot summer day the kids were having a wonderful time in the swimming hole. One of them reported to me that certain daredevils have jumped from the top of the falls into the plunge pool. Hard to believe!

38 MEACHEN FALLS

Rating:	▲▲▲▲△
Type:	Plunge/cascade
Location:	31 km (19 mi) W of Kimberley
Access:	Easy. 11 km (7 mi) on gravel road, 200 m (220 yd) trail
Status:	Provincial forest
When to go:	Spring, summer, fall

Directions: From the Platzl traffic light in Kimberley, drive south on Hwy 95A toward Marysville and Cranbrook. After 3.6 km (2.2 mi) turn right onto St. Mary Lake Road (this junction is 700 m (765 yd) north of the Marysville Falls parking lot. Drive 15 km (9 mi) and then bear left onto Lake Front Road, which becomes St. Mary River Road. Cross the St. Mary River bridge, then bear right onto the Hellroaring Forest Service Road. After 1 km (.6 mi) turn right again onto the Meachen Creek FSR and drive to the km 8 marker. Park here in the wide spot on the right side of the road. The trailhead is at the near end of the parking spot and the trail leads to the natural viewing platform at the top of the falls in less than one minute, and to the lower viewpoint in two to three minutes. Caution is advised at these viewpoints due to the lack of protective barriers atop the rocks and cliffs.

Meachen Falls

Facilities: None

Highlights: Meachen Falls is a beautiful and complex cataract set among the huge green hills of the southern Purcell Range. It has a total drop of about 26 m (85 ft). As the creek approaches the brink of the falls it suddenly surges through a 3 m (10 ft) wide constriction of horizontal strata before plunging and cascading 15 m (50 ft) into a roiling plunge pool with a hydraulic that kicks up into the air like an enormous geyser. It then plunges another 3 m (10 ft) at a lateral angle into a pool with vertical red walls, before rolling transparently down a steep rock and plunging 4 m (13 ft) to a pool of white water. There is a final whitewater torrent down a constricted gulley into another pool before it rumbles through a high-walled canyon that contains a chaotic mixture of gigantic rocks and a jumble of waterborne logs dumped above the tide line. Eventually the creek resumes its peaceful passage. Intrepid visitors can reach the foot of Meachen Falls by continuing beyond the lower viewpoint to a very steep descent and then scrambling back along the edge of the creek.

Snapshot: Three waterfalls (Meachen, Marysville and Perry #1), all in the vicinity of Kimberley, make for a wonderfully relaxing summer's day outing in the beautiful southern Purcell Mountains.

39 BULL RIVER FALLS

Rating:	▲▲▲▲△
Type:	Plunge
Location:	30 km (19 mi) E of Cranbrook, between Galloway and Fort Steele
Access:	Easy. Logging road
Status:	BC Hydro dam site
When to go:	Spring, summer, fall

Directions: From Fort Steele take the Fort Steele–Wardner Road for 20 km (12 mi) and bear left onto the gravel Bull River Road. After 7.6 km (4.7 mi) you will cross a bridge over a flume and, 400 m (440 yd) further, a Bailey bridge over the Bull River. Park here. To exit to Hwy 3 at Galloway, continue past the bridge for 400 m (440 yd) and note the km 20 marker of the Bull River Forest Service Road. Follow this road out to the highway.

Facilities: None

Highlights: The Bull River canyon is a spectacular spot with plenty to see, as the canyon and waterfall now share the site with the Aberfeldie Dam, a BC Hydro generating facility. The dam was completed in 1922 to supply power to nearby Crowsnest Pass coal mines and the town of Fernie. It was rebuilt in 1953 as a run of the river gravity dam, 27 m (90 ft) high and 134 m (440 ft) long. The latest redevelopment and upgrade was planned for completion in October 2008. The Aberfeldie name was given to the dam in 1923 by the president of the company. He decided that he wanted something with more cachet than Bull River, and chose the name after an area of Scotland that he liked.

To see the dam it is best to walk up the road from the parking spot at the bridge. Here the Bull River looks like a fluffy sheet of white cotton candy as it spills down the face of the dam. It then flows through a rugged upper canyon and approaches the main falls, which are virtually underneath the Bailey bridge. The falls can be viewed from the bridge, but better views of both the falls and the canyon beneath the bridge can be had by working your way down the west side of the river.

The falls are a 12 m (40 ft) high plunge into a deep, almost subterranean plunge pool of roiling white intensity. The erosive power of the river is undermining the rock wall and leaving the plunge pool hidden below a massive overhang.

The bridge crosses the river at its narrowest point above a deep canyon whose walls show the elevated, cylindrical erosion patterns of ancient potholes. In the canyon below the falls, the river alternates between a deep, dark, languid flow and the whitewater of a series of cascades and a 4 m (13 ft) plunge. This stretch of the canyon rim can be approached by a short trail from the bridge over the flume, 400 m (440 yd) before the main bridge. Approach the canyon rim with caution.

At the bridge a spillway from the dam releases water in a powerful plunge that cascades 50 m (165 ft) down to the river.

Snapshot: This is one of BC's most spectacular canyons and an extremely powerful waterfall.

40 PEDLEY FALLS

Rating:	▲▲▲▲△
Type:	Cascade
Location:	42 km (26 mi) NE of Canal Flats, 53 km (33 mi) SE of Radium Hot Springs
Access:	Moderate. 42 km (26 mi) logging road, 2 km (1 mi) trail
Status:	Provincial forest
When to go:	Spring, summer, fall

Directions: In Canal Flats turn east onto Grainger Road immediately north of the Hwy 93/95 bridge over the Kootenay River, and then turn right onto the Kootenay River Forest Service Road by passing through the concrete abutments. Proceed along the west side of the river to just before the km 33 marker and bear left onto the Kootenay–Settler FSR. Just beyond km 33 the road crosses the Kootenay River. Nine km (5.5 mi) beyond the Kootenay–Settler junction the road crosses the Pedley Creek bridge, which is the first bridge along the road. The kilometre markers on this road decrease from the junction, and if you reach the km 35 marker you have gone too far.

Park at the bridge and climb the gravel bank 50 m (160 ft) to the north. A faint trail is flagged with faded pink tape (August 2000). The 2 km (1 mi) trail is basically level as far as the rim of the Kootenay River Canyon and can be hiked in approximately 25 minutes. If you lose the trail, it hugs the rim of the upper terrace of Pedley Creek all the way to the falls. For good views of the falls it is necessary to clamber partway down the very steep bank to the left of the brink.

After visiting the falls you can return to Canal Flats the way you came, or continue northwards on the Kootenay–Settler Forest Service Road to reach Radium Hot Springs and the Banff–Lake Louise area. If you are taking the northern route, drive 23.4 km (14.5 mi) and keep left at this junction. It is then a further 12 km (7.5 mi) to Hwy 93, and Radium Hot Springs is 18 km (11 mi) to the west (left) of the junction.

Facilities: None

Highlights: Pedley Creek cascades 30 m (100 ft) into the Kootenay River, which runs in a beautiful white canyon at this point. Pedley Falls tumbles from the plateau into the canyon and is framed by the expansive white headwall. The left side of the falls cascades all the way to the river, but the right side cascades, then plunges, and cascades again. This is a giant waterfall, and surely is particularly impressive at high discharges during the spring runoff.

Snapshot: The trail to Pedley Falls seems little used. However, while I was visiting the falls from above, about 50 people arrived at the foot in rafts, kayaks and canoes along the Kootenay River, suggesting that this is the commonest way of viewing these impressive falls.

41 LOWER BUGABOO FALLS

Rating:	▲▲▲▲△
Type:	Plunge
Location:	35 km (22 mi) NW of Radium Hot Springs, 70 km (44 mi) SE of Golden
Access:	Moderate. Gravel logging road and 15-minute hike
Status:	BC Forest Service Recreation Trail
When to go:	Spring, summer, fall

Directions: From Radium Hot Springs drive 24.7 km (15.3 mi) north on Hwy 95 to the hamlet of Brisco. Turn left (west) onto Brisco Road (it is posted to Bugaboo Provincial Park). After 3.4 km (2.1 mi) bear right onto the Bugaboo logging road, and after a further 1 km (.6 mi) bear right onto Brisco Road again. Then proceed straight ahead for 6.3 km (3.9 mi) and look for the parking lot and trailhead on the left with a sign indicating Lower Bugaboo Falls Recreation Trail. If you reach the km 8 marker you have gone too far.

It is a 15-minute hike, about 1.5 km (1 mi), on a good trail with occasional steep sections to a viewpoint high above Bugaboo Creek. You can continue 5 minutes past this spot to a distant viewpoint of the falls from the creek side. However, the main trail to the falls switches back on itself 20 m (22 yd) before the creek viewpoint (easy to miss) and about 8 minutes hiking brings you to the brink of the falls.

Facilities: None

Highlights: Bugaboo Creek splits at the brink around a rock with two-thirds of the water going to the left and one-third to the right (late July). It plunges 3 m (10 ft) to a ledge and then a further 20 m (65 ft) to the plunge pool, with the right-hand water powering through an arch, almost filling its entire diameter. There are spectacular views, from precarious vantage points, of the white waters falling into the black abyss of the plunge pool. This is the fall line of the Rocky Mountain Trench, and from the brink of Lower Bugaboo Falls you look down the creek across the great rift to the mountains of Kootenay National Park.

The foot of the falls can only be reached by descending down a short but extremely steep, unstable route. This is definitely not a trail and most people will

Waterfalls of British Columbia

Lower Bugaboo Falls

be content to pass on this viewpoint. It does bring you to views from the bottom of the falls, but the plunge pool is largely hidden by a remnant wall of vertically inclined rock, probably a past incarnation of Lower Bugaboo Falls. Clouds of spray blast through this gateway and drift away downstream. A high tide line of detritus indicates much greater flows during the spring freshet.

Snapshot: Few BC waterfalls incorporate arches in their architecture, and for this reason Lower Bugaboo Falls is redolent of another West Kootenay waterfall, Perry Falls. It is a rare and attractive feature.

42 MORRISSEY FALLS

Rating:	▲▲▲△△
Type:	Plunge
Location:	25 km (16 mi) S of Fernie
Access:	Moderate. 12 km (7.5 mi) gravel logging road, short walk to falls
Status:	Provincial forest
When to go:	Spring and summer

Directions: From the bridge on Hwy 3 on the west side of Fernie proceed 12 km (7.5 mi) south and turn left onto Morrissey Road (to the right is Remote Weather Station #36124). Cross the bridge over the Elk River and the railway tracks and continue 4 km (2.5 mi) to the intersection with River Road. Proceed 1.8 km (1 mi) and bear left onto the Morrissey Forest Service Road. Cross the bridge at the km 20 marker, and then look for a big rock on the left at km 24. There are two separate waterfalls, the upper and lower falls, about 200 m (220 yd) apart, between the km 24 and 25 markers. It is easiest to first locate the upper falls at the wide turnout just before the km 25 marker. This trail is level, easy and only 50 m (160 ft) from the road to the rim of the falls. To access the lower falls, walk back along the road for about 200 m (220 yd) to an insignificant widening in the road. A cottonwood sapling has been blazed where the short, steep trail leads from the road to the foot of the falls. The trail involves clambering down and over wet, slippery rock ledges while watching out for devil's club, but no danger is involved.

Just beyond the upper falls look for a small waterfall on a tributary stream at the km 25 marker.

Facilities: None

Highlights: The upper falls consist of two plunges, one of which is 10 m (30 ft) high and drops to a beautiful pool. The lower falls are the main attraction, a wild, dramatic, lonely place that contrasts beauty and chaos. At the falls a 2 m (7 ft) thick

Morrissey Falls

horizontal stratum forms a resistant caprock. Morrissey Creek plunges over this ledge into a classic, vertical-walled plunge pool with a wide overhang behind the falling water. When I visited in early August the falls were a sedate place with two thin ribbons of water, but a log-jam and debris at the tide line 4 m (13 ft) above the August water level indicated the mayhem possible here at high water during the spring runoff.

Boulders as big as cabins are scattered across the rugged canyon below the falls. The geology is of sedimentary origin with conglomerates and even a thin coal seam, suggestive of other areas in the Crows Nest Pass area. A huge rock slab at the foot of the falls is a reminder that occasionally the ongoing erosion reaches a climactic finale.

The wide variety of wildflowers at the foot of the falls among the gigantic rocks and the pools include arnica, aster, harebells, pearly everlasting, yarrow and fireweed.

Snapshot: Lower Morrissey Falls is one of the rare BC waterfalls that allow access behind the curtain of falling water (see Moul Falls, Perry Falls #2 and Findlay Falls). After carefully edging around the far bank, I stood behind the falling water among the wet, black rocks that contrast vividly with the intense green moss and grasses, and pondered life from behind a waterfall.

Further down the canyon below the falls amid the wild secluded scenery, the wildflowers, the butterflies and dragonflies, and the fragrance of the spruce and pine, I was joined by a mother dipper feeding a begging youngster. They became quite agitated when they discovered they were sharing this enchanted spot with me.

Morrissey Falls overhang

43 JOSEPHINE FALLS

Rating:	▲▲▲▲▲
Type:	Cascade
Location:	5 km (3 mi) E of Elkford
Access:	Easy. 2.3 km (1.4 mi) on level, improved trail
Status:	Trail maintained by the Elkford Chamber of Commerce
When to go:	Spring, summer, fall

Directions: At the four-way stop on Hwy 43 in Elkford turn east onto Greenhills Mine Road and proceed 5.2 km (3.2 mi) to the parking lot. Maps and signage are posted at the trailhead. The left-hand trail leads to Josephine Falls and the right-hand one to Lily Lake. There is a connecting path between the two trails and together they form a circular route of 6 km (3.5 mi) with a total hiking time of 80-plus minutes.

Facilities: Map, interpretive signage, outhouses, benches, picnic tables.

Highlights: The placid Fording River winds through the green spruce- and pine-clad mountains until it suddenly tumbles over a 25 m (82 ft) high precipice in an impressive river-wide cascade. The river plunges half the total height of the waterfall to a bench and then cascades/plunges into a strong lateral flow across the face of the falls that collects water from left to right.

It is impossible to see all of this magnificent waterfall from the main viewpoint because of the oblique angle, but the face of the falls can be viewed by continuing 150 m (165 ft) beyond the fenced area and past the Lily Lake turnoff.

At the falls, the valley of the Elk River changes from forested slopes to a Grand Canyon of steep, sliding slopes of loose debris from the crumbling sedimentary strata. A smaller falls is visible downstream.

Waterfalls of British Columbia

Josephine Falls

Josephine Falls acquired its name in 1905 when Professor Fairfield Osborn discovered them while studying big game animals in the area. He named them after his daughter who apparently caught a large trout in the plunge pool. Josephine Falls joins other great BC waterfalls such as Kinuseo and Helmcken that were not discovered until the 20th century. It is a reminder of exactly how remote and uncharted BC still was in the years 1900-20.

Snapshot: While I was admiring this great waterfall from the viewpoint, two buck mule deer appeared to drink at a pool just above the falls. A spruce grouse and a flock of noisy Clark's nutcrackers were encountered on the trail.

44 THE PETAIN WATERFALLS

Rating:	▲▲▲▲▲
Type:	Tiered cascades and plunges
Location:	Elk Lakes Provincial Park
Access:	Difficult. 70 km (43 mi) good gravel road, 10.5 km (6.5 mi) trail
Status:	Elk Lake Provincial Park
When to go:	Summer, fall

Directions: Drive 70 km (43 mi) north of Elkford (the highest town in BC at 1,300 m/4,265 ft above sea level) on the Elk River Forest Service Road to Elk Lakes Provincial Park. The park is just beyond marker 166 on the gravel road. The trailhead with maps and other information is at the parking lot. You may want to pay particular attention to the latest updates on bear sightings that are posted here. The hike to the waterfalls, 10.5 km (6.5 mi) distant, takes 2 to 2.5 hours. From the parking lot Lower Elk Lake is 1.5 km (1 mi) and 20 minutes away, Upper Elk Lake is a further 1.6 km (1 mi) and 20 minutes, and the hike along the shore of the Upper Lake to the campground is 3.4 km (2 mi) and approximately 45 minutes. From the campground it is another 4 km (2.5 mi) to the base of the falls. The trail from the parking lot to the waterfalls only gains 170 m (560 ft) elevation, which is barely noticeable. The condition of the trail is generally good and easy to follow. When I visited on August 5, 2000, Petain Creek was overflowing its banks at the campground, which necessitated paddling (boots off) to reach the bridge across the creek. The trail beyond the waterfall to the Petain Basin is 2 km (1 mi), with a steep gain of 520 m (1,700 ft) elevation.

Facilities: All the usual camping facilities are at Lower Elk Lake campground. The Upper Elk Lake campsite has a pit toilet, a food cache and firewood.

Highlights: The hike to the falls takes you through the classic scenery of the front ranges of the Rockies: imposing mountains and jade green lakes. Immediately before the main viewpoint on an old moraine, you emerge from the forest to a flower-filled meadow, and the thundering sound of the falls becomes evident. From the main viewpoint at 1,830 m (6,000 ft), you are confronted by the Imaxian immensity of the scenery with a stepped but vertical rock wall that leads to the Petain Basin above it. Petain Creek collects the water from about eight (varies) separate waterfalls that cascade from the Castelnau Hanging Glacier and the Upper Petain Basin. The blue ice of the Castelnau Glacier is visible high on the ridge; three separate waterfalls flow from its base and fall down the headwall. The middle fall is deeply incised into the wall, indicating the highly erosive power of the silt-laden water emerging from the glacier. The total height of the falls is 375 m (1,230 ft), with the highest single drop being 61 m (200 ft).

The major waterfall on the main stem of Petain Creek cascades and plunges down the rock wall, and the foot of this impressive falls is accessible by hiking 250 m (270 yd) through the bush alongside the creek. From here, in the spray zone, you can get soaked and experience the full power of the cataract. It is very redolent of Twin Falls in Yoho National Park.

The peaks in this northern portion of the park are named for the French World War I military leaders: Petain, Ney, Nivelle, Joffre, Foch and Castelnau.

The Petain Waterfalls

Snapshot: To visit the Petain Waterfalls is to be immersed in the titanic landscapes of the Canadian Rockies, one of the supreme geologic achievements of our planet. When I visited I was overwhelmed by the immensity of what I was seeing. I stood in awe of the stoic magnificence of the mountains and the sentient power of the falling water weaving through the landscape. In the words of Octavio Paz, "Only the water is human in these precipitous solitudes."

> *A star-filled sky can be compelling,*
> *a snow-capped mountain range can be*
> *awe-inspiring, an after-storm rainbow can*
> *stop you in your tracks, but only a waterfall*
> *can make you feel like you've fallen in love.*
>
> Ann Marie Brown, *California Waterfalls*

YOHO AND KOOTENAY NATIONAL PARKS

This region includes some of Canada's, and indeed the world's most spectacular and acclaimed landscapes. Yoho and Kootenay national parks are synonymous with the expansive mountain panoramas for which the Canadian Rockies are justifiably famous. The Rocky Mountains are a product of uplifted and folded sedimentary strata modified by faulting and recent fluvioglacial action. The titanic orogenic forces that created the Rockies are matched by both the region's magnificent scenery and waterfalls. The highest mountain in the area is Mt. Goodsir at 3,562 m (11,690 ft).

All of the waterfalls in this region except for Thompson Falls are within the two national parks. Plunge falls predominate, as glaciation has played a crucial role in creating the awesome hanging valleys that gave birth to both Takakkaw Falls and Twin Falls in the Yoho Valley. Limestone predominates throughout the area, which gives rise to the waterfall features at Natural Bridge and Marble Canyon that are the products of the chemical solution of limestone.

FALLS 45–54

The high mountains of Kootenay and Yoho National Parks are home to extensive icefields that collect precipitation during the winter and release it during the summer. Consequently, Takakkaw Falls, the queen of the region's waterfalls, may be at its most spectacular during August heat waves. Takakkaw and Helmcken falls in Wells Gray Provincial Park together vie for the title of BC's greatest waterfall.

The concentration of great waterfalls in Yoho National Park is matched in BC only by Wells Gray Provincial Park.

45 THOMPSON FALLS

Rating:	▲▲▲△△
Type:	Punchbowl
Location:	27 km (17 mi) N of Golden
Access:	Moderate. Gravel logging road and trail
Status:	BC Forest Service Recreation Site
When to go:	Spring, summer, fall

Directions: From the traffic lights on the western edge of Golden, proceed west on Hwy 1 for 8 km (5 mi) to Moberly and turn right onto Hartley Road (indicated by the Blaeberry Mountain Lodge sign). After 2.8 km (1.7 mi) turn left at Golden Donald Upper Road and then right after 2 km (1 mi) onto the gravel Moberly School Road. Continue 8.5 km (5.3 mi) to the Blaeberry River bridge, but do not continue straight ahead on the misleadingly named Blaeberry–Thompson Falls Forest Service Road as this will not lead you to the falls. Soon after crossing the bridge note the km 24 marker and proceed 6 km (3.7 mi) to the km 30 marker. Immediately beyond, turn right at an oblique angle onto a spur road marked with a sign announcing BCFS Thompson Falls Recreation Site. It is then 200 m (220 yd) down to the parking lot beside the Blaeberry River. The easy trail follows the west bank of the Blaeberry River with the falls 10 minutes distant. Beware of logging trucks on this access.

Facilities: Picnic tables, outhouse.

Highlights: Beside the parking lot the beautiful aquamarine water of the Blaeberry River flows in a narrow rocky course. The colour is a product of the glacial flour suspended in the water as the river is partially fed by the Mummery Glacier. At low water it is possible to examine the potholes that are being created here. At one spot the river flows through a constriction only 50 cm (20 in) wide (early August). In the summer this is a wonderful spot to sit by the river, an area covered by raging waters during the spring freshet.

Waterfalls of British Columbia

Thompson Falls. Edwina Podemski photo

At high water Thompson Falls becomes an exaggerated horseshoe as water flows into a punchbowl. At low water the river falls 1 m (3 ft) over the rim and then spreads laterally along a ledge before cascading 2 m (6.5 ft) into a rift and powering against the opposite wall.

Below the falls a steep gravel beach forms a wide pool as water backs up from the narrow, deeply incised canyon. A trail leads from the falls down to the beach area and then along the canyon rim for 200–300 m (220–330 yd). Within the canyon logs straddle the narrow walls, hung up 3–4 m (10–13 ft) above the river at its low summer level.

The Blaeberry River was christened in 1859 by Dr. James Hector, who discovered the valley and was impressed by the size of the local blueberries (blaeberry is the Gaelic word for blueberry). The falls are named for explorer David Thompson.

Snapshot: Thompson Falls is a lower echelon waterfall made interesting by its unusual shape. The Blaeberry River is an enchanting spot from the parking lot to the falls and the canyon beyond, with the aquamarine hue of the river matched only by the blue of the harebells that grow here. The Blaeberry River and Thompson Falls are surrounded by dramatic Rocky Mountain scenery as this area borders on the western edge of Yoho National Park. When I visited there was a spotted sandpiper in the immediate area of the falls, for once replacing the ubiquitous waterfall bird, the American dipper.

46 WAPTA FALLS

Rating:	▲▲▲▲▲
Type:	Plunge/cascade
Location:	Yoho National Park
Access:	Moderate. Spur road off Hwy 1, and a 2.3 km (1.5 mi) almost level trail
Status:	Yoho National Park
When to go:	Summer and fall

Directions: The Wapta Falls Road is 31.5 km (19.5 mi) east of Golden, 25 km (15.5 mi) west of Field and 51 km (31.5 mi) west of Lake Louise. Drive 1.8 km (1 mi) to the end of the road. The 2.3 km (1.4 mi) hike to the top of the falls takes 30-plus minutes, and to the foot 40-plus minutes. The trail is virtually level to the top, but quite steep to the bottom.

The trailhead is not posted on Hwy 1 westbound as there is no left turn lane. To reach the trailhead, continue for 3 km (2 mi) to the west entrance of the park and return from there.

Facilities: Picnic tables at trailhead, toilets.

Highlights: If a wide, white, roaring wall of water falling 30 m (100 ft) out of the sky appeals to you, then a trip to the foot of Wapta Falls is called for. This is a major BC waterfall, set amid the wonder of Yoho National Park's incomparable scenery.

Wapta Falls is the result of differential erosion of resistant bands of vertically inclined rock with softer strata. All waterfalls migrate upstream over the millennia, and here previous incarnations of Wapta Falls remain in degraded form as downstream islands. At present the west side of the Kicking Horse River plunges

Waterfalls of British Columbia

Wapta Falls

into a trough against the residual mound of the previous Wapta Falls, and must circumnavigate through 180 degrees to bypass this impediment.

The Kicking Horse River was originally called by the Stony Indian name, the Wapta. However, in 1858 James Hector, who was leading a party from the Palliser Expedition, was kicked unconscious by his horse and the men in his party henceforth referred to the river as the Kicking Horse. By such random events do we acquire the colourful names of our geography.

Wapta Falls has the highest discharge of all BC waterfalls and the third highest in Canada, behind only Niagara Falls, Ontario, and Virginia Falls, NWT.

Snapshot: Wapta Falls is a majestic and inspiring sight framed by forest and the naked upper slopes of Mount Hunter in summer and its snowy heights in spring and fall. Wapta is an extremely popular family hike, and on a blistering hot summer day I watched many people delight in being drenched by the cooling clouds of spray at the foot of the falls, particularly a young Japanese couple who were positively ecstatic in enjoying this wilderness experience.

47 OTTERTAIL FALLS

Rating:	▲▲▲△△
Type:	Tiered plunge
Location:	Yoho National Park
Access:	Moderate. 16.7 km (10.5 mi) one way trail, day outing by mountain bike, long day hike or overnight camp
Status:	Yoho National Park
When to go:	Summer, fall

Directions: The trailhead is a pullout about 100 m (110 yd) east of the Ottertail bridge on the south side of Hwy 1. The Ottertail bridge is 8.3 km (5.2 mi) west of Field and 34.3 km (21.3 mi) west of Lake Louise. The Ottertail Fire Road hugs the east side of the Ottertail River for most of the route and grades are mainly gentle, with one or two steeper sections. The elevation gain is 360 m (1,180 ft) over the 16.7 km (10.4 mi) distance.

The trail, an old road, is very easy to follow. At 2.8 km (1.7 mi) look for some minor hoodoos at a viewpoint over the river. You will cross the Float Creek bridge at 6.2 km (3.9 mi) and the McArthur Creek bridge at 14.6 km (9.1 mi). The McArthur warden cabin is on a bench above the river at 15.1 km (9.4 mi); bikes must be left here for the final 1.6 km (1 mi) hike to the falls. Follow the trail 400 m (440 yd) beyond the cabin to the Ottertail River bridge. After a further 700 m (760 yd) bear left for the trail to the falls and then proceed 500 m (550 yd) to the viewpoint.

Allow about two and a half hours to reach the McArthur cabin by mountain bike, and a further twenty minutes hiking beyond there. The return trip is largely a freewheeling downhill roll that takes less than two hours. The whole excursion can be completed in about six hours.

Facilities: There are no facilities at the trailhead. There is an excellent campsite at McArthur Creek, 15 km (9 mi) along the trail, with the usual backcountry facilities.

Highlights: If you are in Yoho National Park then fantastic scenery is assured. The road to Ottertail Falls is no exception: there are many excellent views across the river to the Ottertail Range peaks such as Mt. Hurd (2,993 m/9,820 ft) and Mt. Vaux (3,319 m/10,890 ft). The McArthur warden cabin is a wonderful place to stop and rest, eat lunch and contemplate the spectacular views of the twin summits of Mt. Goodsir, whose south tower peaks at 3,562 m (11,686 ft), the highest in Yoho National Park.

I had never seen a photograph of Ottertail Falls before visiting so I had no idea what might await me. The falls consist of three consecutive plunges of 3 m (10 ft),

4 m (13 ft) and 4 m (13 ft) into copycat plunge pools, with the falls separated only by their pools. The falls are contained within a rugged canyon and the final plunge pool across from the viewpoint has a high vertical wall that spills house- and car-sized rocks into the riverbed. The time to see maximum water volume here would be in early summer, but the Ottertail River always has plenty of water. Owing to the local topography there is only a single possible viewpoint for these falls.

Spruce grouse are commonly encountered along the trail, and near the falls I was befriended by a confiding flock of boreal chickadees, recognizable by their raspy "cee-dee" calls.

Ottertail Falls

Snapshot: When the weather is fine in early October, the Canadian Rockies possess an incomparable transcendental beauty. The sky is blue, the forests of the deep valleys are either bright green in sunshine or a dark, velvety green in shadow and the colours are offset by the pure white of fresh snow on the high peaks and the surpassing brilliance of the golden aspen and other deciduous species. It is a scene to make grown men cry.

The Ottertail Fire Road is a fine place to partake of this splendour, with the bench at the McArthur cabin strongly recommended as a viewpoint. I sat there in the hot sunshine after visiting the falls, entranced by the presence of Mt. Goodsir, numinous in its north-facing shadows. It was with the greatest reluctance that I finally departed this magical spot for the downhill roll back to the highway.

48 NATURAL BRIDGE

Rating:	▲▲▲▲△
Type:	Punchbowl
Location:	Yoho National Park
Access:	Easy. Spur road off Hwy 1
Status:	Yoho National Park
When to go:	Spring, summer, fall

Directions: Take the Emerald Lake Road 1.6 km (1 mi) west of Field, 55 km (34 mi) east of Golden and 28.5 km (17 mi) west of Lake Louise. Natural Bridge is at 2.4 km (1.5 mi) on the Emerald Lake Road. See also Hamilton Falls, which is at km 9 (5.5 mi) on the same road.

Facilities: Parking lot, outhouses, interpretive signage, viewing platforms, wheelchair accessible.

Highlights: All waterfalls continuously strive for self-annihilation, and Natural Bridge is a fascinating example of a deconstructing waterfall. Over time Natural Bridge has succeeded in downgrading itself from a plunge waterfall to a punchbowl, en route to becoming merely a rapids. As the signage indicates, "Yesterday's waterfall is today's bridge, becoming tomorrow's chasm."

At Natural Bridge the vertically inclined strata first created the original impediment to the flow of the Kicking Horse River. The erosive forces at work now are both mechanical and chemical, as the river enlarges cracks in the rock by both

Natural Bridge

solution of the limestone and by the abrasive power of its silt-laden water. Presently, the river flows beneath the base of the former waterfall, leaving the base suspended as a bridge.

At high water the river powers into a punchbowl, a watery holocaust immediately before the bridge, and the constricted and falling waters pass beneath the bridge and pour forth in a fearsome pile of seething water that crashes against the far wall of the gorge. Interestingly, the rectangular dissolution of the rock has created a second incomplete channel for the river that operates as a blowhole, with pent-up water splashing out from the cavity on an irregular basis and posing an interesting photographic challenge.

At extreme high water Natural Bridge still functions as a regular waterfall with some of the water flowing over the bridge, rather than beneath it. At low water it is possible to observe the river dropping 3 m (10 ft) from its punchbowl into the slot beneath the bridge.

Snapshot: Punchbowls are an uncommon waterfall type. Natural Bridge and The Mushbowl in Wells Gray Provincial Park are the provincial archetypes. Both provide excellent examples of a waterfall in a late stage of its devolution.

49 HAMILTON FALLS

Rating:	▲▲▲△△
Type:	Plunge
Location:	Yoho National Park
Access:	Easy. Spur road off Hwy 1, steep 800 m (875 ft) trail
Status:	Yoho National Park
When to go:	Summer and fall

Directions: Take the Emerald Lake–Natural Bridge Road 1.8 km (1 mi) west of Field or 55 km (34 mi) east of Golden. Proceed 9 km (5.5 mi) to the parking lot at Emerald Lake. The trailhead is off the side of the parking lot. It is a 20-minute hike to the foot of the falls and an additional 10 minutes on an ever-steeper trail to the top.

Facilities: Emerald Lake is one of the most visited spots in the Rockies, with a complete range of visitor facilities including accommodation, restaurant, concession with canoe rentals, toilets, etc.

Highlights: Hamilton Falls is a dramatic spot within the channel of Hamilton Creek as it drops from Hamilton Lake to the Emerald River. The falls are about 100 m (330 ft) in total, but only the lower 30 m (100 ft) is actually visible, as the

Hamilton Falls. Nick Riemondi photo

creek is deeply incised into a massive headwall that shows the synclinal folding for which the Rockies are the textbook example. The visible falls plunge from a slot in the headwall to a pool before falling over a final step.

The foot of the falls is in a dark, forested gorge an area somewhat adulterated by the construction of a concrete weir, a relic of an abandoned water system. Below the weir is a pothole, hollowed like a gourd into the sedimentary layers by pebbles and filled with crystal clear water. By climbing the trail to the top of the falls you will earn expansive views of the loveliness of Emerald Lake and of the great massif of Mt. Burgess (2,599 m/8,527 ft) of Burgess fossil fame to the east, and Mt. Vaux (3,320 m/10,890 ft) and Mt. Goodsir (3,562 m/11,686 ft) to the south.

The trail continues to the alpine environs of Hamilton Lake, 5.5 km (3.4 mi) one way from the trailhead at Emerald Lake.

Snapshot: The hike to the top of the falls is recommended for the view, but those with vertigo will not relish looking down into the chasm of the falls. It is also a potentially dangerous spot and caution is advised as there are no fences.

The trail to the foot of the falls traverses a forest that contains most of BC's main coniferous tree species. I noted Douglas fir, western hemlock, western red cedar, balsam, Engelmann spruce, lodgepole pine and western yew, an uncommon diversity for any forest in BC.

50 TAKAKKAW FALLS

Rating:	▲▲▲▲▲
Type:	Plunge
Location:	Yoho National Park
Access:	Easy. Blacktop, five-minute walk to base
Status:	Yoho National Park
When to go:	Late June to October 1

Directions: The Yoho Valley Road is 3.5 km (2.2 mi) east of Field and 23.5 km (14.5 mi) west of Lake Louise on Hwy 1, the Trans-Canada Highway. It is 14 km (9 mi) from the highway turnoff to the parking lot. Note that trailers and large RVs must be left at the parking lot at the bottom of the Yoho Valley Road because of severe switchbacks. Information on access can be obtained from the Parks Canada offices at either Field or Rogers Pass.

Takakkaw Falls is not a place for solitude, as this is one of the most popular locations in the entire Canadian Rockies, and on summer days the parking lot is frequently full to capacity. Maximum flows over the falls are in late spring when the snow is melting and on hot summer afternoons. The falls can be viewed from the parking lot or a level, easy trail leads 300 m (330 yd) to the base of the falls, less

Takakkaw Falls

than 10 minutes walking. The more adventurous can also climb a steep, rocky trail that approaches the spray zone of the falls.

Facilities: Interpretive signage, toilets, camping and picnic tables. The trail to the foot of the falls is wheelchair accessible. The Whisky Jack Hostel is adjacent.

Highlights: Takakkaw Falls is one of North America's pre-eminent waterfalls. Not only is it one of the highest, but its location within the spectacular scenery of Yoho National Park in the heart of the Canadian Rockies ensures its iconic status in the consciousness of the nation.

The Yoho Valley is a classic glacial U-shaped trough with numerous tributary hanging valleys and their attendant waterfalls, including Laughing and Twin falls. The flow of Takakkaw Falls is produced by the meltwater from the Daly Glacier, part of the Waputik Icefield. The glacier approaches within about 350 m (380 yd) of the brink of the falls. During the summer when water flows are high the creek spews through a narrow cleft in the headwall, pulverizes on a ledge and descends in roiling clouds of whitewater and spray to the valley below, where it joins the Yoho River. At low flows in the fall it is possible to see that the waterfall actually consists of a cascade to the ledge that creates a roostertail, a plunge to another ledge, another plunge and a final cascade down a sloping rock wall. In the winter the falls are reduced to narrow ribbons of ice that climbers scale.

For many years Takakkaw carried the title of "the highest waterfall in Canada." This accolade is now conceded to Della Falls on Vancouver Island, with Takakkaw considered the third highest with a total drop of 384 m (1,260 ft). It also has the second highest vertical plunge of 254 m (833 ft), behind only Helmet Falls at 352 m (1,155 ft).

The first recorded visit to Takakkaw was in 1897 by the German explorer Jean Habel, and his visit encouraged William Van Horne, president of the Canadian Pacific Railway, to follow. It was Van Horne who conferred on the falls the name *takakkaw*, a Cree word for awesome. Van Horne also famously stated that "if we can't export the scenery, then we'll import the tourists," and so began the birth of tourism in the Canadian Rockies.

It is well worth climbing to the foot of the falls and looking up into the plummeting maelstrom of pulverized water. Mountain goats are often seen on the rocky slopes near the falls, elk along the access road and Clark's nutcrackers, gray jays and ravens patrol the picnic tables for crumbs and handouts.

A different perspective on the falls and their wider setting can be achieved by hiking the famous Iceline Trail high on the west side of the Yoho Valley. From here there are awesome views of Takakkaw Falls, the Waputik Glacier, high mountain peaks and the Yoho Valley.

Snapshot: Yoho is a Cree word that expresses awe and wonder, and it really encapsulates the whole experience of this incomparable valley and its great waterfall. Everything is built on a grand scale, with sweeping views of classic Rocky Mountain scenery and the centrepiece of the magnificent, magnetic Takakkaw Falls. To stand before Takakkaw Falls on a hot August afternoon when it is in full spate, and to mingle with awestruck visitors from around the world who have come to pay homage, is to stand before the central icon, the myth personified, of the Canadian Rockies. The metaphor could be extended to all of Canada, but Niagara Falls, Ontario, might have something to say about that.

The Yoho Valley is redolent of Yosemite Valley in California not only in the magnificence of the scenery and the famous high waterfalls, but also in the esteemed position the two valleys hold in the consciousness of the two respective nations.

The world waterfall stage is shared by the famous river-wide plunges such as Niagara, Iguazu and Victoria falls and high, ribbon plunges such as Angel Falls in Venezuela, Yosemite Falls in California and Takakkaw Falls in the Canadian Rockies.

51 LAUGHING FALLS

Rating:	▲▲▲▲△
Type:	Plunge
Location:	Yoho National Park
Access:	Moderate. 3.9 km (2.4 mi) hike one way
Status:	Yoho National Park
When to go:	Summer and early fall

Directions: As for Takakkaw Falls. There is no access until the snow clears in the spring and Parks Canada may close the road as early as October 1. Information is available from Parks Canada at either Field or Rogers Pass.

The access to Laughing Falls is along the Yoho Valley Trail, which leaves from the north end of the Takakkaw Falls campsite. The busy trail is initially wide and level, followed by a steeper, rougher section beyond the km 1.9 marker. The falls are 3.9 km (2.4 mi) distant and hiking time is 65-plus minutes. The base of the falls can be closely approached along either side of the creek.

Facilities: See Takakkaw Falls. Laughing Falls has its own popular, primitive campsite located between the foot of the falls and the banks of the Yoho River.

Highlights: The hike from Takakkaw to Laughing Falls will actually reward you with four waterfalls. Angel's Staircase and Point Lace Falls are situated midway along the trail; Twin Falls is 2.4 km (1.5 mi) beyond Laughing Falls and is strongly

Laughing Falls

recommended. The trail ends at the Yoho Glacier at 8.3 km (5.2 mi). Angel's Staircase, 100 m (110 yd) to the right of the main trail at the km 1.9 marker, is a cascading creek that flows strongly in early summer, but is almost dry by September. Only 10 m (30 ft) beyond the turn to Angel's Staircase on the main trail, a 150 m (165 yd) side trail on the left leads to Point Lace Falls, which cascades lacily down an angled 13 m (43 ft) rock face. Beyond the Point Lace turnoff the trail climbs steeply away from the Yoho River for a short distance before rejoining the riverbank.

Laughing Falls is a 30 m (100 ft) plunge that is created as the Little Yoho River thunders out of a narrow throat in the craggy headwall to its plunge pool.

Snapshot: I visited Laughing Falls on a morning in early August when a heat wave was producing a high discharge. The trail on the left-hand side of the creek leads to a spray-soaked vantage point immediately downstream of the plunge pool. On that morning I witnessed the most intense waterfall rainbow I have ever seen. The Yoho Valley is a Shangri-La at any time of the year, but a visit in late September with blue skies, fresh snow sprinkled on the high peaks and the golden deciduous trees is particularly magical.

52 TWIN FALLS #2 (YOHO VALLEY)

Rating:	▲▲▲▲▲
Type:	Plunge
Location:	Yoho National Park
Access:	Moderate. 8.5 km (5.3 mi) trail one way from Takakkaw Falls campsite
Status:	Yoho National Park
When to go:	Summer and early fall

Directions: See Takakkaw and Laughing falls. Twin Falls is 8.5 km (5.3 mi) beyond the Takakkaw Falls campsite and 4.6 km (2.9 mi) beyond Laughing Falls, with an elevation gain of 300 m (980 ft).

Facilities: See Takakkaw Falls. The seasonally operated Twin Falls Chalet, an old Canadian Pacific building, is dramatically located near the foot of the falls. Lunch and/or drinks can be purchased here and lodging is available for small groups with reservations.

Highlights: You can discern the first distant views of Twin Falls through the trees on the trail between Laughing Falls and the Twin Falls campground. Closer views must wait until you reach Twin Falls Chalet.

Twin Falls is a major BC waterfall and is at its most impressive at maximum discharge during summer heat waves. It is well named: Twin Falls Creek plunges 80 m (260 ft) from a hanging valley through twin notches at the brink and the two streams fall side by side down an enormous limestone rock wall before joining together on their way to the Yoho River in the valley below. An interesting but salutary story concerning Twin Falls dates back to 1924, when trail workers decided they could improve upon nature by making the two falls equal in volume. Their foolhardiness was repaid when debris from the blast blocked the left-hand notch and created the opposite effect to that intended. Fortunately the workers were able to rectify their ill-advised scheme with another blast.

Access to the foot of the falls is along the north (right) bank of the creek where you can experience the full elemental power of this mighty waterfall. When you reach the cliff beside the torrent, it is possible to look down into the plunge pool, a maelstrom of falling white water, roiling clouds of pulverized spray and the ongoing rush of the creek as it races downstream to more gigantic cascades that are major waterfalls in their own right.

Snapshot: To stand close by this giant waterfall in full flow with the roar of the water and the periodic crack of water-borne rocks impacting on the creek bed is

Twin Falls #2

a thrilling experience of the first magnitude. I noticed from certain points on the trail that the roar of the falls sounded like the approach of a low-level jet fighter. As I stood looking down into the plunge pool being pounded incessantly by tons of water per second, I decided that this must be the most hostile spot in BC.

The outing to Twin Falls is one of the most intense waterfall experiences possible in BC, as the 8.5 km (5.3 mi) trail includes three of the province's great falls, Takakkaw, Laughing and Twin, plus other minor falls. In addition, the hike amid the absolute splendour of the Yoho Valley is guaranteed to leave a lasting impression.

53 MARBLE CANYON

Rating:	▲▲▲▲△
Type:	Plunge
Location:	Kootenay National Park
Access:	Easy. Short trail beside highway
Status:	Kootenay National Park
When to go:	Spring, summer, fall

Directions: From Radium Hot Springs drive north on Hwy 93 through Kootenay National Park for 89 km (55 mi). The Marble Canyon trail is an easy walk beside the canyon of Tokumm Creek. The trail criss-crosses the creek over seven bridges in a distance of 800 m (875 yd). The two waterfalls are at the end of the trail.

Facilities: Parking, toilet facilities, trail information and interpretive signage.

Highlights: Confusingly, although the area is called Marble Canyon, Tokumm Creek actually drains an area known as Prospectors Valley. Marble Canyon is an exquisite place that got its name when the dolomite was mistaken for marble. The trail builders here have done an excellent job of incorporating the paths and bridges into the landscape to accommodate the thousands of people who visit each year.

The Tokumm Creek waterfalls have been on the move because of erosion by both solution and abrasion along fractures within the dolomite and limestone of Marble Canyon. Interpretive signage on the trail shows the estimated position of the falls after the last Ice Age 11,000 years ago, when Tokumm Creek became a hanging valley to the main channel of the Vermilion River. A further marker estimates where the falls were 9,000 years ago and their present location is 600 m (660 yd) from the presumed starting point. The upstream migration of the falls, along with the downcutting (the canyon is up to 37 m (120 ft) deep), indicates the dynamic geomorphologic processes at work here.

Waterfalls of British Columbia

Marble Canyon

The aquamarine waters of Tokumm Creek flow deep down within the narrow confines of the eroded canyon, in many places only a few centimetres wide. The creek has even left a natural bridge suspended high above it at the site of the falls 9,000 years ago. The sculpted walls of the silvery limestone and dolomite are patterned with tubular potholes, potholes within potholes and moss gardens growing in abandoned potholes and on ledges.

At the head of the canyon the main drop is preceded by a step, and from the final bridge you can peer down into the confusion of a 21 m (69 ft) waterfall confined by encompassing walls, ledges and darkness. Doubtless this waterfall is a wild place at the height of the spring freshet.

Over the years there have been multiple fatalities at Marble Canyon from people inadvertently backing over the canyon edge while taking photographs.

Snapshot: Marble Canyon is one of the most beautiful and enthralling spots in the Rockies, but is the antithesis of much of the Rocky Mountain scenery. Instead of the Imax-ian immensity of many Rocky Mountain landscapes this is an intimate place on a human scale where rock gardens grow a profusion of wildflowers and mosses, and where the subalpine firs eke out a bonsai existence on the precarious soils of the abandoned ledges and potholes.

While I was standing on one of the bridges I heard a familiar sound coming from below, deep within the canyon. It was a dipper calling, the sound strangely amplified by the confines of the narrow canyon.

During my visit on a beautiful sunny morning in late July Marble Canyon was populated with visitors from around the world speaking with Greek, French, British, German and American accents. Maybe there were even a few Canadian nationals there, along with me, bursting with nationalistic pride at this enchanting spot.

54 HELMET FALLS

Rating:	▲▲▲▲▲
Type:	Tiered plunge
Location:	74 km (46 mi) N of Radium, 45 km (28 mi) S of Lake Louise and 50 km (30 mi) W of Banff
Access:	Difficult. 16 km (10 mi) hike one way
Status:	Kootenay National Park
When to go:	Spring, summer, fall

Directions: The trailhead is at the Paint Pots parking lot, 74 km (46 mi) north of Radium Hot Springs and 19.6 km (12.2 mi) south of Castle Junction on Hwy 1. For the first kilometre the trail follows the Paint Pots Nature Trail through the ochre beds and crosses the Vermilion River on a bridge to the "cones" created by the high iron content in the water. Immediately beyond the cones the trail enters the forest, but all junctions and campsites are signed. The significant spots are at km 3.7 (mi 2.3) where the Tumbling Creek trail branches left, km 6.2 (mi 3.9), the Helmet–Ochre Junction campsite and km 6.5 (mi 4.0), the Helmet Creek bridge, which is followed by a short steep section of switchbacks as you climb away from the creek. At km 12 (mi 7.5) a second bridge crosses Helmet Creek and the first distant views of Helmet Falls are attained at km 13.5 (mi 8.4). At km 14.3 (mi 8.9) the trail intersects with the Rockwall Trail and the Helmet warden cabin is only 300 m (330 yd) away to the left, with the campground just beyond across a bridge. The viewpoint at the base of Helmet Falls is about 1 km (.6 mi) beyond the cabin along the trail that passes through the campsite.

Hiking southward on the Limestone Summit Trail will open up different perspectives on the falls.

The 16 km (10 mi) trail is in very good condition and is easy to follow. It is generally level, except for the relatively short climb away from Helmet Creek. I hiked to the falls in 3 hours and 40 minutes, and out again in 4 hours. It is a long, tiring day and the 32 km (20 mi) should only be attempted as a day hike by strong hikers confident of their ability and endurance.

Facilities: The Paint Pots trailhead has parking, toilets and trail information. The backcountry Helmet Falls campground has tent sites, barbecues, picnic tables, outhouses and bear caches.

Highlights: Helmet Falls trail is not particularly distinguished as it mostly travels beneath a forest canopy with little in the way of scenery until you reach the vicinity of the falls. The Helmet trail also serves as access to the spectacular Rockwall Trail and Goodsir Pass.

Helmet Falls has a total drop of 352 m (1,155 ft) and is the fifth highest waterfall in Canada. The falls are fed by the meltwater streams of two separate glaciers, the Sharp and the Washmawapta, which merge in mid-fall high on the headwall. The unified stream then falls into a narrow slot canyon from which the second tier of the falls plunges to the base.

The monumental amphitheatre at Helmet Falls is formed by Limestone Peak (2,878 m/9,443 ft), Helmet Mountain (3,138 m/10,296 ft) and Sharp Mountain (3,049 m/10,004 ft). The three mountains form part of the Rockwall, the limestone eastern escarpment of the Vermilion Range that extends 53 km (33 mi) through Kootenay and Yoho national parks. The Rockwall Trail traverses the foot of the massive, 1,000 m (3,280 ft) high escarpment for nearly 30 km (20 mi) and crosses three alpine passes in the process. Look for mountain goats on the headwall cliffs.

A Guide to BC's Best 100 Falls

Helmet Falls

Snapshot: Helmet Falls is redolent of the Petain Waterfalls: both share the common feature of a meltwater stream that plunges down a giant headwall from a glacier. The viewpoints are similarly located in open terrain on old moraines at the foot of the falls with enormous vertical headwalls and spectacular peaks.

Although the trail is long and lacks scenery my hike was relieved by the wildlife I encountered along the way. A pine marten perched in a tree just beyond the Paint Pots, a spruce grouse insisted on sharing the trail with me and only flew off when I came within 2 m (6 ft) of it and I spotted a mountain goat on a bluff from the km 12 (7.5 mi) bridge. On my return trip a grizzly bear was feeding in the last avalanche chute before the Helmet Creek switchbacks. I spotted the bear about 250 m (275 yd) away as I entered the chute and it immediately seemed to sense me too as it became uneasy. I froze and watched it feeding for five minutes, but as soon as I resumed walking the bear bolted into the bushes. This was the only on-trail grizzly I encountered while researching this book.

They left their home of summer ease
Beneath the lowland's sheltering trees
To seek, by ways unknown to all,
The promise of the waterfall.

Some vague, faint rumour to the vale
Had crept—perchance a hunter's tale—
Of its wild mirth of waters lost
On the dark woods through which it tossed.

Somewhere it laughed and sang; somewhere
Whirled in mad dance its misty hair;
But who had raised its veil, or seen
The rainbow skirts of the Undine?

John Greenleaf Whittier, "The Seeking of the Waterfall"

WELLS GRAY PROVINCIAL PARK & AREA

Wells Gray Provincial Park, "the waterfall park," is the waterfall capital of British Columbia. It is one of BC's largest parks at over 5,000 sq km (3,000 sq mi) and is located on the Yellowhead Highway, north of Kamloops, in south-central BC. The park is the product of the old triumvirate of landscape-forming processes: fire, ice and water and is the epicentre of past volcanism in BC. Lava flows from the present Trophy Mountains have resulted in extensive basalt plateaus modified by more recent glacial and fluvial processes. Volcanism on this scale is something of an anomaly in BC, where metamorphic and sedimentary geology dominates the landscape. The fluvial erosion of basalt is the premier mechanism for the creation of classical plunge waterfalls and the Wells Gray area is the paradigm.

The high, rugged backcountry of Wells Gray Park rises to 2,860 m (9,380 ft) at Garnet Peak. The mountains capture heavy snowpacks during the winter, and the melt is released as runoff that maintains high discharges in the rivers and waterfalls through the summer months.

The present landscape of Wells Gray Provincial Park revolves around the glacial overdeepening of the Clearwater River valley and the consequent creation of the hanging valleys of its tributaries, especially the Murtle River. The Murtle is notable for the series of seven major waterfalls along its 36 km (22 mi) course from Murtle Lake. Its final plunge toward the Clearwater River has produced BC's greatest waterfall, Helmcken Falls, a continentally significant feature. Wells Gray Park is home to a significant concentration of BC's most impressive waterfalls: Helmcken, Dawson, Spahats, Sylvia/Goodwin, Osprey, Moul and others are all crowded into a small area. It is deserving of its title as BC's waterfall capital.

Waterfalls of British Columbia

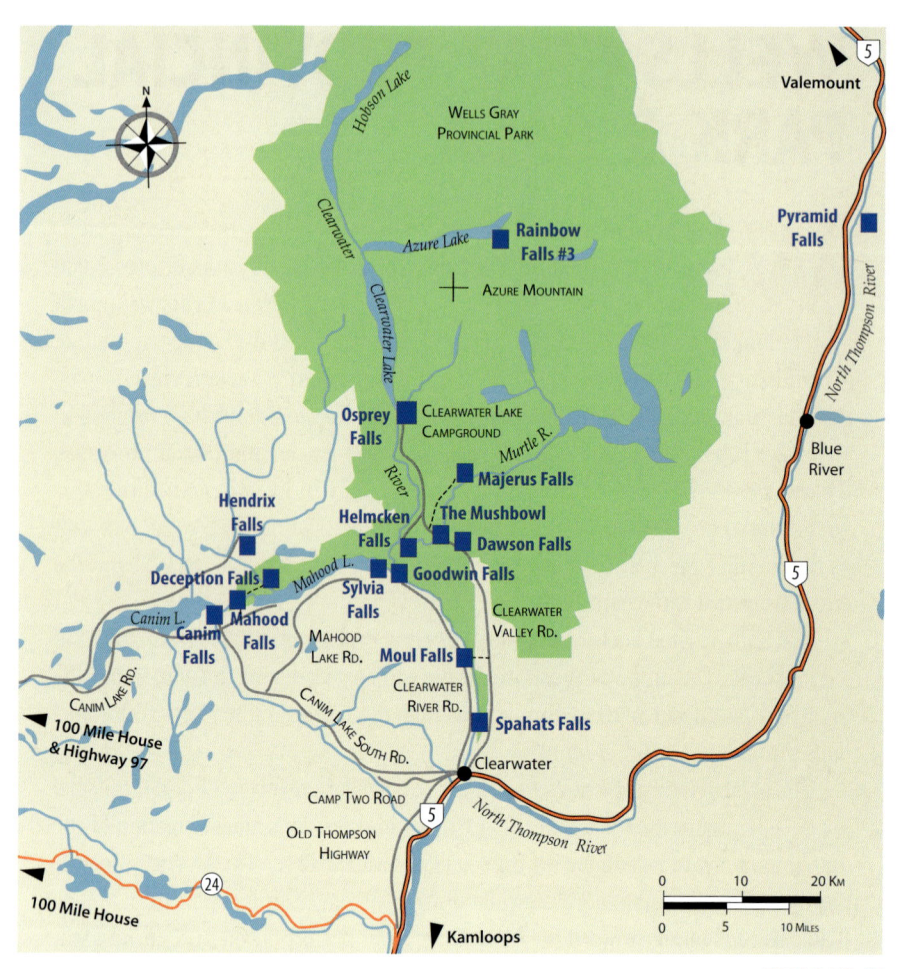

FALLS 55–71

55 HENDRIX FALLS

Rating:	▲▲▲▲△
Type:	Plunge
Location:	70 km (44 mi) northeast of 100 Mile House
Access:	Easy. Gravel logging road and short trail
Status:	Forest Service Recreation Trail
When to go:	Spring, summer, fall

Directions: Drive north on Hwy 97 from 100 Mile House and turn right after 2 km (1 mi) onto the road to Forest Grove, which is 21 km (13 mi) distant. At Forest Grove turn right onto the Canim Lake Road. After 12.8 km (8 mi) continue straight ahead and proceed along the west side of Canim Lake through the small community of Eagle Creek to where the road becomes the gravel 6000 Road (now 46 km

(29 mi) from Hwy 97). Watch the roadside kilometre markers and proceed 18 km (11 mi) to 6018. Take the right fork onto the 7000 Road, the Hendrix Creek–Deception Creek Forest Service Road, and after 700 metres (765 yd) cross the bridge and then immediately bear right onto the 710 Road where a sign indicates Hendrix Falls. This road passes through a plantation then enters standing timber and at 2.8 km (1.7 mi) the trailhead is marked on the right.

Facilities: None

Highlights: The short, level trail to the falls through a mixed coniferous forest of spruce, lodgepole pine, red cedar, Douglas fir and subalpine fir can be hiked in 5 to 10 minutes. The shrub understory contains thimbleberry, red osier dogwood, high bush cranberry and box, with flowers such as pearly everlasting, columbine and false Solomon's seal. Listen for the "yank, yank" call of red-breasted nuthatches. There is ample evidence that moose frequent the trail area.

Hendrix Falls. Chris Harris photo

Hendrix Falls is a classic Cariboo–Wells Gray type waterfall, sculpted in basalt as the waters of Hendrix Creek fall 20 m (65 ft) into the perfectly round plunge pool. The upper stratum of the headwall is formed of basalt pillars with a typical undercut behind the falls. Water volume is greatest during the spring snowmelt; when the water flow is low later in the year, the waterfall splits into three separate columns.

Hendrix Falls and the associated creek and lake are named for John "Slim" Hendrix (1870–1938), who lived in the Canim Lake area and ran a trapline in the Hendrix Creek drainage.

Snapshot: The logged area of the access road immediately before the falls is an old clear-cut with a healthy plantation of new trees. When the area was logged the unwanted aspen trees were left standing. Today, this patch of forest could easily pass for the model for Emily Carr's famous painting, *Scorned as Timber, Beloved of the Sky*.

Waterfalls of British Columbia

56 & 57 CANIM AND MAHOOD FALLS

Rating:	▲▲▲▲△
Type:	Plunge
Location:	70 km (44 mi) NE of 100 Mile House
Access:	Easy. 30 km (19 mi) of good gravel road, 1 km (.6 mi) of level trail
Status:	Wells Gray Provincial Park
When to go:	Spring, summer and fall

Directions: From downtown 100 Mile House drive north on Hwy 97 for 2 km (1 mi) and turn east on the Canim Lake Road. At Forest Grove, 23 km (14 m), turn right (east) toward Canim Lake. After 13 km (8 mi) bear right onto the Canim Lake South Road, also called the 8100 Road. The road becomes gravel after 6 km (4 mi). Proceed to the T-junction at Mahood Lake Road, turn left and after 10.5 km (6.5 mi) watch for the trail signs on the left.

Facilities: Pit toilet.

Highlights: Wells Gray Provincial Park has two sites that allow you to kill two birds with one stone. This is one; the other is Sylvia and Goodwin falls. The Canim River flows from Canim Lake to Mahood Lake in a braided course and Canim Falls and Mahood Falls are on different branches of the river. The two waterfalls can be viewed from the same trail within 200 m (220 yd) of each other. Canim Falls on the main stem of the Canim River is the major falls. The geology here is typical of the Wells Gray area as the river has carved an impressive canyon through the basalt

Canim Falls

lava flows. The trail passes through a mixed forest of Douglas fir, red cedar, lodgepole pine and spruce, with kinnikinnick and queen's cup growing on the floor.

Mahood Falls

A five-minute hike along the trail brings you to the canyon rim and the viewpoint for Mahood Falls, which is framed by the forest in the mid-distance. Mahood Falls is a 15 m (50 ft) twin plunge that tumbles down to meet the main stem of the Canim River. The falls, river and lake are named for James Adam Mahood, a surveyor for the Canadian Pacific Railway, who was active in the area in the 1870s.

Canim Falls

Mahood Falls

A further five-minute hike beyond Mahood Falls alongside the rim of the Canim River canyon leads to the 30 m (100 ft) Canim Falls. From the main viewpoint the falls can only be viewed from a slightly oblique angle, but the volume of water and the great plunge pool carved in basalt is impressive. By circumventing the far end of the safety fence the brink of the falls can be approached but extreme caution is advised on the slippery rocks. From the rim there is a clear view down the Canim River valley.

At high flows Canim Falls is a twin plunge. During the spring runoff a weeping wall forms across the canyon as water seeps between layers of basalt and then flows down the canyon wall. The base of Canim Falls can be accessed by a rough trail that descends from the main trail midway between the two viewing areas.

Snapshot: I have visited Canim and Mahood falls on spring mornings when the high flow created a spectacular white wall of water contrasting with the wet, black rocks and the bright green mosses and grasses of the spray zone. I have also visited late on a November afternoon when the walls of the plunge pool were decorated with icicles like stalactites. Even at that late time of the year a dipper still sang and bobbed above the falls.

58 DECEPTION FALLS

Rating:	▲▲▲▲△
Type:	Plunge
Location:	81 km (50 mi) NE of 100 Mile House
Access:	Easy. Logging road and short trail
Status:	Wells Gray Provincial Park
When to go:	Spring, summer, fall

Directions: Follow the directions to Canim and Mahood falls. At 4.2 km (2.6 mi) beyond the Canim–Mahood trailhead stay left; go left again after another 20 m (22 yd) on to Mahood Lake North Road. Drive 5 km (3 mi) to the trailhead on the left (note that the park sign incorrectly indicates 8 km). The road ends at a turnaround 200 m (220 yd) after the trailhead. The 800 m (875 yd) trail ascends gradually to the fenced viewpoint, about a 15-minute hike. It continues along the rim of the gorge toward the brink of the falls, but only poor views can be had from here.

It is possible to reach the foot of the falls by descending a wet and slippery route into the creek bed and proceeding upstream on dangerously slick rocks.

Facilities: None

Highlights: The creek was so named after twice deceiving railway surveyors, the first time in 1873, into believing they were exploring the Clearwater River. The name was bestowed by the second unfortunate explorer, Joseph Hunter.

The lower part of the trail is in a trembling aspen and paper birch forest that gives way to Douglas fir and lodgepole pine as you ascend. In June the forest floor is carpeted with bunchberry and twinflower, and the songs of Cassin's, warbling and red-eyed vireos and Swainson's thrush abound.

Deception Creek flows through an upper gorge and makes an

Deception Falls. B.D. Davis / Backpack Photography

initial small plunge of 3–4 m (10–13 ft) to a foamy pool before the main plunge of 40 m (130 ft). From the viewpoint the foot of the falls is hidden at high water in June in a veil of imploding spray that drifts away to the south wall of the gorge. Closer to the brink the angle becomes oblique and trees obscure the view.

Snapshot: From the brink of the falls the views downstream to Mahood Lake created an optical illusion of the lake appearing higher than the falls.

59 & 60 SYLVIA AND GOODWIN FALLS

Rating:	▲▲▲▲▲
Type:	Block plunge / cascade
Location:	Wells Gray Provincial Park
Access:	Moderate. 40 km (25 mi) of gravel road, 3 km (2 mi) on trail
Status:	Wells Gray Provincial Park
When to go:	Spring, summer, fall

Directions: Across from the Wells Gray Inn on Hwy 5 in Clearwater, turn onto Old Thompson Highway, which leads into the commercial centre of Clearwater. After 1 km (.6 mi) cross the Clearwater River bridge and immediately bear right on to Camp Two Road. Proceed 2 km (1 mi) and at the end of the blacktop turn right onto the Clearwater River Road. Follow this road 39 km (24 mi) to its dead end at a campsite at the confluence of the Mahood and Clearwater rivers. The trail follows the south side of the Mahood River for 3 km (2 mi) to Sylvia Falls, about 45 minutes hiking time. Sylvia Falls can also be accessed by a 2 km (1 mi) trail from the mouth of the Mahood River on Mahood Lake.

Facilities: None at the falls, but the trailhead is a primitive campsite with a picnic table and outhouse.

Highlights: The 40 km (25 mi) drive from Clearwater along the Clearwater River is well worth the trip alone. There is much to see, including some spectacular rapids. For a detailed log of this drive refer to *Exploring Wells Gray Park* by Roland Neave.

The trail beside the Mahood River initially winds through an Interior wet belt forest of Douglas fir, massive western red cedars, hemlock, birch and cottonwood, with an understory of thimbleberry, devil's club, skunk cabbage and wild mint. Indian pipe is also present. After 30 minutes hiking you will be tantalized by a distant view of the right side of Goodwin Falls. The trail leads directly to the brink of Sylvia Falls and it is easiest to visit here first and work back to Goodwin Falls. The two falls are less than 100 m (110 yd) apart, with Sylvia upstream of Goodwin.

Waterfalls of British Columbia

Sylvia Falls

Goodwin Falls and Sylvia Falls

    Sylvia Falls is one of the premier waterfalls of Wells Gray Park, reminiscent of the bigger and grander Kinuseo Falls in northeastern BC. Sylvia is a block plunge 10 m (30 ft) high and 50 m (160 ft) wide, although technically it plunges at both sides and cascades in the centre. The waterfall tumbles over a ledge of compacted glacial till that is less resistant to erosion than the basalt that predominates elsewhere in this region. Consequently, Sylvia Falls is migrating upstream faster than any other Wells Gray waterfall.

There are three possible spots from which to view and photograph the falls: at the brink, from the middle of the falls and at the plunge pool (the latter two along short spurs from the main trail).

To reach Goodwin Falls retrace your steps for about 100 m (110 yd) from the foot of Sylvia Falls. At the bottom of a hill listen for the sound of the falls and locate a Douglas fir and a red cedar that grow as twins, seemingly from the same root. A faint trail through the trees leads to the falls and, for the best views, you may have to clamber through and along some windfall trees.

> In 1940 Chess Lyons, best known for his classic book, *Trees, Shrubs and Flowers to Know in British Columbia*, was assigned by the BC Forest Service to map the trails and features of Wells Gray Park. Wellesley Gray, the Minister of Lands for whom the park is named, presented Lyons with a list of his friends whose names were to be used in naming the natural features of the park. Lyons, however, had his own agenda. He believed that the features should be named for people who had made a direct contribution to the park. Lyons circumvented this tricky conundrum with a brilliant sleight of hand: he named insignificant features from Gray's list and used his own for the big creeks, waterfalls and peaks. Over the years most of Gray's names have faded away while Lyons' have persisted. Brilliant!
>
> Goodwin Falls is actually an exception to this rule. As Lyons tells it, this is the most significant feature in the park named from Gray's list, and he used it as a subterfuge to cover his own plan. For many years no one knew for whom Goodwin Falls was named. The mystery was solved by Helen and Philip Akrigg, authors of *BC Place Names*, when they learned from Gray's niece that Goodwin was a Spokane dentist and a friend of her uncle. Ironically, the intrigue continued with Sylvia Falls. Despite the fact that Goodwin's wife's name was Sylvia, they are actually named for Sylvia Lyons (Chess's wife).

Goodwin Falls is a 4–5 m (13–16 ft) block plunge, perhaps the purest example of this waterfall type in BC. Across the width of the river and across the entire face of the falls, the plunge attribute is unsullied by any suggestion of cascading. The falls are located at the juxtaposition of a glacial moraine and bedrock that is clearly visible on the far side of the river. Some 10 m (30 ft) downstream the river is constricted by an impediment (which is the best viewing spot) and is suddenly confined to a narrow, turbulent canyon.

This optimum spot below Goodwin Falls allows a full frontal view of the plunging water from a distance of about 15 m (50 ft), and 50 m (160 ft) upstream Sylvia Falls frames Goodwin.

Snapshot: The viewpoint below Goodwin Falls offers a perspective that is unique in BC, as the two great block plunge falls appear stacked one above the other. In addition, the perfect symmetry of its plunge makes Goodwin Falls an aesthetic masterpiece. While I was admiring Goodwin Falls, I was surprised to see a female common merganser lead her family of five flightless young into the turbulence at the foot of the falls. The young birds had to paddle and flap their rudimentary wings frantically, but they bobbed like corks even when swept into the fiercest maelstroms.

61 SPAHATS FALLS

Rating:	▲▲▲▲▲
Type:	Plunge
Location:	Wells Gray Provincial Park
Access:	Easy. Five-minute hike
Status:	Wells Gray Provincial Park
When to go:	Spring, summer, fall

Directions: From the Wells Gray Information Centre at the junction of Highway 5 proceed due north along the Clearwater Valley Road for 10 km (6 mi). Turn left into the posted Spahats Falls area and left again for the falls parking lot and trail. It is a five-minute walk on a level trail to the observation deck.

Facilities: Picnic tables, toilets, observation deck, interpretive signage.

Highlights: The word *spahats* means bear in the local First Nations dialect. Spahats Falls is one of the major attractions of Wells Gray Provincial Park and it epitomizes the breathtaking geomorphologic forces at work in the area. The trail from the parking lot hugs the top of the gorge as Spahats Creek hurtles toward its destiny at the falls. The interesting interpretive signage at the observation deck explains the volcanic, glacial and fluvial history of the falls over the last 400,000 years.

Spahats Falls

Spahats Creek emerges from a narrow slot in the headwall and plunges 85 m (280 ft) in a thin ribbon into the huge amphitheatre of sheer basalt walls over 100 m (328 ft) high. The creek then hurries through its eroded creation to the confluence with the Clearwater River 500 m (1,600 ft) downstream. The dramatic canyon at Spahats Falls is the product of post-glacial erosion at a time when the creek was much bigger. Today the small creek flows in an outsized canyon, a phenomenon known as a misfit creek.

In winter an ice cone frequently extends halfway up the falls and in extreme weather all the way to the top like an enormous icicle.

Snapshot: As you walk along the trail there is a heart-stopping first view of the stupendous nothingness that is the eroded amphitheatre of Spahats Falls. From the observation platform the wonderful symmetry of the Spahats amphitheatre with the creek tumbling out of the green forest into the basaltic abyss makes this one of the most impressive scenic spots in all of British Columbia.

Base of Spahats Falls

Spahats Falls is a breathtaking sight from the observation platform, but to experience this waterfall at really close quarters it is possible to visit the foot of the falls within the canyon. From the viewing platform proceed along the canyon rim to a fork in the trail that descends steeply into the canyon. When this trail intercepts another trail bear left toward the falls. Caution is advised on the wet, slippery talus blocks. This trail is about a 2 km (1 mi) return trip, but progress is slow so allow two to three hours.

A visit to the foot of Spahats Falls is redolent of excursions within the canyons of both Helmcken and Brandywine falls. All three falls are confined within classic columnar basalt amphitheatres. Each is awe-inspiring from their respective observation platforms at the canyon rims, but to stand close to these high waterfalls as they plunge from high in the sky with terrifying force, dwarfed in the immensity of the canyons, will add magnitudes of significance to the experience.

62 MOUL FALLS

Rating:	▲▲▲▲△
Type:	Plunge
Location:	Wells Gray Provincial Park
Access:	Moderate. 40-minute hike on a generally level trail
Status:	Wells Gray Provincial Park
When to go:	Spring, summer, fall

A Guide to BC's Best 100 Falls

WELLS GRAY PROVINCIAL PARK

Directions: From the Wells Gray Information Centre on Hwy 5 proceed north on the Clearwater Valley Road for 20.6 km (12.8 mi) to the posted trailhead on the left (west) side of the road. This spot is also 2.7 km (1.7 mi) north of the Fage Creek bridge. If approaching from the north it is 3.7 km (2.3 mi) south of the Grouse Creek bridge.

The 2.9 km (1.8 mi) trail to the brink of the falls is well posted and level until a short steeper section just before the falls. The access to the foot of the falls is down a steep but well-constructed wooden staircase.

Facilities: None. The staircase to the foot of the falls has rustic seats at strategic viewing locations.

Moul Falls

Highlights: The 40-minute hike through an attractive spruce–pine, birch–aspen forest meanders along the edge of Grouse Creek. In summer the trail is colourful with wildflowers such as oxeye daisies, pearly everlasting and self-heal, and in the forest look for the ghostly, saprophytic Indian pipe. In early August I noted northwestern fritillary, pearl crescent, white admiral, pine white and painted lady butterflies. Dark-eyed juncos are common birds and spruce grouse have been observed. The trail delivers you to the brink of the 35 m (115 ft) falls. From this spot there is a vista of the falls dropping off into nothingness and of Grouse Creek wending its way to the Clearwater River through an impressive canyon.

A visit to the foot of the falls is highly recommended as it allows a totally different perspective on the falls, the plunge pool and the canyon. The overwhelming reason for the adventurous to visit here is that Moul Falls is one of the few BC waterfalls with easy access behind the falling water. Simply follow the trail as it disappears behind the curtain of water. This is not dangerous, but be prepared to get wet from the spray. Navigating the path behind the waterfall will bring you to a large grotto undercut into the headwall.

Snapshot: Moul Falls is an outstanding place to visit. It has great beauty in the symmetry of the single sheet of falling water. It is also a waterfall you can fully experience: it can be admired from near, far and every angle, even behind. Being within touching distance of the relentless cascade of 35 m (115 ft) of falling water is thrilling as your senses are assaulted by the unfamiliar sensations, the noise, the spray and the encompassing atmosphere of the grotto.

On an October visit I stood at the back of the grotto looking out toward the sunshine while the golden leaves of fall drifted leisurely down into the plunge pool, the last butterflies of the year danced against the cavern wall and a dipper bobbed on the rocks in the creek. On the trail to the falls the carpet of fallen leaves exuded the heady aroma of decay as summer gave way to winter.

63 DAWSON FALLS

Rating:	▲▲▲▲▲
Type:	Plunge/cascade
Location:	Wells Gray Provincial Park
Access:	Easy. Short walk on trail
Status:	Wells Gray Provincial Park
When to go:	Year-round

Directions: From the Wells Gray Park Information Centre at the junction of Hwy 5 proceed due north on the Clearwater Valley Road for 40 km (25 mi). The parking lot and trailhead are posted on the right. The level trail is well maintained; it takes less than five minutes to walk to the main viewpoint and a further five minutes to the viewpoint at the brink of the falls.

Facilities: Parking lot, pit toilets. The Dawson Falls campground is located 500 m (550 yd) beyond the trailhead.

Highlights: The Murtle River on its descent from Murtle Lake to the Clearwater River falls over seven major waterfalls. Above Dawson Falls are McDougall, Meadow, Horseshoe and Majerus falls, while below Dawson are the Mushbowl and finally Helmcken Falls.

Dawson Falls is a major waterfall with a large volume of water flowing over its 90 m (295 ft) width. Even before the falls come into sight on the trail the thunder of the river tumbling 20 m (66 ft) over a lava ledge builds anticipation. Dawson Falls is a Niagara-type waterfall–the entire river spills over a single ledge. The falls plunge on the far side of the river, cascade on the near side and drop to a wide platform in the centre. Dawson Falls was formerly famous for a cave that allowed dramatic access behind the roaring water of the falls. However, the cave collapsed in 1990, the end result of the slow erosive process.

A Guide to BC's Best 100 Falls

Dawson Falls

Two observation places can be accessed. From the parking lot the trail follows the canyon rim to the main viewpoint (less than five minutes), and continues to a point beside the very brink of the falls. The falls can also be approached on the north side via an unsigned and rough trail, about a 45-minute return trip. The trailhead is 1.3 km (.8 mi) beyond the Dawson Falls trail, just beyond the Mushbowl.

The forest here is a transitional type between the wet and dry belt forests, and most of BC's conifer trees can be identified beside the trail: white spruce, Douglas fir, western red cedar, lodgepole pine, balsam and western hemlock.

In winter Dawson Falls is generally frozen except for the fastest flowing water in the centre. They are named for George Herbert Dawson, surveyor general of BC from 1912 to 1917.

Snapshot: From the main viewpoint Dawson Falls presents a classic Canadian river scene of sky, mountain, forest, river and falls. From the viewpoint at the brink of the falls it is thrilling to watch the clear water of the Murtle River transposed to a white effervescence at your feet. In the early morning of a late July day a fine rainbow was suspended in the spray zone.

64 THE MUSHBOWL

Rating:	▲▲▲△△
Type:	Punchbowl
Location:	Wells Gray Provincial Park
Access:	Easy. The Mushbowl is beside the road
Status:	Wells Gray Provincial Park
When to go:	Usually seasons other than winter

Directions: Follow the directions to Dawson Falls. The Mushbowl is 600 m (660 yd) beyond the Dawson Falls parking lot or 41.2 km (25.5 mi) from Clearwater. The Mushbowl is immediately to the right of the bridge that crosses the Murtle River.

Facilities: Dawson Falls campground is 500 m (550 yd) before the Mushbowl.

Highlights: The road bridge crosses the Murtle River directly above the Mushbowl. Park on the far side. As you walk back across the bridge you can feel the spray from the foaming waterfall as it careens around both sides of a central rock anchored in midstream. The falls are 4.5 m (15 ft) in height. The name Mushbowl derives from the swirling whirlpool at the foot of the falls, which is at its maximum during the spring freshet.

Roland Neave in *Exploring Wells Gray Park* gives a detailed description of the geology here, a fascinating story of 500 million years portrayed in the canyon wall below the falls. The Mushbowl is a residual feature in the migration of Dawson Falls from a point 700 m (765 yd) downstream of the bridge to its present location 500 m (550 yd) above the bridge.

The Mushbowl. Dianna Smith photo

Present-day visitors to the Mushbowl might have the opportunity to observe the new breed of extreme athlete at play here, as kayakers plunge vertically down the waterfall and bury themselves in the churning cauldron at the bottom.

On the south-facing outcrops on the north side of the Mushbowl northern alligator lizards have been reported. This location is near the northern extremity of the range of this, the most northerly occurring lizard in North America. Any sightings should be reported to the Wells Gray Visitor Centre.

In the summer of 1940 BC Minister of Lands Arthur Wellesley "Wells" Gray, for whom the park is named, visited the recently created park. While crossing the footbridge over the Murtle River Gray almost fell into the Mushbowl, apparently after some serious imbibing the previous evening.

Snapshot: Eroded into the bedrock beneath the bridge are textbook examples of the pothole phenomenon. These perfectly formed potholes are up to 2 m (6.5 ft) wide and 2 m (6.5 ft) deep with smooth rounded walls.

In July 2001 I was standing on the bridge at the Mushbowl when a female common merganser and one of her young were paddling around in the falls. Suddenly the pair was swept through beneath the bridge, but they were totally unfazed, riding the torrent as if it were the easiest thing in the world.

65 MAJERUS FALLS

Rating:	▲▲▲▲△
Type:	Segmented cascade
Location:	Wells Gray Provincial Park
Access:	Difficult. Level 10.5 km (6.5 mi) trail, just over two hours one way
Status:	Wells Gray Provincial Park
When to go:	Spring, summer, fall

Directions: From the Wells Gray Information Centre drive north on the Clearwater Valley Road toward the Dawson Falls–Helmcken Falls area. Dawson Falls is at km 40 (mi 25) with the Mushbowl bridge 600 m (660 yd) further, and the turnoff to Majerus Falls (posted to Pyramid Mountain) 700 m (765 yd) beyond that. The trailhead is 1.2 km (.75 mi) along this road on the left, and the trail to the falls is straight ahead.

Facilities: The Pyramid campground is close by the trailhead. There is a good wilderness campsite atop the bank of the Murtle River at 8 km (5 mi) along the trail, and another above Horseshoe Falls beyond Majerus Falls. Otherwise, there are no facilities along this wilderness trail.

Majerus Falls

Highlights: Majerus Falls, 12 km (7.5 mi) north of Dawson Falls on the Murtle River, is a 12 m (40 ft) cascade that spans the full 90 m (100 yd) width of the river. The river has breached the strata on either side of a large residual rock that sits midstream as a treed island. Erosion at Majerus Falls is proceeding such that the river cascades in a stepped or tiered format over the rocky impediment.

The falls and other local features are named for Michael Majerus. He first came to the Clearwater Valley in 1911 and worked with the survey crew of Robert Lee, who discovered Helmcken Falls. Majerus stayed on to become a homesteader and trapper in the area.

Horseshoe Falls, 3.5 km (2 mi) beyond Majerus Falls, is reached by continuing along the same trail. Here the river cascades 14 m (46 ft) over a double step. Majerus is the fourth of the waterfalls on the Murtle River (Helmcken being the first), Horseshoe is the fifth, Meadow Falls (10 m/30 ft high) the sixth and McDougall Falls (14 m/45 ft high) the seventh. Meadow Falls is 4 km (2.5 mi) beyond the trail's end at Horseshoe Falls and can only be reached by bushwhacking. McDougall Falls can be reached by a 5 km (3 mi) trail along the river and is accessed from Murtle Lake to the north. Be aware for bears on the trail.

Snapshot: Though Majerus Falls is a major waterfall, it is accessed by a fairly long hike on an uninspiring trail through a small-tree forest with only occasional views of the river. In addition it suffers by comparison with similar Wells Gray falls such as Dawson Falls or Sylvia Falls that are easier to access.

66 HELMCKEN FALLS

Rating:	▲▲▲▲▲
Type:	Plunge
Location:	Wells Gray Provincial Park
Access:	Easy. Blacktop
Status:	Wells Gray Provincial Park
When to go:	Spring, summer, fall

Directions: From the Wells Gray Park Information Centre on Hwy 5 proceed 42 km (26 mi) due north on the Clearwater Valley Road. One km (.6 mi) after crossing the bridge over the Murtle River at the Mushbowl turn left on the posted road that takes you 4 km (2.5 mi) to the falls. A short trail leads from the parking lot to the observation deck.

Facilities: Parking lot, picnic tables, toilets, interpretive signage. The short trail to the observation platform is wheelchair accessible.

Highlights: Helmcken Falls is formed as the Murtle River tumbles over the western edge of the Murtle Plateau into Helmcken Canyon and flows on to the Clearwater River 10 km (6 mi) distant. The 141 m (463 ft) drop is three times the height of Niagara Falls and Helmcken has the sixth highest single plunge in Canada.

After the main drop the Murtle River just recovers its composure before it falls over the lower 15 m (50 ft) step. An enormous black grotto extends back more than 50 m (165 ft) behind the main plunge. From the observation deck you have clear views of the main plunge, the great amphitheatre of the plunge pool, the lower falls and the perfectly sheer, chiselled south wall of the canyon. At the foot of the canyon walls the forested talus slopes are dwarfed by the enormity of the canyon. In the spray zone around the plunge pool moss and grasses sparkle amid the greenness.

Helmcken ice cone. Jon Weaver photo

Helmcken Falls

There is a strong imperative for a late January or February visit as a spectacular ice cone forms at the base of the falls. The cone reaches 50 m (165 ft) in height (as high as Niagara Falls) or even higher in exceptionally cold winters, and remains into early summer.

Interpretive signage at the observation deck explains that 500,000 years ago volcanoes spewed lava through the existing river valleys, and that after the last Ice Age silt-laden water from melting glaciers carved Helmcken Canyon through the layers of lava. The canyon is still enlarging today.

Incredibly, this continentally significant landform and major scenic and tourist attraction was only discovered on July 24, 1913, when government land surveyor Robert Lee stumbled upon the falls. He was so excited by his discovery that he wrote a letter that same evening to the premier of British Columbia, Sir Richard McBride, to suggest the name McBride Falls. McBride altruistically declined, and instead suggested it be named after Dr. John Sebastian Helmcken, an English surgeon with the Hudson's Bay Company. Helmcken was a pioneer BC politician, one of three men who negotiated the terms of BC's confederation with Canada. He never saw his eponymous natural wonder.

Snapshot: The two serious contenders for the title of BC's premier waterfall, Helmcken and Takakkaw, are diametric opposites. Helmcken is a high discharge block plunge into a cavernous, shady plunge pool that can only be viewed at a distance from its brink; Takakkaw is a ribbon of water that falls from high in the sky down a sheer, bare, sunny cliff and can be closely viewed from its base. Helmcken has the dark, misty, mystical ambiance of a great Gothic cathedral, while Takakkaw brazenly displays its wares in the full light of day. Takakkaw is mightily impressive, but to stand in the presence of Helmcken Falls is to stand before the Great High Altar of BC waterfalls.

The lower 15 m (50 ft) plunge would easily make the list of 100 best BC waterfalls if it stood by itself, but it pales to insignificance at the foot of its overwhelmingly dominant parent.

The view from the north observation deck displays the great waterfall in its spectacular setting, but for a more involving interaction with the falls, hike the south rim trail or the trail to the foot of the falls.

Helmcken Falls, South Rim

Facilities: Outhouse, interpretive trail signage.

Directions: A short spur to the left 200 m (220 yd) beyond the parking lot for Dawson Falls leads to the parking lot that is the trailhead for the hike to the south rim. The level trail is 4 km (2.5 mi) one way, and can be hiked in about 45 minutes.

Highlights: The falls signage describes the hurricane force winds that hit Wells Gray Park on August 31, 1996, and blew down thousands of trees in a few minutes. The start of the trail passes through areas of fallen trees from that day and leads to the rim of Helmcken Canyon at the brink of the falls. The road to the north viewpoint and the present observation deck was built in the early 1960s; until then the south rim trail was the only way to view the falls.

Snapshot: Nothing prepares you for the enormity of this place. Helmcken wears a pervasive air of unreality: it is at once one of the most beautiful yet terrifying places I have ever trodden. It is mesmerizing and discombobulating to peer over the rim and feel your senses being overwhelmed as you follow the hypnotic column of falling water 141 metres (463 ft) down, down, inexorably down into the miasma of pulverized water. When I visited on an afternoon in late July, an intense rainbow was suspended in the upper spray zone within the amphitheatre.

The Utmost Caution is Advised

This is an exceedingly dangerous place. If you contemplate peering over the edge at the south rim, you would be well advised to lie down on your stomach, or at least to make sure your feet are firmly planted while you grasp one of the small trees that grow along the edge. Also, be extremely careful if other people are present, as the slightest nudge or loss of attention could result in catastrophe. It is not just a case of being physically aware here; dizziness, craziness or feelings of being overwhelmed or disoriented are all possible.

At once, it seems that there should be a fence here, but a barrier would preclude anything but unsatisfactory views of the falls, and might induce even more dangerous activity. Be careful of yourself and others.

Base of Helmcken Falls

Access: Fairly strenuous hike, about 2.5 hours one way

Directions: The trail begins at the main viewpoint at the north rim (see above). From the viewing platform hike about 2 km (1 mi) downstream along a

A Guide to BC's Best 100 Falls

Helmcken Falls grotto

good trail that follows the canyon rim. After 25–30 minutes look for an obvious, well-worn trail that descends straight down into the canyon. The trail is flagged with blue paint on a pine tree to the right of the trail and a red diamond on a tree 10 m (30 ft) further on.

On the new trail immediately bear left along the foot of the canyon wall. Do not follow a trail that proceeds straight down the gulley to the Clearwater River, unless you specifically wish to pursue this optional side trip, which is about one hour return.

The route to Helmcken Falls essentially follows the foot of the canyon wall the entire way, but the trail is not always obvious, especially where it crosses a number of talus slides. The best advice is to stay close to the foot of the canyon wall as best you can and ignore any temptation to head downhill toward the river. For much of the distance the trail is easy to follow as you walk along on level ground, sometimes on the shale-like detritus fallen from the canyon walls towering above you.

As you approach the falls an undercut appears in the canyon wall, and a glimpse can be had of the top of the falls through an opening in the trees. The north rim viewing platform is 150 m (500 ft) directly overhead, but two hours hiking away unless you can levitate. The trail immediately cuts steeply uphill to again join the foot of the canyon wall in the vicinity of Cougar Creek, which flows down the canyon wall as an ephemeral waterfall. Soon after the trail emerges from the forest at the grassy slope that you will have observed from the upper viewing platform before starting out.

Highlights: The surroundings are spectacular as you proceed ant-like into the maw of Helmcken Canyon with vertical walls that rise 150 m (500 ft) overhead. The forest is initially a dry ecotype of Douglas fir and birch, but as you approach the spray zone of the falls it undergoes a radical transition to the Interior wet zone species of western red cedar, western hemlock and western yew.

The grassy bank onto which you emerge at the foot of the falls is in the immediate spray zone and is too wet and cold to support trees. The grass is augmented by wild mint, arnica, pearly everlasting, aster and fringed grass of Parnassus. The aromatic mint adds a fragrant element to the other sensations that regale your senses at this incredible spot. The knoll is assaulted by intermittent blasts of cold spray from the falls and warm rushes of air from the canyon, and when I was there an intense rainbow was fixed in the depths of the plunge pool as the sun shafted through the spray.

Snapshot: As you walk along the trail at the foot of the canyon walls it is probably best to not dwell on exactly how all that detritus arrived at its present location.

The base of Helmcken Falls and the fantastic 141 m (463 ft) column of water falling from the sky is quite simply one of the most exhilarating, inspiring, intimidating and unique spots in BC. During my visit the exploding watery supernovas around the falling water seemed to me an allegory of cosmic cataclysm or creation itself. When not being awed by its cosmic attributes I lapsed into frivolity, thinking of the waterfall as the Mother of All Showers.

While I stood entranced before the falls a hummingbird suddenly appeared, flew two circles around the amphitheatre and departed, inspired or intimidated I know not.

I spent a couple of hours alone on the grassy bank, enamoured of the solitude. A few people at the distant north rim waved at the crazy speck of a person dwarfed against the enormity of the canyon and the falls. It was with great reluctance that I disengaged myself from the spectacle and turned for the long walk home, elated to have fulfilled a long-time fantasy of standing at this incomparable spot.

67 OSPREY FALLS

Rating:	▲▲▲▲△
Type:	Plunge
Location:	Wells Gray Provincial Park
Access:	Easy. Gravel road and short walk
Status:	Wells Gray Provincial Park
When to go:	Spring, summer, fall

Directions: From the Wells Gray Information Centre on Hwy 5 proceed north along the Clearwater Valley Road for 65 km (40 mi), almost to the end of the road at 68 km (42 mi). Turn left into the Clearwater Lake campground and find the path along the river's edge. Osprey Falls can be viewed from here.

Facilities: Clearwater Lake and Falls Creek campgrounds are both adjacent to Osprey Falls and have the full complement of facilities found in provincial park campgrounds.

Highlights: Osprey Falls forms an inverted dam between Clearwater Lake and the Clearwater River. It is an L-shaped falls over 500 m (1,600 ft) wide and is easily the widest of all BC waterfalls. At low water from August through April the drop is about 4 m (13 ft). The falls are the product of a lava flow that flooded out of the nearby tributary Falls Creek and dammed the main Clearwater River. The present falls are receding through this lava plug and within a century a possible breach would substantially lower Clearwater Lake.

An unusual feature of Osprey Falls, and unique for all BC waterfalls, is its penchant for disappearing. This feat is accomplished when the water volume in the Clearwater River is so high from meltwater that the water backs up through the canyon below the falls and submerges them. Consequently, a visit in May or June risks missing the falls. Osprey Falls is not accessible after the first snowfall of winter, as the Clearwater Valley Road is not plowed beyond the Helmcken Falls turnoff.

The falls are named for the ospreys that nest here each year.

Snapshot: Though not one of the province's most impressive waterfalls, Osprey Falls has proven to be the deadliest. Roland Neave in *Exploring Wells Gray Park* reports that 18 people have gone over the brink, with only three survivors, a salutary lesson about the extreme danger around all waterfalls. When I think of accidental deaths around waterfalls, I am reminded of the myth of the Siren, whose song lured the obsessed but unwary to their death.

Waterfalls of British Columbia

Osprey Falls. Jeremy Staveley photo

68 RAINBOW FALLS #3 (AZURE LAKE)

Rating:	▲▲▲△△
Type:	Plunge
Location:	Wells Gray Provincial Park
Access:	Difficult. Boat access only via Clearwater and Azure Lakes
Status:	Wells Gray Provincial Park
When to go:	Summer and fall. High water is in June

Directions: Your own watercraft, power or self-propelled, can be launched on Clearwater Lake. Clearwater Lake Tours (phone 250-674-2121 or see www.clearwaterlaketours.com for current prices) run twice-daily trips from the south end of Clearwater Lake (adjacent to the BC Parks campground) lasting four hours, to Rainbow Falls. They also operate a water taxi service on the lake. There is time to walk from the beach about 500 m (550 yd) along the trail to the falls. Tours operate from May 15 to October.

Facilities: Clearwater Lake campground at the northern end of the Clearwater Valley Road and the southern tip of Clearwater Lake has the full range of BC Parks facilities. The Rainbow Falls wilderness campsite beside the falls has primitive tent sites and outhouses.

Highlights: To reach Rainbow Falls you must navigate Clearwater Lake, Azure Lake and the Clearwater River that joins the two. Clearwater Lake is 23 km (14 mi) long, the river is 2.9 km (1.8 mi) long and Azure Lake 24 km (15 mi) in length. The east side of Clearwater Lake is dominated by Azure Mountain (2,495 m/8,185 ft), and the north side of Azure Lake by Garnet Peak (2,860 m/9,380 ft), the highest summit in Wells Gray Park. Garnet Falls is on the north shore of Azure Lake and almost directly opposite on the south shore is Roostertail Falls. Clearwater Lake Tours will closely approach both of these falls.

Rainbow Falls, on Angus Horne Creek near the head of Azure Lake, is situated 200 m (220 yd) up the creek from the lake and a short, easy trail links the campsite and the falls. Above the falls the creek makes a right-angled turn and flows as a rapids then a cascade before plunging 10 m (30 ft) down the main falls.

Rainbow Falls #3

In early August twinflowers, fringed grass of Parnassus and the exotic-looking prince's pine flowered close to the falls. The bunchberries already sported their red berries.

Snapshot: If you take advantage of Clearwater Lake Tours, this is a leisurely half-day trip through great scenery to the geographic heart of Wells Gray Park, and to one of the most remote waterfalls in this book (in terms of distance from road access).

69 PYRAMID FALLS

Rating:	▲▲▲△△
Type:	Plunge/cascade
Location:	Between Blue River and Valemount
Access:	Easy. Pullout beside Hwy 5
Status:	Pyramid Creek Falls Provincial Park
When to go:	Spring, summer, fall

Directions: At 30.5 km (19 mi) north of the Husky gas station in Blue River or 58 km (36 mi) south of Valemount, look for a small pullout on the west side of the highway. The falls are visible on the mountainside, across the river on the east side of the North Thompson. There is no vehicle access to the falls or to the park. It may be possible to bushwhack to the falls.

Facilities: None

Highlights: Pyramid Creek descends via a hanging valley from the snowy alpine heights of an icefield dominated by Mt. Lempriere (3,208 m/10,525 ft), with Mt. Cheadle looming on the south side of the forested gulley. Pyramid Falls consists of two main plunges and a final wide cascade and it flows strongly all year fuelled by the perennial meltwater from the icefield.

In past times CN trains would stop at the foot of the falls to allow passengers to take photographs, and this may still happen on the Rocky Mountaineer train.

Snapshot: On one visit to Pyramid Falls I was driving south when I pulled over to admire the falls and take a photograph. It was raining and there were bands of fleecy stratus cloud draped over the mountainside with the tumbling white falls sharply offset against the dark green of the forest. Up the gulley of Pyramid

A Guide to BC's Best 100 Falls

Creek directly above the falls the distant snow cone of Mt. Lempriere was visible, and a flock of twittering Vaux's swifts careened around the valley. Suddenly an intense double rainbow appeared, with Pyramid Falls serendipitously dead centre in the middle of the bow.

Pyramid Falls, viewed from the Rocky Mountaineer train. R.G. Daniel photo

WELLS GRAY PROVINCIAL PARK

CENTRAL

This disparate region is based on geography rather than any other unifying feature, and stretches from the Coast Range in the vicinity of Bella Coola, through the Chilcotin Plateau to the Cariboo Mountains and the Rockies in the east. Hunlen Falls in the Coast Range is the fourth highest vertical waterfall in Canada and is this region's premier waterfall. The Chilcotin Plateau, a vast area with little in the way of relief, is not conducive to waterfall creation. Six of the Central region's falls are in the central Rockies, either within or close to Mt. Robson Provincial Park. Emperor Falls, Falls of the Pool and White Falls are actually successive tiered waterfalls on the Robson River. Rearguard and Overlander Falls are both on the upper Fraser River.

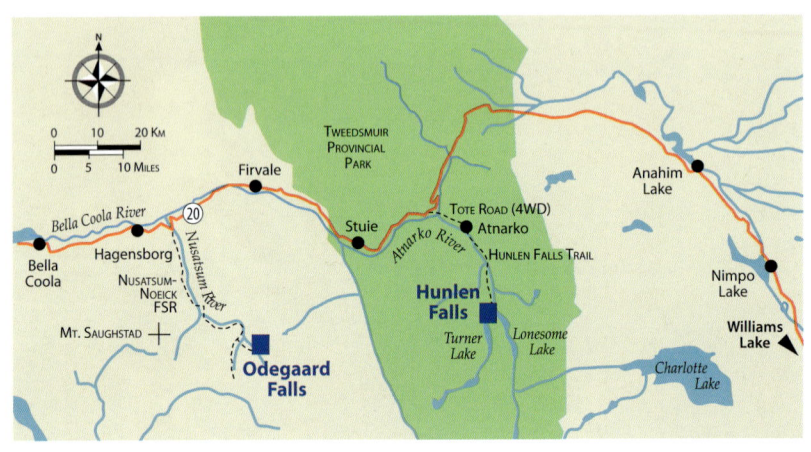

FALLS 70–71

70 ODEGAARD FALLS

Rating:	▶▶▶▶▶
Type:	Cascade
Location:	39 km (24 mi) SE of Bella Coola
Access:	Moderate. 25 km (15 mi) of rough, 2WD road, 2 km (1.5 mi) trail one way
Status:	Provincial forest
When to go:	Summer, fall

Directions: From Bella Coola, drive east on Hwy 20 for 16 km (10 mi) to Hagensborg. Exactly 8 km (5 mi) east of Hagensborg and immediately before the bridge, locate the Nusatsum–Noeick Forest Service Road on the right. After

13.5 km (8.5 mi), cross the Nusatsum River bridge and take the right-hand fork. The Odegaard Falls picnic area and viewpoint is at km 24.2 (mi 15). After a further 700 m (765 yd), cross the Nusatsum River again. The recreation site and trailhead are on the left. A 20-minute hike brings you to the viewpoint near the foot of the falls.

Facilities: The Nusatsum River Recreation Site at the trailhead has a picnic table, barbecue pit, outhouse and space for camping or parking.

Highlights: The drive along the FSR affords spectacular views of high mountains such as Mt. Saughstad (2,908 m/9,540 ft). The viewpoint at km 24.2 (mi 15) has a view of Odegaard Falls across the valley of the Nusatsum

Odegaard Falls

River, amid a setting of magnificent Coast Range peaks with hanging glaciers and snowfields. The falls are fed by the Odegaard Glacier, visible above the timberline.

The hike to Odegaard Falls has the immediate bonus of Nusatsum Falls beside the trail in the first few metres. This is a 10 m (33 ft) plunge followed by a cascade in a rugged, steep walled canyon. The path to Odegaard Falls is a beautiful woodland trail through a mossy, old-growth hemlock forest with ferns and devil's club. Typical birds to listen for include varied thrush, winter wren and golden-crowned kinglet.

The trail ends at a viewpoint from where you can sit on the bench and watch the Nusatsum River tumble 280 m (918 ft) from the heights in a magnificent confusion of plunges, cascades, twists, turns, pools, spray and shafting sunlight.

Snapshot: This huge and infinitely complex waterfall is one of BC's outstanding falls. On a sunny summer morning when the discharge is high, and the falls are at their most unrestrained with drifting clouds of spray mingling with the shafting sunlight, then is the time to realize that this is one of BC's peak waterfall experiences. Bryan Swan, a world waterfall expert, wrote on his website (www.waterfallsnorthwest.com), "Odegaard Falls is probably the best waterfall in all of Canada."

The falls are located in a valley of unearthly beauty. They are also remote with few visitors, so this is a wilderness experience of the highest order.

When I visited on July 27, 2004, smoke from the huge Charlotte Lake forest fire was obscuring the peaks surrounding the Nusatsum Valley, and the fragrance in the air was tinged with the sweet aroma of distant fire.

71 HUNLEN FALLS

Rating:	▲▲▲▲▲
Type:	Plunge
Location:	70 km (40 mi) E of Bella Coola, 320 km (200 mi) W of Williams Lake, 45 km (28 mi) W of Nimpo Lake (by air)
Access:	Very difficult. Access by strenuous trail, float plane and short hike, or fly-by
Status:	South Tweedsmuir Provincial Park
When to go:	Summer, fall

Directions: Hunlen Falls can be accessed via a strenuous trail that begins in the Bella Coola Valley. The easier way to access the falls is by float plane from Nimpo Lake to Turner Lake, and then by a short trail to the falls viewpoint. It is also possible to take a fly-by flight from Nimpo Lake that allows good views of the falls from the air. This option is considerably cheaper than landing and hiking.

1. Hiking: From Bella Coola, drive east on Hwy 20 for 70 km (40 mi) to the Tote Road, which begins at the Young Creek picnic site at the base of "the Hill." The four-wheel-drive Tote Road parallels the Atnarko River; follow it 11 km (7 mi) to the trailhead of the Turner Lake trail. Turner Lake campsite is a strenuous 16.4 km (10 mi) distant, with an 800 m (2,600 ft) elevation change and an intimidating 78 switchbacks. Allow six to nine hours to complete the trail. This is prime grizzly bear habitat and camping is prohibited outside of the designated campground for that reason. Hiking is advised in the late morning and early afternoon to minimize possible bear encounters.

Hunlen Falls. Philippe Henry photo

2. By air: From Nimpo Lake the flight to the Turner Lake campsite takes 20 minutes. You can either camp here, or the float plane can hold over while you make the short hike to the falls viewpoints.

Facilities: BC Parks maintains a staffed campsite at Turner Lake, where it is possible to rent canoes for travel on the Turner Lake chain. The scenic and well-maintained campsite is located on the lakefront and has raised tent sites, tables, a bear-proof food cache, firepits, firewood, an outhouse and drinking water from the lake. The camp warden has a satellite phone for calling the airline company when you wish to leave. He can also lead guided hikes to the falls.

Highlights: Hunlen Falls is one of Canada's greatest waterfalls. With a plunge of 253 m (830 ft) it ranks as the fourth highest vertical falls in the nation, after Helmet, Harmony and Takakkaw falls. Hunlen was originally known as Mystery Falls, but now takes its name from a native trapper, Hana-Lin, who ran traplines in the vicinity of the falls. The first recorded visit to the falls was in 1909 by George Turner, a local trapper. When Don Munday, the doyen of BC mountaineers, visited in 1939, he reported that since 1909 not more than "a score" of people had visited the falls owing to their inaccessibility.

The spectacular flight into Turner Lake allows you to take in the magnificent high mountains of the Bella Coola area. The inbound flight also treats you to a view of Hunlen Falls that puts the great falls into its larger context as the outfall of Hunlen Creek as it plunges toward the Atnarko River from Turner Lake. The lake and Hunlen Falls are at an altitude of 1,100 m (3,600 ft) above sea level. Also obvious from the air is how close the falls came to being burned over by the great 2004 conflagration, with the dividing line between the green timber and the burned trees a mere 200 m (220 yd) away from the falls.

The short trail from the campsite to the main falls viewpoint takes between 10 and 15 minutes. It crosses a footbridge at a narrow neck of Turner Lake and soon emerges into a clearing with burned timber. Here you can observe the rapid post-fire recovery of the forest under way, as tall fireweed and healthy lodgepole pine seedlings begin anew the perennial cycle of fire and regeneration that has characterized Chilcotin forests for millennia.

The trail proceeds through a green forest to an unprotected cliff-edge viewpoint. Walking toward the edge and looking across the enormous chasm, the silver glimmer of the creek emerges from the forest and begins its long fall. More and

Aerial view of Hunlen Falls. Jane Little photo

more of the white plume becomes visible as you approach the edge of the chasm, but there is no end to the falling water until you finally peer over into the nothingness (best to do this on your stomach). Only then does the enormity of the vertical 253 m (830 ft) plunge take on any real meaning. This vantage point gives excellent views of the limestone headwall over which Hunlen Falls now flows. On the way back to the footbridge I recommend that you follow the loop trail that climbs a low ridge and gives views of the now-burned valley of Lonesome Lake, made famous by the exploits of Ralph Edwards and his trumpeter swans.

As you return toward the footbridge, look for a faint path on the right, 20 m (22 yd) before the bridge. This short trail leads to the brink of the falls and from here you can lie on your stomach, look over the edge and watch the plumes of spray cascading down to infinity. Be careful!

By returning toward the campsite and taking the Hunlen Falls Trail to the right, you can reach a third falls viewpoint. A 15-minute walk from this junction brings you to a flagged trail to the right, and a further 5 minutes brings you to the viewpoint. From here you look directly at the falls and can watch the successive plumes of spray chasing each other to the bottom.

Clark's nutcrackers are abundant and noisy birds in the vicinity of Hunlen Falls and your campsite may be visited by grey jays, so keep an eye on your food. During our two nights camping at Turner Lake, great horned owls were quite vocal after dark.

Snapshot: Even though Hunlen Falls is one of the "big five" of BC waterfalls, it was one of the last falls that I visited in my research for this book. In July 2004, my hiking partner and I drove the 900 km (560 mi) from Vancouver to Nimpo Lake with the intention of flying into Turner Lake and hiking to the falls. As we approached Nimpo Lake we cast an uneasy eye on the growing clouds of smoke that emanated from the entire area south of the highway, centred on Charlotte Lake. To our dismay the airline informed us that the forest fire was out of control and that no one would be flying anywhere. After the long and now abortive drive, we moved to plan B—hiking into the Rainbow Range on the north side of Hwy 20.

The following day we sat on a ridge looking south toward Hunlen Falls. A spectacular 6,100 m (20,000 ft) cumulus cloud of smoke dominated the sky, and we were left wondering if it was too late to ever see Hunlen Falls in its forested splendour. We know now that the falls were spared by the narrowest of margins.

Waterfalls of British Columbia

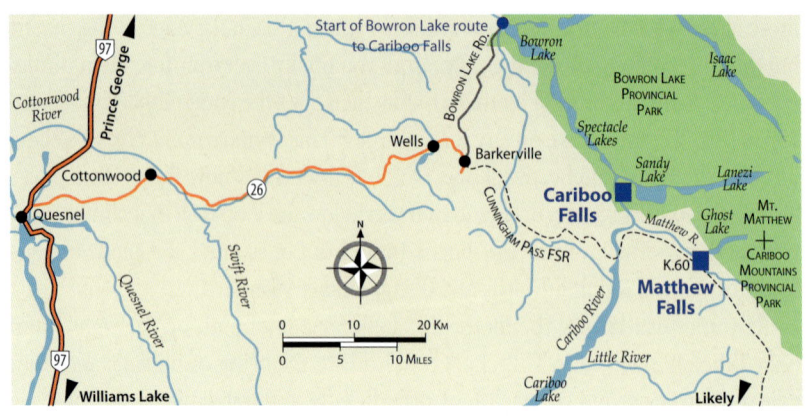

FALLS 72–73

72 MATTHEW FALLS

Rating:	▲▲▲▲△
Type:	Cascade
Location:	142 km (88 mi) E of the junction of Hwys 97 and 26, the Barkerville Hwy, 64 km (40 mi) E of the Wells–Barkerville area
Access:	Moderate. Gravel logging road
Status:	Cariboo Mountains Provincial Park and provincial forest
When to go:	Summer and fall

Directions: From the junction of Hwys 97 and 26 proceed 74 km (46 mi) east to Wells. Drive 4.3 km (2.7 mi) beyond the Wells gas station and general store, turn left onto the Bowron Lake Road, and after 200 m (220 yd) bear right onto a road signposted to Likely. This is the 3100 Road, the Cunningham Pass Forest Service Road. A sign here warns of log hauling from 4 a.m. to 6 p.m. Monday to Friday, and that vehicles without the appropriate radio channels must stop and follow a vehicle with a radio. The kilometres are marked on the 3100 Road and thus at 3139 you cross the Cariboo River on a major bridge. At 3160, after 60 km (37 mi) on the logging road, a faded sign indicates Ghost Lake and falls. It is 4.3 km (2.7 mi) from here to the lower falls, which are immediately above and below a bridge on the logging road. To reach Ghost Lake and the upper falls, bear right on the road immediately beyond the lower falls and proceed 1.5 km (1 mi) to the parking lot. Various short, rough trails lead to Ghost Lake and frontal and side views of the falls.

Facilities: There are picnic tables and an information sign at the Ghost Lake parking lot.

Highlights: The Matthew River drops out of Ghost Lake at the upper falls in a magnificent mountain setting with the snowcapped Mt. Matthew (2,595 m / 8,500 ft) looming above the jade green waters of the lake. The upper falls, a complex, segmented cascade, spills from Ghost Lake in four separate spillways 8 to 10 m (25 to 30 ft) in height, and is framed by the mountain and the lake.

The lower falls can be seen from either side of the bridge that crosses the river at its narrowest point. Above the bridge the river is a rushing cascade, and below is a complex segmented cascade that divides around a midstream rock. These falls can be better seen by clambering down on a rough trail along their south side to view the 8 m (25 ft) cascade and the long, extended race on the north side. From the bridge at the lower falls the scene is of the rounded foothills of the Cariboo Mountains with extensive clear-cuts, now green again with regenerating plantations of spruce and pine.

Upper Matthew Falls

Snapshot: On a hot Sunday afternoon in early July, a good variety of butterflies including swallowtails, blues and white admirals were present. On a different visit we were privileged to watch a northern goshawk, an icon species of northern wilderness, fly out of an orange sunset in the west and disappear over the ridge toward Ghost Lake.

In the course of a conversation with a couple from Kansas whom I met at the lower falls, the man wistfully commented, "I'm not sure why I live in Kansas." His was a memorable comment voiced at a special location, even within the pantheon of BC's many outstanding beauty spots.

Waterfalls of British Columbia

73 CARIBOO FALLS

Rating:	▲▲▲▲▲
Type:	Plunge/cascade
Location:	On the Cariboo River, 120 km (75 mi) E of Quesnel, 30 km (19 mi) N of Barkerville
Access:	Very difficult. There are two options, both water-based: 1) Canoe the Bowron Lake chain 2) Chartered jet boat up the Cariboo River
Status:	Bowron Lake Provincial Park
When to go:	May 15 to the end of September

Directions: The put-in for the Bowron Lake Canoe Circuit is at Bowron Lake, 30 km (19 mi) north of Barkerville. There are two possible routes to the falls. The first entails paddling the entire Bowron Lake circuit, a total of 116 km (72 mi), 108 km (67 mi) paddling and 8 km (5 mi) portaging, with a time commitment of six to ten days. The alternative is the shorter Westside Route, which entails paddling 45 percent of the entire circuit, or 54 km (34 mi) round trip over two to four days.

Canoes can be rented at businesses in the immediate area. Reservations are mandatory to enter the circuit, with a charge of $60 per person for the full circuit and $30 for the Westside Route. Commercial operators also offer fully outfitted and guided canoe expeditions around the circuit. The park is open from May 15th to the end of September. Full information concerning the park can be viewed at the BC Parks website, www.env.gov.bc.ca/bcparks.

Cariboo Falls. Michael Maughan photo

Cariboo Falls is accessed from the south end of Unna Lake (on the canoe circuit) by a 1.2 km (.75 mi) trail that leads to the falls. Access to the falls by canoe along the Cariboo River is forbidden because of the danger of being swept downstream and over the falls.

Facilities: There is a BC Parks campsite at the put-in to Bowron Lake. There are also lodges in the vicinity with cabins, stores and other facilities. The canoe circuit is a total wilderness environment and complete self-sufficiency is required. Campsites on the circuit have wilderness facilities such as outhouses and bear caches; some have cabins available on a shared basis.

Highlights: The Bowron Lake Canoe Circuit is ranked among the top 10 canoe trips in the world. About 5,000 people avail themselves of the experience each year. The circuit encompasses a rectangular chain of lakes connected by rivers and creeks on the western slope of the Cariboo Mountains. Those who complete the entire circuit will also get to see Isaac Falls, an 11 m (36 ft) cascade at the south end of Isaac Lake that must be portaged.

Cariboo Falls is a major BC waterfall that cascades and plunges 24 m (79 feet). The falls are on the Cariboo River, which drains from the Cariboo Glacier through Lanezi and Sandy lakes and joins the Quesnel River and eventually the Fraser River. There can be very high water volumes in the river and at the falls during the freshet, with a declining discharge as summer progresses.

The trail to the falls, like other trails in the Central Region, has suffered from the depredations of the mountain pine beetle. The trail leads to the top of the falls, but it is also possible to visit the base where the roar of the water, the spray and frequent rainbows deliver the essential waterfall experience.

It should be noted that there is another waterfall in the area that also goes by the name of Cariboo Falls. In the absence of a completely different name that would avoid further confusion, I refer to this second waterfall as Cariboo River Falls.

Snapshot: In the early 1970s an acquaintance of mine, Dave Carmezind, visited the Bowron Lakes and Cariboo Falls. Dave was canoeing alone along the Cariboo River above the falls when he was inadvertently swept over the brink. People standing on the riverbank reported that when he realized he was going over the falls he stood up in his canoe, raised his hands to the heavens and accepted his fate. He did not survive. I have always admired this heroic gesture.

Waterfalls of British Columbia

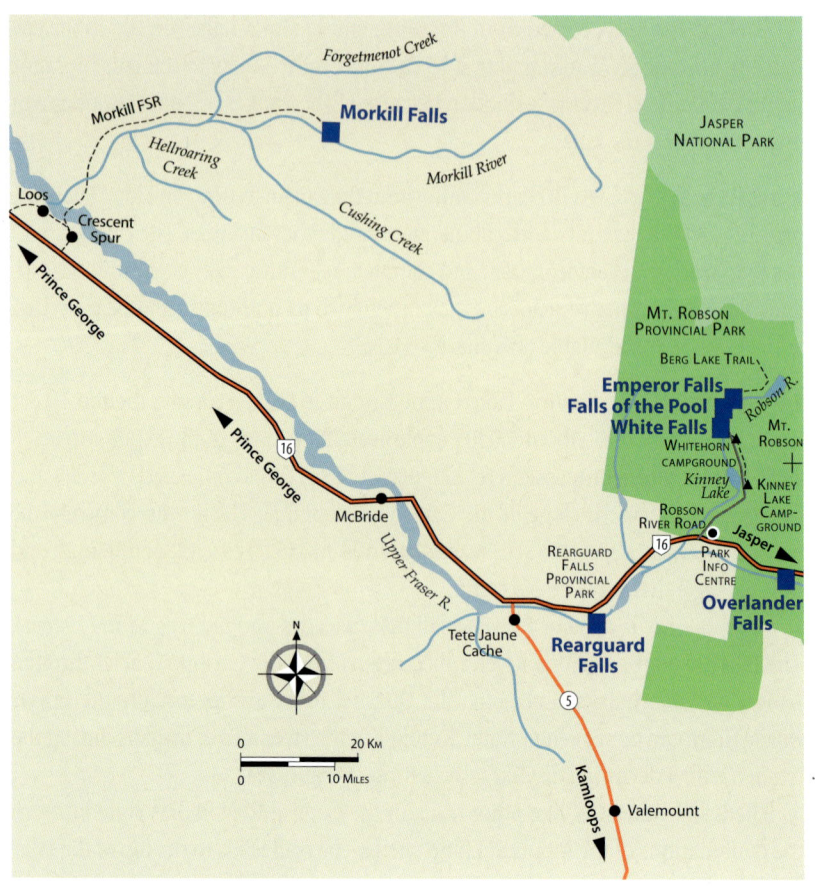

FALLS 74–79

74 MORKILL FALLS

Rating:	▲▲▲▲△
Type:	Plunge
Location:	160 km (100 mi) E of Prince George, 50 km (30 mi) W of McBride
Access:	Moderate. 2WD logging road, 100 m (110 yd) walk
Status:	Provincial forest
When to go:	Summer, fall

Directions: Look for the road sign to Crescent Spur along the Yellowhead Highway east from Prince George or west from McBride. Turn north off the highway onto a gravel road and proceed 7.3 km (4.5 mi) to the Morkill Forest Service Road. This mainline logging road is in reasonable condition for any two-wheel-drive vehicle, but has been inactive for some time and has an unkempt appearance. The

Morkill Falls. Rand Rudland photo

road is posted with the occasional kilometre marker. Proceed to the bridge over the Morkill River at km 34 and park there. Immediately before the bridge a spur leads into a gravel pit. A 100 m (110 yd) trail leads through the trees to the brink of the falls. You can view the river disappearing over the rim from here, but it does not allow views of the waterfall itself. It appears to be impossible to gain access to the foot of the falls from the west side due to impassable cliffs.

To reach the foot of the falls and the only location where a view of the entire waterfall is possible, it is necessary to cross the bridge and hike in along the east side of the river. The short distance, about 400 m (440 yd), requires bushwhacking over fallen timber and through neck-high devil's club and is not for everyone. Those who decide to proceed will be rewarded in spades. If you do go, a machete to clear a way through the devil's club would be useful, but not mandatory.

Morkill Falls is situated around a bend in the river. As you near the falls, locate the single route down the cliff line (fairly easy to spot), which delivers you to the spray zone at the foot of the falls.

Facilities: None

Highlights: The Morkill River is a major drainage from the western face of the Rockies on the BC–Alberta border, north of Mt. Robson. Morkill Falls is one of BC's great waterfalls, but is little known or visited. The river rounds a bend just below the bridge on the Morkill FSR and flows through a 10 m (33 ft) raceway before plummeting over the brink in a powerful, confused, whitewater plunge. Visitors to the foot of the falls are rewarded with close-up views of the 30 m (100 ft) plunge. In the spray zone at the foot, water droplets are constantly propelled by the force of the plunge, making it necessary to pick your moment to take photographs.

Morkill Falls is the result of a resistant band of limestone. The river has found a route over the brink of the escarpment, leaving a virtually impregnable line of cliffs on either side of the falls. At the brink, the river has worn the rock to a smooth surface with Henry Moore sculpture-like shapes and weathering along the horizontal fault lines. Along the canyon below the falls cabin-sized slabs of rock have fallen from the cliffs.

There are actually three waterfalls to view at this location. In addition to the main attraction, two tributary streams cascade down high, precipitous gulleys on the east side of the river. One can be viewed from the main viewpoint at the top of Morkill Falls on the west side of the bridge; the other can only be seen by bushwhacking along the east side of the river on the way to the foot of the main falls.

The drive along the Morkill FSR traverses rugged, steep-sided mountains cloaked in the greenness of the Interior wet belt ecosystem. Much old-growth timber remains and the area is recovering from both logging and forest fires. On our drive to the falls we saw two black bears, and grizzlies are common inhabitants of the valley. In late August there was a memorable hatch of Compton tortoiseshell butterflies, and the entire length of the logging road was populated by hundreds of the winged creatures.

Morkill Falls, along with the river and mountain of the same name, is named for Dalby Brooks Morkill, a BC land surveyor who worked in the area in 1912–13, and on the BC–Alberta boundary surveys north of Yellowhead Pass in the early 1920s.

Snapshot: Morkill Falls is virtually unrecorded in the literature and its presence seems known to few. Prior to visiting I had been unable to find any images of this great waterfall and really did not know what to expect. It was one of the last waterfalls I visited in researching this book, so to see this remote, well-guarded and impressive waterfall was a special thrill. On my visit on a sunny afternoon in late August, a double rainbow was suspended in the spray zone below the falls.

75 REARGUARD FALLS

Rating:	▲▲▲△△
Type:	Low cascade
Location:	Hwy 16, 27 km (17 mi) NE of Valemount, 3.3 km (2 mi) E of Tete Jaune Cache, 12.2 km (7.5 mi) W of Mt. Robson Provincial Park, 95 km (60 mi) W of Jasper
Access:	Easy. Beside Hwy 16, walk in 300 m (330 yd)
Status:	Rearguard Falls Provincial Park
When to go:	Spring, summer, fall

Directions: The parking lot for the falls is on the south side of Hwy 16 between Tete Jaune Cache and Mt. Robson Provincial Park. The trail leads downhill toward the river. After 50 m (55 yd) take the T-junction 20 m (22 yd) to the right for a peekaboo view through the trees of one half of the falls. The main trail goes to the left and the viewing platform is reached in less than five minutes.

Facilities: Roadside pullout parking lot, toilets.

Highlights: The Fraser River flows over a 2 m (6.5 ft) step and then riffles down a canyon of horizontally stratified sedimentary deposits.

The Fraser is the largest salmon-producing river in the world. It rises in the nearby Mt. Robson area and flows 1,378 km (856 mi) to the Pacific Ocean. An interpretive sign at the viewpoint states, "Only a few Chinook, largest and strongest of the salmon, come this far. Look for them here in late summer." Despite the sign, the actual upper limit of migration on the Fraser River is at Overlander Falls, a few kilometres upstream. It has been estimated that about 90 percent of the fish that attempt to leap Rearguard Falls fail, with only between 350 and 550 fish per year succeeding. Most of the fish spawn just below the falls after their 11-week migration up the river.

Snapshot: The viewing platform provides a thrilling, hypnotic, close-up view of the green river as it approaches the brink, flows fluidly over the step and transposes into white foam.

Rearguard Falls. Nathen Jantzen photo

76 OVERLANDER FALLS

Rating:	▲▲▲△△
Type:	Plunge
Location:	Hwy 16, 17 km (10.5 mi) E of Tete Jaune Cache, 1.4 km (1 mi) E of Mt. Robson Visitor Centre, 80 km (50 mi) E of Jasper
Access:	Easy. Short trail beside highway
Status:	Mt. Robson Provincial Park
When to go:	Spring, summer, fall

Directions: The parking lot is on the south side of the highway 1.4 km (1 mi) east of Mt. Robson Visitor Centre. The easy trail leads downhill to the falls viewpoint, five minutes away.

Facilities: Interpretive signage.

Highlights: The green, glacial waters of the Fraser River plunge 6 m (20 ft) into a wide pool, then over a minor drop, before entering a canyon and heading toward Rearguard Falls about 14 km (9 mi) distant. A parks sign states that these falls are "the final unattainable challenge" for the few Chinook salmon that conquer Rearguard Falls. Today, kayakers may be seen challenging the falls.

Overlander Falls

The falls are named for the Overlanders, a group of 175 men and one woman who attempted to travel across the continent from Ontario to the Cariboo goldfields at a time when the usual route was via Cape Horn. They passed through the Yellowhead Pass and by this waterfall, en route to Tete Jaune Cache, in late August 1862. At Tete Jaune the party split, with some continuing on down the Fraser to Quesnel and others going south down the North Thompson to Fort Kamloops. Both parties endured fatalities on the rivers and after all their hardships, few made it to the goldfields.

Snapshot: It is fascinating to stand at Overlander Falls and contemplate the history and the name of the place. In the space of less than 150 years Overlander Falls has witnessed the progression from the first overland migrants to BC with all the attendant hardships, dangers and uncertainties they endured, to the post-industrial world tourists who fly in from far continents. During this whole period, the Fraser River has continued to flow over the falls, a never-ending symbol of continuity.

77, 78, 79 WHITE FALLS, FALLS OF THE POOL, EMPEROR FALLS

Type/Rating:	White Falls–Cascade/plunge ▲▲▲▲△
	Falls of the Pool–Plunge/cascade ▲▲▲▲△
	Emperor Falls–Plunge ▲▲▲▲▲
Location:	On the Robson River, 17 km (11 mi) E of Tete Jaune Cache, 80 km (50 mi) W of Jasper
Access:	Difficult. 15 km (9 mi) hike (one way) on the Berg Lake Trail
Status:	Mt. Robson Provincial Park
When to go:	Summer, fall

Directions: The three falls are reached via the Berg Lake Trail, one of the most famous and heavily used hiking trails within the Canadian Rockies. The three falls are stacked one above the other on the Robson River, with Emperor Falls the uppermost at 1,500 m (4,920 ft) elevation and 15 km (9 mi) from the trailhead, Falls of the Pool at 13.5 km (8 mi) and White Falls at 12.5 km (7.75 mi). The trailhead is at 850 m (2,790 ft) elevation.

From the Mt. Robson Visitor Centre drive 2 km (1.2 mi) up the west side of the adjacent Robson River Road to the Berg Lake Trail parking lot. Kinney Lake is 4 km (2.5 mi) distant, the Kinney Lake campground at 7 km (4.4 mi), Whitehorn campground at 11 km (6.8 mi) and the bridge across the Robson River at 12 km (7.5 mi). To this point the trail is relatively level, with short, lumpy sections. After the bridge it climbs steeply, gaining 365 m (1,200 ft) elevation between the bridge and

Emperor Falls. This section of the trail is known as Heartbreak Hill, for reasons that become obvious for those who attempt it.

White Falls and Falls of the Pool are beside the trail, with a short, well-signed side trail to the Emperor Falls viewpoint. The Emperor Falls campground is 700 m (765 yd) beyond the viewpoint trail and Berg Lake a further 3 km (2 mi), where there is a choice of campsites at Marmot or Berg Lake.

Facilities: All facilities are available at the park headquarters and Visitor Centre, including restaurant, gas station, campground, extensive displays about the history and wildlife of the park and any information or permits that may be required for the Berg Lake Trail. The trail itself has a series of well-spaced campsites along its 22 km (13.5 mi) length, with tent pads, toilet facilities, shelters with tables and bear-proof food storage caches.

Highlights: The Berg Lake Trail is world famous and one of the most popular hiking routes in the Canadian Rockies, attracting about 50,000 hikers per year. The trail circumscribes the great western base of Mt. Robson, the highest peak in the Canadian Rockies at 3,954 m (12,973 ft). It then traverses an old-growth western red cedar forest, passes along the eastern shore of jade green Kinney Lake, "the mirror of the mount," enters the Valley of the Thousand Falls with White, Falls of the Pool and Emperor at trailside, and finally reaches Berg Lake, with its unparalleled views of Mt. Robson and the Berg Glacier carving icebergs into the lake.

In 1863, Lord Milton and Dr. Cheadle, two English adventurers, reported that "On every side the snowy heads of mighty hills crowded round, whilst, immediately behind us, a giant among giants, and immeasurably supreme, rose Robson's Peak." (http://www.env.gov.bc.ca/bcparks/explore/parkpgs/mt_robson)

White Falls

White Falls is made up of four separate drops: a 7 m (23 ft) cascade, a 15 m (50 ft) plunge, a second 15 m (50 ft) plunge and a final 15 m (50 ft) cascade. On the opposite side of the Robson River the Valley of the Thousand Falls rises dramatically, sheer and craggy. It is an easy 200 m (220 yd) walk up the east side of the river from the bridge to better observe and photograph the lower cascade. From the main viewpoint on the trail a short side trail leads to better and closer views of the upper falls. As you walk across the talus here, spray from the falls flies by and there are good views of the scoured channel of the river as it races over clean bedrock between the second and third drops.

White Falls

Falls of the Pool

This waterfall combines beautiful architecture and an unbelievable setting, framed against the sheer, northern ramparts of Mt. Robson. The falls plunges 10 m (33 ft) within an enclosed tube or chimney to a minor ledge, cascades 10 m (33 ft) to its beautiful toponymic pool and drops down a second 15 m (50 ft) segmented cascade before barrelling down a long, narrow, deeply incised canyon toward White Falls. These latter two features are only visible by walking down along the rim of the canyon from the viewpoint.

Emperor Falls

The side trail leads 200 m (220 yd) to the spray-blasted plateau of bare rock, grasses and krummholz, the legacy of the Robson River plunging 45 m (150 ft) over a cliff. The

Falls of the Pool

river initially cascades 10 m (33 ft) before hitting an impediment and exploding outwards in an enormous roostertail known as the Emperor's Leap. The waterfall appears to land partly on a flat bed of rock, which creates tremendous volumes of spray that are blasted away from the foot of the falls. The river drains away from the falls in a more recent course, leaving the older "captured" channel dry, except when it still receives overflow water at flood stages. This feature is the result of the upstream migration of Emperor Falls as erosion has progressed.

The foot of Emperor Falls is a hostile environment of blasting spray and is very chilly after the sweaty exertions of the trail. It is possible to sneak in to the base of the falls by staying close against the cliff and forest in a narrow, spray-free zone. Some hikers may even feel inclined to take a cold shower here.

Snapshot: It is a rare privilege to have three major, named waterfalls in such close proximity to each other on the same river. The falls are entirely different from one another, and they encompass a wide array of the structural elements of waterfalls.

The Berg Lake Trail rightly deserves its fame, and while it is not a place for solitude, a wonderful camaraderie exists along the way from its international clientele of pilgrims.

Finally, there is the enduring image of Emperor Falls, of the Monarch and the Emperor–Mt. Robson, the Monarch, highest peak in the Canadian Rockies, hovering over the fabulous roostertail of its offspring Emperor Falls. Of all the iconic images in the scenic wonderland that is the Canadian Rockies, this is perhaps the apotheosis, combining as it does the two features synonymous with the public perception of the area, great mountains and great waterfalls.

Emperor Falls

Waterfalls of British Columbia

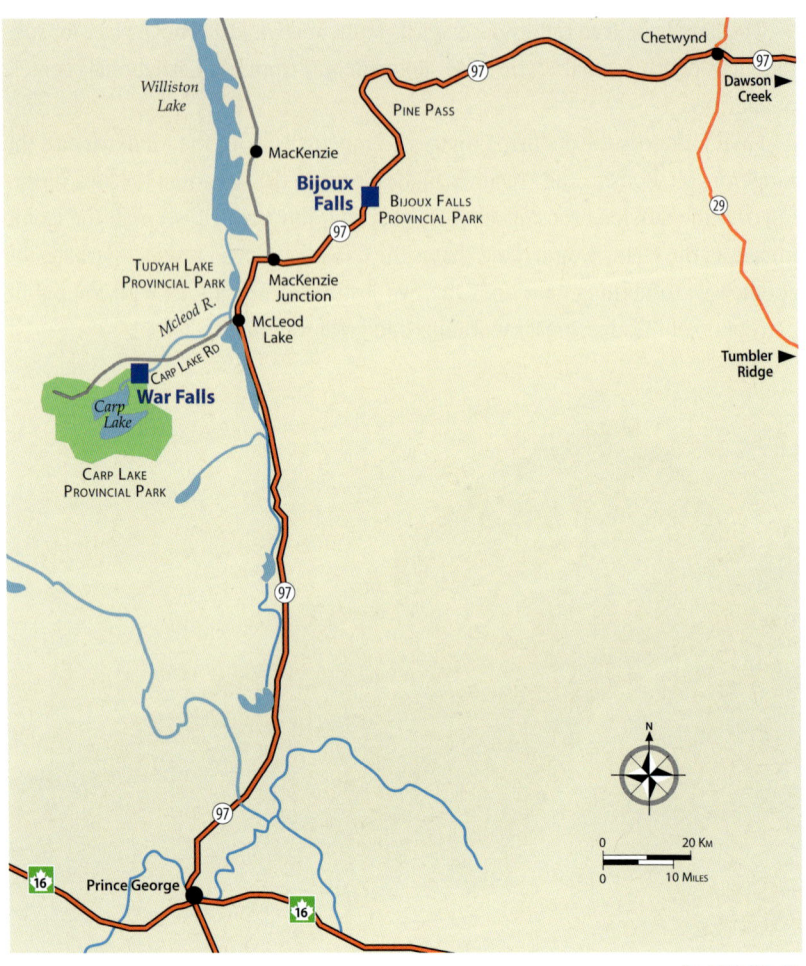

FALLS 80–81

80 WAR FALLS

Rating:	▲▲▲▲△
Type:	Tiered cascade
Location:	McLeod River in Carp Lake Provincial Park, 141 km (88 mi) N of Prince George, 16 km (10 mi) S of Mackenzie Junction
Access:	Moderate. 23 km (14 mi) gravel logging road, 600 m (650 yd) of park trail with stairways
Status:	Carp Lake Provincial Park
When to go:	Spring, summer, fall

Directions: From Hwy 97 turn onto the well-signed Carp Lake Road at McLeod Lake and drive 23.2 km (14.4 mi) to the War Falls trailhead on the right,

War Falls

100 m (110 yd) beyond the Carp Lake Provincial Park sign. The easy trail leads past a series of falls and cascades to War Falls, which is 600 m (650 yd) from the trailhead.

Facilities: Pit toilet at the trailhead, interpretive signage along the trail. Carp Lake, just ahead, is a full facility park with a boat launch, swimming, picnic shelters and adventure playground.

Highlights: The trail leading downstream alongside the McLeod River passes four distinct cascade waterfalls. The uppermost falls is a 7 m (23 ft) segmented cascade and each of the two segments divides again into two. A minor cascade is followed by a 6 m (20 ft) falls and the main attraction, 12 m (39 ft) War Falls. May and June are the optimum months to visit to see the maximum flow, but the falls are still respectable even in late summer.

The trail weaves through a boreal white spruce forest with a subalpine fir component. The shrub understory contains alder, high-bush cranberry, red osier dogwood, kinnikinnick, spirea and sarsaparilla, and other plants and flowers to look for include bunchberry, aster, palmate coltsfoot, oak fern and club moss. The signage indicates that bird species include ruffed grouse and black-backed woodpecker. Mammals such as porcupine, moose, fox and bears are present. On an August visit belted kingfisher, spotted sandpiper and American dipper were noted in the pools and along the river.

As a point of interest, Carp Lake is at the exact geographical centre of British Columbia.

Snapshot: This short side trip and hike is well worth a visit as you drive from Prince George towards the Pine Pass. For those from the south the distinctive fragrance of the boreal spruce forest will welcome you to northern BC.

81 BIJOUX FALLS

Rating:	▲▲▲▲△
Type:	Cascade
Location:	Beside Hwy 97, 188 km (117 mi) N of Prince George, 117 km (73 mi) S of Chetwynd
Access:	Easy. Parking lot at the foot of the falls
Status:	Bijoux Falls Provincial Park
When to go:	Spring, summer, fall

Directions: The park is 32.5 km (20 mi) north of Mackenzie Junction, and 11.5 km (7 mi) south of Azouzetta Lake Lodge, at the summit of the Pine Pass.

Facilities: Large parking lot with a lawn and picnic tables at the foot of the falls. Tudyah Lake Provincial Park, a full-facility park with camping, is about 40 km (25 mi) to the south.

Highlights: Bijoux Falls is a series of four cascades with a combined height of 40 m (130 ft), confined within a narrow, jagged chasm between horizontal strata of shale. A steep, slippery, rugged path ascends the slope on the east side of the falls, allowing a more intimate exploration of the falls than can be seen from the viewing area at the base. The upper cascades are invisible from the foot of the falls and can only be seen by climbing the trail. Caution on the steep, slippery trail is advised. The highest of the individual falls, at about 10 m (30 ft), flows through a huge culvert from beneath railway

Bijoux Falls

tracks into a wide plunge pool. Dippers can be frequently observed either on the waterfall itself or on rocks in the swift flowing creek below the falls. Steller's jays, BC's provincial bird, patrol the picnic tables in search of handouts or crumbs.

Bijoux is the French word for jewels, so this is a well-named falls.

Snapshot: This is more or less a mandatory stop in any season or weather on the long drive from Prince George over the Pine Pass. On a hot summer's day the cool rush of air and the fine mist at the foot of the falls mingled with the smell of spruce and fir is the intoxicating essence of the Rocky Mountains.

> *It is wearisome to be in a fresh rapture at every turn of the road. And as I have before said, you must be that or nothing.*
>
> Charles Darwin's Beagle Diary

NORTHWEST

Significant waterfalls are poorly represented in this vast region. There are waterfalls, but most are small and unprepossessing. The landscape of the region covers the gamut from the high, heavily glaciated Coast Range mountains to the rolling interior plateaus. Twin Falls #3 near Smithers and Cheslatta Falls southwest of Vanderhoof are the prime waterfalls of the region. Perhaps there are unknown and wondrous waterfalls hidden away in the remote wildernesses of northwestern BC?

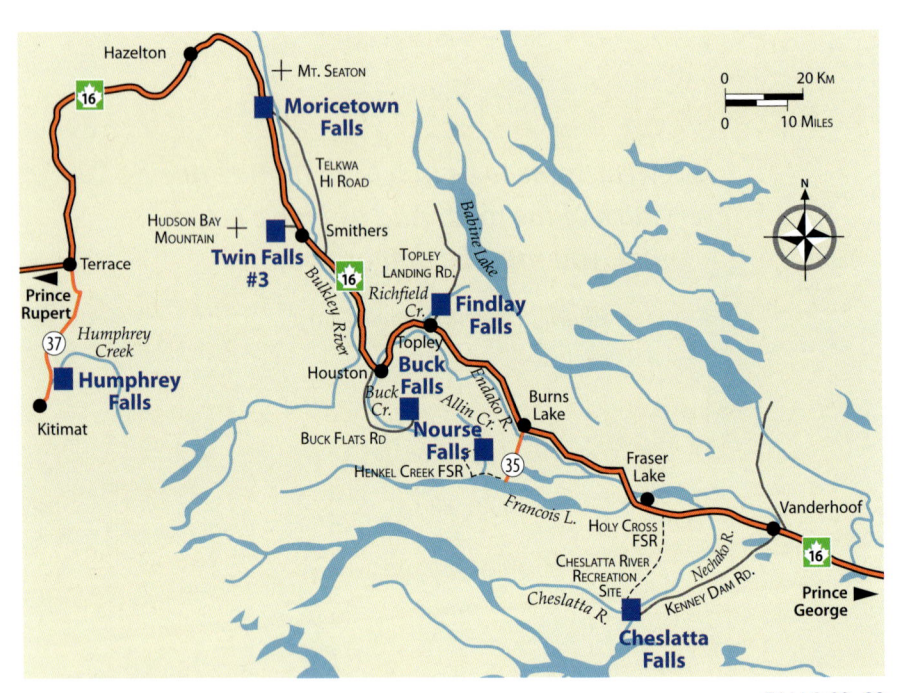

FALLS 82–88

82 CHESLATTA FALLS

Rating:	▰▰▰▰▱
Type:	Tiered block plunge
Location:	On the Cheslatta River, SW of Vanderhoof
Access:	Moderate. 59 km (37 mi) gravel logging road, 1.2 km (.75 mi) trail
Status:	BC Forest Service trail
When to go:	Maximum flow is in the spring

A Guide to BC's Best 100 Falls

Cheslatta Falls

Directions: The closest town is Vanderhoof. There are two possible routes to the falls, and they can be combined into a circle route (I would recommend this option). From Vanderhoof drive 52.4 km (32.5 mi) west on Hwy 16, past Fort Fraser, and turn left (south) onto the Holy Cross Forest Service Road. The community of Fraser Lake is 6.3 km (3.7 mi) west of the Holy Cross Road. Proceed to km 59 (signed as 159) and park at the bridge across the Cheslatta River. The trailhead is on the left (east) side immediately after the bridge. It is 1.2 km (.75 mi) one way (about 20 minutes) to the top of the main falls on a good trail with some short, steep pitches. The trail is a loop, so return by completing the circle.

Once at the falls, it is possible to scramble down the rocks, and through the bush for an up-close view of the two drops. Extreme caution is advised and this climb is not recommended for children. Another trail leads down a short, steep incline to the foot of the falls and the dry bed of the old Nechako River.

Returning to your vehicle you can either drive back to Hwy 16 the way you came, or continue south for 7 km (4.5 mi) to the Kenney Dam and back to Vanderhoof on the Kenney Dam Road, a distance of 93 km (58 mi). All junctions are signposted.

Facilities: The trail begins at the Cheslatta River Recreation Site, which has campsites, picnic tables and outhouses.

Highlights: Just upstream from the bridge at the start of the trail, a set of rapids descends over successive basaltic sills toward the main falls. Cheslatta Falls is a duo of block plunges–enormous piles of water tumble a total of 18 m (59 ft) in two drops separated by a roiling pool of white foam. The main plunge pool below the lower falls is an amphitheatre of vertical basalt columns. Here at the foot of the falls is the ancient confluence of the Cheslatta and Nechako rivers, a dry plain of sand and willows since the Nechako River was diverted.

The completion of the Kenney Dam in 1952, 7 km (4 mi) beyond the southern end of the Grand Canyon of the Nechako, cut off the entire flow of the Nechako River and diverted about one-third of the total discharge westward through an extensive lake system that includes Ootsa and Eutsuk lakes. Eventually, after passing through a 16 km (10 mi) tunnel beneath the Coast Range mountains, the water reaches the Kemano hydro facility that powers the aluminum smelter at Kitimat. At 90 m (295 ft) high, the Kenney Dam was the largest rock-filled dam in the world at the time. The reservoir behind the dam gradually filled over the five-year period from 1952 to 1957. The Cheslatta River is now fed by the Skins Lake spillway, which controls the level of Ootsa Lake and maintains discharges in the Cheslatta and Nechako rivers. At the start of the trail an earthen dam blocks an old branch of the Cheslatta River, leaving a dry falls.

Between the Kenney Dam and Cheslatta Falls the now abandoned Grand Canyon of the Nechako is preserved as the Nechako Canyon Protected Area. This 7 km (4 mi) long area protects the unique erosional features of the canyon and First Nations archaeological sites.

Snapshot: A friend of mine who grew up in Fort Fraser and made frequent fishing expeditions in his youth to Cheslatta Falls told me a story. One day he was fishing in the pool at the foot of the falls when to his unmitigated amazement he watched a black bear be swept along in the river, go over the falls, disappear in the maelstrom and climb uninjured out of the plunge pool. My correspondent informs me that the bear tried to make light of the incident, as if it was a regular occurrence, with no bear fallibility implied.

83 FINDLAY FALLS

Rating:	▲▲▲▲△
Type:	Plunge
Location:	On Richfield Creek, N of Topley between Burns Lake and Houston
Access:	Moderate. Short walk on a very steep, loose, unimproved trail
Status:	Provincial forest
When to go:	Spring, summer, fall

Directions: The hamlet of Topley is 51 km (32 mi) west of Burns Lake and 30 km (19 mi) east of Houston. At Topley turn north onto the Topley Landing Road, also known as the Granisle Highway. Proceed 6.8 km (4.2 mi) to the bridge across Richfield Creek. Park here and walk back 150 m (160 yd) from the bridge on the southwest side of the road, along a wide, flat expanse of gravel, and look for a trail leading into the timber. The upper viewpoint is just inside the timber, but there are no views of the actual falls from here, only of the plunge pool and a minor, 2 m (6.5 ft) upper falls with a pool immediately before the main drop. The falls can be fully observed from the lower viewpoint, but the short trail is very steep, loose and potentially dangerous. It should only be negotiated by the active and is not recommended for young children. A faint side trail leads down to the plunge pool.

Facilities: None

Highlights: Findlay Falls has cut a deep notch in the igneous rock before it plunges 17 m (55 ft) into its large plunge pool. The sheer, bare headwall is undercut behind the plunge in the classic fashion of basalt waterfalls. A convenient horizontal ledge allows easy access behind the falling water with no danger from the main plunge, although you may get sprayed in the process. There are good views downstream of the impressive canyon. Findlay Falls is ensconced in a spruce–pine forest with saskatoon, bunchberry and showy Jacob's ladder in the understory. Moose prints and droppings were noted and a warbling vireo was singing when I visited.

Snapshot: This is one of the few BC waterfalls with access behind the plunge. It is redolent of Moul Falls in Wells Gray Provincial Park.

84 NOURSE FALLS

Rating:	▲▲▲▲△
Type:	Lower: Tiered cascade; Upper: Plunge
Location:	39 km (24 mi) SW of Burns Lake, 110 km (70 mi) SW of Houston
Access:	Easy. 37.4 km (23.2 mi) of blacktop, 1.6 km (1 mi) of gravel, short hike
Status:	Provincial forest and BC Forest Service Recreational Trail
When to go:	Spring, summer, fall

Directions: At the main intersection in Burns Lake turn south off Hwy 16 onto Hwy 35 toward Francois Lake. Bear right (west) at the lake and proceed past the ferry terminal at 23 km (14 mi) for a further 13.4 km (8.3 mi) to the Nourse Creek bridge. One kilometre past the bridge turn right (north) onto the Henkel

Creek Forest Service Road, which is also posted to Nourse Creek Falls. Beware of possible logging traffic on this road. Turn right after 1.4 km (.87 mi) onto a side road posted "Nourse Creek Trail." The parking lot and trailhead is a further 200 m (220 yd) and a sign reads "1.5K to Lower Falls, 3.4K to Upper Falls" (actual distances are shorter).

Facilities: Outhouse at the trailhead, picnic tables at the Upper Falls and another table about 500 m (550 yd) along the trail.

Highlights: I visited Nourse Falls on a hot, mid-June afternoon. The drive through lake country takes you by lakes of a blue rarely seen on this planet, densely green meadows filled with dandelions and the distant white snowcaps of Tweedsmuir Park.

The forest is a dry spruce–pine–aspen–juniper ecosystem with a profusion of wildflowers. In June, clematis, heart-leaved arnica, early blue violet, showy Jacob's ladder, clasping twistedstalk, fairyslipper orchid and wild strawberry were all in bloom. Songbirds I recognized included ruby-crowned kinglet, warbling vireo and Swainson's thrush. Butterflies noted were swallowtails, Stella's orangetips and blues.

The first 300 m (330 yd) of trail offers two distant views of the Lower Falls and a glimpse of the hoodoos on the opposite side of the creek. At the 500 m (550 yd) mark, the views down the canyon to Francois Lake open up. The main viewpoint for the Lower Falls is about a 10-minute hike, and allows long-range views of Nourse Creek on its wild tumble through a steep-walled canyon. The highest drop at the lower falls is a 15 m (50 ft) plunge/cascade that is only partially visible. Further cascades rush around car-sized rocks. Isolated in the canyon downstream of the falls sits an immense sheer wall with pinnacles of a reddish-coloured rock. The viewpoint gives panoramic views of the pristine valley of Nourse Creek and its canyon, hoodoos and waterfalls. Do not attempt to go below the viewpoint; the incline is steep, loose and dangerous.

The trail continues for another 10 minutes to a picnic table at the canyon rim above upper Nourse Falls. The trail down to the foot of the falls is steep and loose. The falls are a 3 m (10 ft) plunge divided in midstream by a basaltic horn with a foamy pool at its base.

Nourse Creek is also known as Allin Creek, and both names commemorate early homesteaders on Francois Lake. The Nourse homestead was at the mouth of the creek that bears this name.

Snapshot: Nourse Canyon is a delightful destination on a sunny day with lots to occupy the botanist, the birder, the lepidopterist, the geologist and the waterfall lover.

85 BUCK FALLS

Rating:	▲▲▲▲△△
Type:	Tiered plunge
Location:	34 km (21 mi) S of Houston
Access:	Easy. Good gravel logging road and 300 m (330 yd) level trail
Status:	Provincial forest
When to go:	High water is in May and June

Directions: From the traffic lights at the mall in downtown Houston drive westward on Hwy 16 for 2.2 km (1.4 mi). Turn left (south) onto Buck Flats Road, which immediately becomes gravel. Proceed 28.5 km (17.7 mi) to a Y in the road and bear left onto the Goosly Road (note the km 26 marker). After 2.2 km (1.4 mi) turn left onto K10 Creek Road and drive 1.2 km (.75 mi) to the bridge across Buck Creek. Park here, and the best viewing trail is on the far (north) side of the bridge. Walk in 300 m (330 yd) on the level trail to view the two falls.

Facilities: None

Highlights: The drive to Buck Falls will take you through the regenerating forests of the catastrophic 1982 "Swiss Fire" (named for the nationality of the culprits), in which $2 billion worth of prime timber was burned. The huge burn is now green with deciduous brush and planted pine trees, but the telltale burnt snags remain, testimony to both the destruction wrought by fire, and also the great regenerative power of the forest.

Buck Falls

Buck Falls is a tiered falls with consecutive 3 m (10 ft), 3 m (10 ft) and 2.5 m (8 ft) plunges, and a fourth step as a rapids. It is about 100 m (330 ft) between the second and third plunges.

Snapshot: I intended to make a brief visit to Buck Falls, but stayed for hours, on a stunningly gorgeous mid-June morning. Buck Creek was running high in freshet on its way from Goosly Lake to the Bulkley River. The blue, blue sky and the fragrance of the warm spruce and pine forest mixed with cooler draughts of air by the creek. Many wildflowers were in bloom, including showy Jacob's ladder, arnica, white pussytoes, purple-leaved willowherb and, on the rocks at the lower falls, leather-leaved and three-toothed saxifrage. There were also blooming fairyslipper orchids, *Calypso bulbosa*, which take their Latin name from the goddess daughter of Atlas who was Homer's beautiful nymph hidden in the woods. It may be a long way from classical Greece to the sub-boreal forest of Houston, British Columbia, but this all had a great resonance on an exquisite spring morning by beautiful Buck Falls.

86 MORICETOWN FALLS

Rating:	▲▲▲▲△
Type:	Punchbowl
Location:	29.5 km (18 mi) W of Smithers, 160 km (100 mi) E of Terrace and 36.5 km (22.5 mi) E of Hazelton
Access:	Easy. Beside Hwy 16
Status:	Wet'suwet'en Indian Reserve
When to go:	Spring and summer

Directions: The falls can be viewed from a rest area beside Hwy 16. For a more intimate visit take Telkwa Hi Road immediately west of the rest area and park at the bridge.

Facilities: There is a roadside rest area beside the highway, and a picnic site just beyond the bridge.

Highlights: The wide, brown Bulkley River swirls in a huge, leisurely eddy before it approaches the canyon where its waters are compressed through a narrow gorge, about 10 m (30 ft) wide, beneath the bridge. At high water there are four separate drops into the canyon, all 2–3 m (6.5–10 ft) high. The canyon is a bucking maelstrom of heaving white water, with debris spinning in the swirling whirlpools.

The location is surrounded by beautiful scenery: Hudson Bay Mountain (2,560 m/8,400 ft) off to the south, dramatic peaks to the west and Mt. Seaton (2,036 m/6,680 ft) to the northeast. In June the grassy banks of the river are colourful with dandelions, Jacob's ladder, field chickweed and lance-leaved stonecrop.

A Guide to BC's Best 100 Falls

Moricetown Falls. Thomas Gotchy photo

Moricetown Falls is an ancestral fishing spot for the local Wet'suwet'en people, who gaff or net salmon as they stand on ledges of the canyon walls. Concrete fishways have been constructed to help the salmon migrate upstream beyond the falls.

Snapshot: This is an idyllic spot to linger on a sunny day, with views of the canyon, the mountains and the white clapboard church on the west bank. It is an exciting place during the high water of the spring freshet, and is a good spot to observe traditional native fishing practices when the salmon are running in July and August.

87 TWIN FALLS #3 (SMITHERS)

Rating:	▲▲▲▲△
Type:	One plunge and one cascade
Location:	10 km (6 mi) NW of Smithers, 190 km (120 mi) E of Terrace
Access:	Easy. Gravel road, 10-minute trail
Status:	BC Forest Service Recreation Site
When to go:	Spring, summer, fall. Ice climbing in the winter

193

Waterfalls of British Columbia

Twin Falls #3 Gareth Jones photo

Directions: From the traffic light in downtown Smithers drive west on Hwy 16 for 3 km (2 mi) to the left turn at Lake Kathlyn Road. Follow this road and note the signage for the falls. Bear left onto Glacier Gulch Road for 6.3 km (4 mi) to the parking lot of the BCFS Recreation Site. The trail is straight ahead. After 200 m (220 yd) the trail splits to Glacier Gulch on the left and to the Twin Falls viewpoint on the right, and splits again 50 m (55 yd) beyond this point. You can either follow the official trail to the viewpoint or take a short path that goes up the creekbed.

The Glacier Gulch trail leads you on a two-hour hike through forest and then open scree to the lower parts of Hudson Bay Glacier. The molybdenum deposit below the ice has been mined since the 1950s.

Facilities: The recreation site at the trailhead has campsites, tables, barbecue pits and outhouses. The viewpoint is a wooden observation deck.

Highlights: Twin 183 m (600 ft) high waterfalls drain from the cirque of Hudson Bay Mountain (2,560 m/8,400 ft). To the left, the Hudson Bay Glacier gives birth to a plunge waterfall; to the right, a cascade drains Toboggan Glacier. In mid-June an additional minor cascade with dribbles to the left and right forms down the central headwall. The enormous cirque that feeds Twin Falls is best viewed from a roadside rest area 5.5 km (3.5 mi) west of the East Kathryn Lake Loop or 1.7 km (1 mi) west of the West Kathryn Lake Loop.

From the viewing platform the wide, U-shaped glacial valley surrounds you. The falls flow down the vertical headwall with rugged snow-capped ridges and peaks above. A dwarf krummholz forest of small, broken hemlocks and balsams attests to the heavy and active snowloads here. The gulley to the right of the trail is filled with deep snow into late summer and its surface is littered with the debris and rocks typical of glacial terrain.

Mountain goats are sometimes present on the steep walls of the valley.

Snapshot: This is a two-for-one experience. Other waterfalls in this book where there are two falls together include Sylvia and Goodwin Falls in Wells Gray Provincial Park and Belcourt Falls in the Tumbler Ridge area.

88 HUMPHREY FALLS

Rating:	▲▲▲△△
Type:	Plunge
Location:	On Hwy 37, 43.6 km (27 mi) S of Terrace, 20.5 km (12.7 mi) N of Kitimat
Access:	Easy. 2.5 km (1.5 mi) gravel road, 100 m (110 yd) trail
Status:	Provincial forest
When to go:	Spring, summer, fall

Directions: From the junction of Hwys 16 and 37, 3 km (2 mi) east of Terrace, proceed 40.6 km (25.2 mi) south on the Kitimat Highway. The Humphrey Road is on the left (east) and is unmarked. If you reach the Humphrey Creek bridge you have gone 1 km (.6 mi) too far. After 300 m (330 yd) on the Humphrey Road bear right and drive a further 2.1 km (1.3 mi) to the second road on the right. Park here and walk in 100 m (110 yd) to the trailhead. The trail itself is only 100 m (110 yd), with the upper path leading to the top of the falls and the lower path to the base. It is a short scramble up the rocks to the brink of the falls.

Facilities: None

Highlights: Though not one of BC's major waterfalls, Humphrey Falls is an exceptionally beautiful spot. From the middle viewpoint the creek powers through a notch in the rock, roostertails 10 m (33 ft) directly into an opposing wall that confronts it at right angles and rushes down the canyon, an eroded cleft in the granite. It then plunges 3 m (10 ft) through a narrow constriction before a final 3 m (10 ft) cascade.

Snapshot: I visited Humphrey Falls during a mid-June heat wave and the resulting freshet created at the foot of the falls one of the angriest tumults in BC waterfalldom. This display was in total contrast to the extravagant display of bunchberries blooming at trailside and the rainbow suspended in the drifting spray of the canyon.

TUMBLER RIDGE

The Tumbler Ridge area in the foothills on the eastern side of the northern Rocky Mountains is blessed with an abundance of waterfalls, much like the Wells Gray Park area. Both places have geological conditions specifically favourable to the creation of waterfalls. At Wells Gray it is the presence of basalt, while in the Tumbler Ridge area the waterfalls are sculpted in both the sandstone

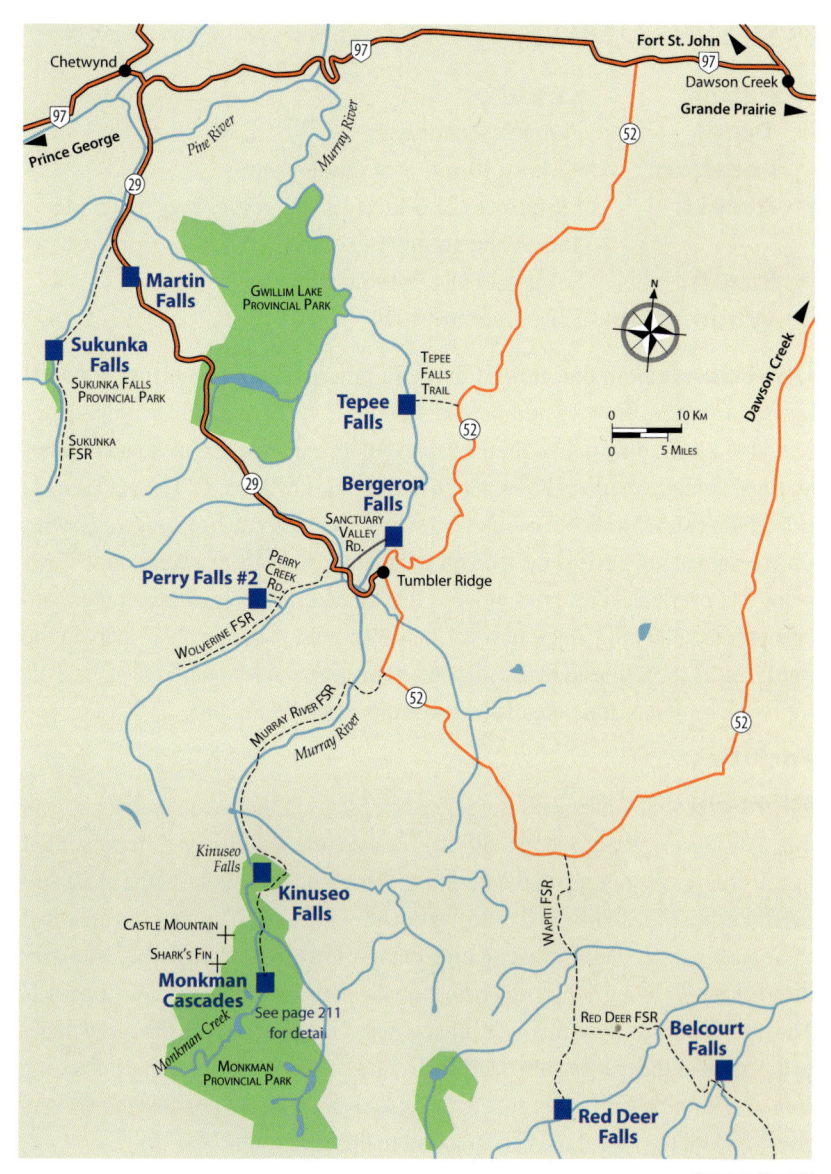

FALLS 89–97

Waterfalls of British Columbia

and limestone associated with the nearby Rockies. Over much of the area the strata are generally horizontal; where waterfalls occur through faulting or simple erosion, the result is usually a plunge waterfall. The Tumbler Ridge area has recently become notable as a hotbed of paleontology and the fossil seeker and the waterfall aficionado share a common interest in the sedimentary geology.

The region is home to one of BC's greatest waterfalls at Kinuseo Falls. It also has the unique Monkman Cascades, a difficult to access scenic and geologic wonder that is truly one of the great places to visit in all of North America.

89 SUKUNKA FALLS

Rating:	▲▲▲▲△
Type:	Plunge/cascade/step
Location:	47 km (30 mi) S of Chetwynd
Access:	Moderate. 21.5 km (13 mi) gravel logging road and short, steep trail
Status:	Sukunka Falls Provincial Park
When to go:	Spring, summer, fall

Directions: From downtown Chetwynd proceed 3 km (1.8 mi) east toward Dawson Creek on Hwy 97 and bear right onto Hwy 29 to Tumbler Ridge. After 22.6 km (14 mi) turn right onto the gravel Sukunka Forest Service Road and follow the kilometre markers 21.5 km (13.4 mi) to the km 221 sign. The road is wide enough for two vehicles, but caution is advised due to oil patch and logging traffic. On the right at km 221 a short loop off the main road leads to a panoramic viewpoint that overlooks the series of steps that is Sukunka Falls. To reach the main falls proceed 300 m (330 yd) beyond the viewpoint to another short loop on the right. This is the trailhead for the descent down a very steep path to the falls. This trail is slick, muddy and potentially dangerous in wet conditions.

Facilities: None

Highlights: Sukunka Falls is a series of 10 steps in the Sukunka River, spread over a distance of about 300 m (330 yd). The steps are walls of tilted strata; the flat face acts as a resistant cap to the flow of the river and thus protects the more vulnerable exposed seams from the erosive power of the water. The river has breached these faces at each step, the biggest drop being a 4 m (13 ft) plunge where the river diverts laterally along a rock wall before finally pouring through in a wide breach. The trail leads directly to this wall and it is possible to walk out on the rocky finger to the brink of the plunge with the river around you on three sides, an exhilarating spot to commune with the beauty of Sukunka Falls. It is also possible to reach the river's edge at the foot of the falls, adjacent to this rock wall.

Sukunka Falls

On a visit in late August a trout was attempting to jump the main falls, but fell back each time. A late spotted sandpiper bobbed along the water's edge and a belted kingfisher was very vocal in its fishing attempts.

In October 1914 Samuel Prescott Fay discovered Kinuseo Falls on the Murray River. He thought that the Murray River was probably the Sukunka, then mistakenly travelled upstream on the Sukunka, believing it to be the Pine River. In the process he found and photographed Sukunka Falls and later wrote: "At this point the river goes through a rocky canyon, above which are a series of very pretty cascades and small, symmetrical falls, so much so as to be almost artificial." (Helm, p.213)

A panoramic view of the 10 steps of Sukunka Falls can be viewed from the road, but the descent to the river is recommended for those able to negotiate the steep trail.

Snapshot: An exquisite time to visit Sukunka Falls is in the fall when the leaves of the birch, balsam poplar and aspen are at their golden best, late September and early October being the peak. At this season the river and the falls framed by the green spruce and pine and the brilliant golden foliage of the riparian deciduous species is simply breathtaking. It is a photographer's dream, and a highlight of any appreciation of BC waterfalls.

90 MARTIN FALLS

Rating:	▲▲▲△△
Type:	Tiered plunges
Location:	66 km (41 mi) N of Tumbler Ridge, 29 km (18 mi) S of Chetwynd
Access:	Moderate. Hike to top of the upper falls, steep bushwhack to the middle and lower falls
Status:	Provincial forest
When to go:	Summer and fall

Directions: Both accesses are from Hwy 29, the Tumbler Ridge Highway. To reach the upper falls drive north for 65.6 km (40.7 mi) from Tumbler Ridge and park at a creek that passes beneath the road in a large culvert. Walk down the creek for 300 to 400 m (330 to 440 yd) until it reaches the larger Martin Creek, then bear right and follow Martin Creek to the brink of the falls in about 1 km (.6 mi). This is only possible at low water during the summer and fall. You may be able to keep your feet dry by dexterous rock hopping, but shallow wading in the creek is the other option. From the brink of the falls it is best to bushwhack straight up the steep bank back to the highway. Your vehicle will be about 700 m (765 yd) back along the road.

A Guide to BC's Best 100 Falls

TUMBLER RIDGE

Martin Falls

To reach the middle and lower falls watch for a gravel side road 700 m (765 yd) north of the parking spot for the upper falls. Park your vehicle on the shoulder of the road 300 m (330 yd) north of here. By bushwhacking straight down the slope in extremely steep terrain a single possible gulley accesses Martin Creek between the middle and lower falls. Extreme caution is advised on this slope. The middle falls are 200 m (220 yd) upstream and the lower falls 200 m (220 yd) downstream from this access point.

Facilities: None

Highlights: The upper falls is an 8 m (26 ft) plunge. At high water Martin Creek spills over the entire ledge, but during lower flows it laterals to the left against the overhanging cliff before spilling down the headwall. About 100 m (110 yd) separates the upper and middle falls, but the inaccessible cliffs make it impossible to access one from the other. The middle falls is a 7 m (23 ft) cascade surrounded by enormously high canyon walls. The intriguing feature here is a cave on the west side, partway up the cascade, where the creek makes a turn. The cave is a fascinating spot to sit and view the waterfall and is easily reached by crossing the creek and wading. In 2002 a dipper's nest was built in a cavity on a ledge in the roof of the cave.

The lower falls, about 300 m (330 yd) downstream is a 2.5 m (8 ft) plunge/cascade where the creek flows through a 50 cm (20 in) notch. Again there is a cave on the far side of the creek, and a circular plunge pool that makes a good swimming hole. Downstream from the falls a fine example of a recumbent fold can be seen in the strata of the high canyon wall.

Snapshot: Martin Creek Falls is another among the impressive list of imposing waterfalls and canyons near Tumbler Ridge. The Martin Creek canyon is a wonder, but drivers passing along the highway a few metres away are blissfully ignorant of its existence. And even knowing of its existence, it is still a difficult place to access.

91 PERRY FALLS #2 (TUMBLER RIDGE)

Rating:	▲▲▲▲△
Type:	Rare double plunge
Location:	30 km (19 mi) WNW of Tumbler Ridge
Access:	Moderate. 20 km (12 mi) gravel logging road and short, steep descent to foot of the falls
Status:	Provincial forest
When to go:	Spring, summer, fall

A Guide to BC's Best 100 Falls

Directions: From the Tumbler Ridge Visitors Centre drive 0.8 km (.5 mi) to Hwy 29. Proceed north toward Chetwynd for 8.9 km (5.5 mi) and turn left on to the gravel road. At 300 m (330 yd) from the highway zero your odometer at the official start of the Wolverine Forest Service Road. At km 5.6 (mi 3.5) cross the Two Creek bridge and then the rail tracks. Stay right and go uphill at the major junction at km 8.3 (mi 5.2). At km 10.2 (mi 6.3) cross the rail tracks again and the Perry Creek bridge at km 11.9 (mi 7.4), before the Spieker Mountain Snowmobile Trail System signage. Immediately beyond here at the km 12 marker take the Perry Creek road uphill to the right. Proceed to the km 7 road sign; the trailhead is 100 m (110 yd) beyond here at a cleared spot on the right

Perry Falls #2

with piles of dirt. There is a bridge across Perry Creek at km 7.4.

A faint but discernible trail leads directly downhill to the only access down the steep canyon wall to the creek bed below the falls. The access requires scrambling down the last 100 m (110 yd) while hanging on to bushes and saplings. It is steep, but not dangerous if care is taken. Hiking time is about five minutes.

While you explore around the foot of the falls or find spots for photography, be aware of slippery logs in the log-jam, and also of precariously balanced and wobbly slabs of moss-covered rock.

Facilities: None

Highlights: Perry Falls is a rare example of a perfectly formed tiered or double plunge. Perry Creek pours through a deep notch in the sandstone strata and plunges 8 m (25 ft) to a ledge before making a second leap of 10 m (30 ft) to the plunge pool that, with the canyon below the falls, creates a large amphitheatre.

The intermediate ledge of more resistant rock is topped by softer strata that have eroded behind the falls to create a huge grotto that extends 10 m (30 ft) back into the headwall. By crossing the log-jam at the foot of the falls and clambering along the right side wall it is possible to enter the grotto and walk behind the curtain of falling water. Perry is one of the few BC waterfalls that allows this particular activity.

Below the falls a series of log-jams and the woody debris at the tide line high above the summer flow level indicate mayhem at the spring freshet or periodic floods. The lower levels of the amphitheatre are a jumble of moss-covered slabs of detritus that have fallen from the fractured walls of the canyon. These wobble disconcertingly and contain hidden holes, so caution should be exercised if you attempt to walk over them.

Watch for that ubiquitous denizen of waterfall plunge pools, the dipper, at this lonely spot. The Perry Creek canyon is notable as the northernmost recorded site in the world for black swifts, "which almost certainly breed here." (Helm, p.179) Look for the swifts in June, July and August.

Snapshot: Perry Falls is the only perfect tiered plunge waterfall in this book. It is also notable as one of the few BC falls where access is possible behind the falling water, the others being Moul, Findlay, Canim and Morrissey.

92 TEPEE FALLS

Rating:	▲▲▲▲△
Type:	Plunge
Location:	Hwy 52, 35 km (22 mi) N of Tumbler Ridge
Access:	Easy. 3 km (2 mi) hike one way
Status:	Provincial forest
When to go:	Spring, summer, fall

Directions: From Tumbler Ridge proceed north on the Heritage Highway for 35 km (22 mi). There is a wide pullout on the right (east) side of the road with a large information sign. The trail begins directly across the road and is level and easy to follow. Hiking time to the junction down to the falls is 35 minutes, plus an additional 5 minutes to reach the falls.

Facilities: None, except for map at trailhead.

Highlights: Tepee Creek has eroded a notch through the sandstone strata, much like at nearby Bergeron Falls. The creek plunges 8 m (26 ft), cascades a further 8 m (26 ft) into a jumble of gigantic talus, flows to a long, gentle, 45 degree angled cascade and then proceeds in a spectacular canyon toward the Murray River through a

A Guide to BC's Best 100 Falls

Tepee Falls

hellish jumble of fallen rock slabs, some as big as cabins.

The best spot from which to observe the falls is a small knoll that projects out into the canyon. This viewpoint is small, narrow and exposed; extreme care is required. Not everyone will feel comfortable venturing out here. A few aromatic pasture sage plants grow atop the knoll.

From this viewpoint it appears that the downcutting action of Tepee Creek is proceeding slowly as it wrestles with a monolithic stratum of sandstone about 7 m (23 ft) thick that forms a sheer polished wall on the far side of the falls.

The downstream canyon has high vertical walls with basal slopes of talus forested with conifers on the north-facing aspects, and grassy knolls and scattered deciduous species, birch and balsam poplar, facing south. This beautiful viewpoint is surely at its best during the fall colour season.

Snapshot: Bergeron and Tepee falls make a memorable duo of pleasant hikes with the finest examples of sandstone waterfalls in the Tumbler Ridge area at trails' end. Both trails were completed in 2001–02 by the Wolverine Nordic and Mountain Society, which is doing a wonderful job of opening up previously unknown waterfall wonders in the region.

93 BERGERON FALLS

Rating:	▲▲▲▲△
Type:	Plunge/cascade
Location:	14 km (9 mi) N of Tumbler Ridge
Access:	Moderate. 8 km (5 mi) of gravel road, 5 km (3 mi) hike one way
Status:	Provincial forest
When to go:	Spring, summer, fall

Directions: From Tumbler Ridge drive north on Hwy 29 toward Chetwynd. After 6.5 km (4 mi) turn right onto the Sanctuary Valley Road and drive to the end of the road, which is in a large gravel pit. The trailhead is at the entrance to the pit on the left-hand side. The trail is initially quite steep, but then levels out for the rest of the way. The total elevation gain is 110 m (360 ft). Hiking time is about an hour and a quarter. As you near the falls, Bergeron Creek can be crossed by either rock hopping or wading at low water, or by balancing on a large spruce log felled across the creek as a bridge. Caution should be exercised at high water in the springtime. Just ahead at the rim of the canyon are numerous spots to observe the falls and its spectacular amphitheatre. Extreme caution is paramount here especially with children, as there are 100 m (330 ft) vertical drops and no fences or safety barriers.

Bergeron Falls

It is also possible to canoe or boat up the Murray River and then hike the 1 km (.6 mi) up Bergeron Creek.

Facilities: None, other than a map at the trailhead.

Highlights: The initial steep section of the trail leads through aspen up to a lodgepole pine forest on the plateau. Along the way a 10 m (11 yd) side trail leads to the minor Vomer Falls. In late August some late-blooming wildflowers including great northern aster, Canada goldenrod and tall larkspur still stood, but flowers were giving way to fruit. I noted five kinds of red berries beside the trail: bunchberry, kinnikinnick, Hooker's fairybell, highbush cranberry and rosehip. On our hike to the falls we disturbed a cow moose that was grazing close below the trail, and at the canyon rim a Townsend's solitaire flitted about.

Bergeron Falls is a spectacular example of a hanging valley. The tiny "misfit" Bergeron Creek emerges from a notch in the horizontal sandstone strata and plunges down toward the glacially overdeepened Murray River valley. The enormous and magnificent amphitheatre created by the creek ranks alongside that of the well-known and much-visited Spahats Falls in Wells Gray Provincial Park. At Bergeron Falls, however, you will almost certainly be alone.

At 100 m (330 ft) in height Bergeron Falls is the highest waterfall in northern BC. On its way from the brink to the foot the creek plunges down the vertical upper cliff, then cascades down an inclined section of the headwall, plunges again and finally cascades through talus at the base. The canyon walls, 100 m (330 ft) high and formed of almost perfectly horizontal strata, extend about 500 m (1,600 ft) downstream, with Bergeron Creek flowing placidly for about a kilometre to its confluence with the Murray River.

Mt. Bergeron, Bergeron Creek and its namesake falls commemorate P.O. John Bergeron of Pouce Coupe, a small settlement just east of Dawson Creek, who was killed in action in 1944.

Snapshot: Over the course of my research for this book I have been amazed by how I continued to learn of major waterfalls that were previously unknown to me. I learned about Bergeron only in 2001 from Charles Helm's excellent guide, *Tumbler Ridge–Enjoying its History, Trails and Wilderness*. Bergeron is only the most impressive of the Tumbler Ridge region's previously unheralded waterfalls (Kinuseo excepted), and the town is now a BC waterfall hotspot to compare with the better-known Wells Gray Provincial Park and Yoho National Park.

94 KINUSEO FALLS

Rating:	▲▲▲▲▲
Type:	Cascade
Location:	160 km (100 mi) S of Chetwynd, 64 km (40 mi) S of Tumbler Ridge
Access:	Easy. Good gravel logging road beyond Tumbler Ridge, 200 m (220 yd) trail
Status:	Monkman Provincial Park
When to go:	Spring, summer, fall

Directions: From Hwy 97 at Chetwynd take Hwy 29 to Tumbler Ridge. At Tumbler Ridge continue south on the extension of Hwy 29 for 13.5 km (8 mi) before turning right onto the Murray River Forest Service Road, also signed to Monkman Provincial Park. Watch for logging trucks. Stay on the main road for exactly 50 km (31 mi) and once inside the boundary of the park watch for the right turn posted to Kinuseo Falls. It is a further 1 km (.6 mi) to the parking lot. A 200 m (220 yd) wheelchair-accessible trail leads to the viewing platform at the brink of the falls, and a separate trail, 250 m (270 yd) long and somewhat steep, leads to a viewpoint

Kinuseo Falls

further downstream that allows a more panoramic view of the falls. This same trail also leads in 1.5 km (1 mi) to the banks of the Murray River for river level views of the falls.

It is also possible to access the foot of the falls by jet boat. Tours can be arranged in Tumbler Ridge.

Facilities: At the Kinuseo Falls parking lot there are picnic tables beside the river and toilet facilities. The upper viewing platform at the brink of the falls has interpretive signage. The Kinuseo Falls campground is large with 42 sites and a full range of facilities including a gazebo.

Highlights: Kinuseo Falls is one of Canada's premier waterfalls, and on the grandeur scale is one of the four major waterfalls in BC (the others being Helmcken, Hunlen and Takakkaw). It is a classically beautiful cascade, an impressive 69 m (226 ft) high, that tumbles over a resistant wall of limestone at an angle of about 60 degrees. Above the falls the unsuspecting Murray River drops in small steps over resistant ledges. Directly across the falls, engraved in the side of the canyon, is a fine example of a recumbent fold, which illustrates the process that built not only the Rockies themselves but also the orogenic origin of Kinuseo Falls. The steepness of the falls is decreasing as the erosive power of the water and ice of the river is greatest at the brink of the falls. Downstream the Murray River resumes its leisurely progress to its confluence with the Pine River east of Chetwynd, and from there to the Peace River. An osprey frequents the great plunge pool at the foot of the falls in the summer.

The first record of European visitation to Kinuseo was Jim Dixon in 1907, but it was Samuel Prescott Fay on September 20, 1914, who first described and photographed the falls and announced its existence to the world. Fay's response to the falls was equal in "wow factor" to that of Robert Lee, who stumbled upon Helmcken Falls two years earlier. Fay wrote, "It gave me an inspired sensation as I stood there alone at the foot of the falls, covered with spray, to think that only two or three parties had ever beheld this magnificent sight. They are fine enough if they were accessible to be a sight such as tourists would travel a long distance to see." (Helm, p. 263) Six years later in 1920, Fay made application to name the great cascade Kinuseo Falls. *Kinuseo* was the Cree word for many fish, which he chose based on the abundance of trout in the vicinity of the falls. When Fay applied to register the name with the Geographical Board of Canada, the board commented that he was "lucky" to have the name accepted, as "the Board generally looks with disfavour on names suggested by tourists." Their singularly inappropriate remark reflected the monumental shortsightedness of the government bureaucrats who sat behind desks in Ottawa. Fay and his party suffered brutal tribulations exploring an uncharted wilderness to reach the falls and in fact, Fay was congratulated by the U.S. Biological Survey for "clearing up one of the blank spaces on the map of North America." (Helm, p. 83) In 1927 Prentiss Gray took the second photographs and the first moving pictures of the falls. Gray, like Fay before him, suffered mightily in reaching the falls and what had been planned as a day trip on horseback turned into a three-day epic as Gray and his guides hauled heavy camera equipment on their backs through miles of windfall timber. Although Fay had registered the name Kinuseo Falls, Gray records that there was an existing Cree name for the falls, *Kapaca tignapy*, meaning falling water. Thus, we are left to ponder that this magnificent landform might have lived out its fame under a name other than the Kinuseo Falls with which we are now familiar.

By 1939 the tourism potential of Kinuseo Falls was beginning to be realized. Cabins and a restaurant were built at the location of the present parking lot, and it was recorded that on one weekend in that year there were 200 visitors to the falls.

Snapshot: The first time I visited Kinuseo Falls was, coincidentally, October 29, 1998, the thirtieth anniversary of my arrival in Canada as a landed immigrant. The majesty and solitude of Kinuseo Falls framed by the wilderness foothills of the Rocky Mountains on that October afternoon was an inspiring place to reminisce on that momentous personal anniversary. Kinuseo Falls lay before me in all its glory, a stunning symbol of all that conspires to keep me entranced by Beautiful British Columbia.

95 THE MONKMAN CASCADES

Rating:	▲▲▲▲▲
Type:	Tiered plunges separated by wide pools
Location:	Monkman Provincial Park
Access:	Very difficult. Overnight backpacking expedition or long mountain bike trip
Status:	Monkman Provincial Park
When to go:	Summer and fall

Directions: From Tumbler Ridge follow the directions for Kinuseo Falls. The trailhead for Monkman Lake and the Cascades is at the Kinuseo Falls campground at the northern edge of Monkman Provincial Park. The road terminates at the Murray River in a large parking lot that is also the trailhead. The trail is easy to follow and there are kilometre markers to assist your progress.

The trail follows the east bank of the Murray River for the first 6.5 km (4 mi). At 1.5 km (1 mi) from the trailhead the trail passes beneath a bridge on the Imperial Creek Forest Service Road. It is possible to drive to this point and begin your hike here, thus saving 3 km (2 mi) in total.

A Guide to BC's Best 100 Falls

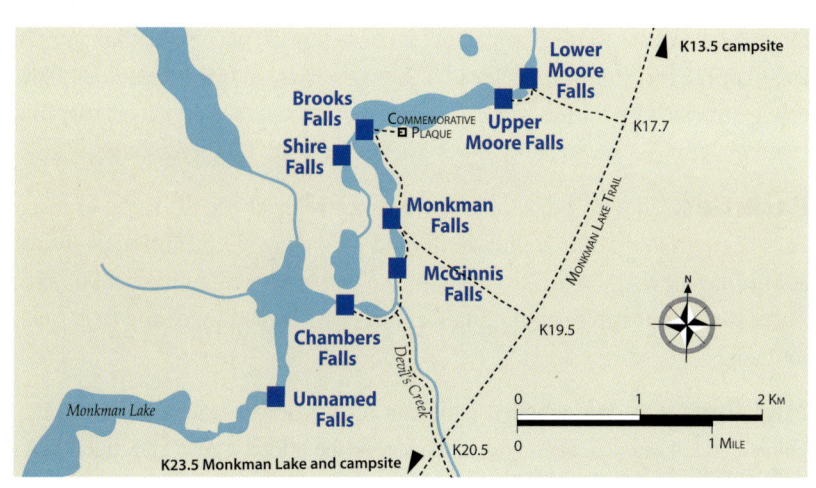

THE MONKMAN CASCADES

Directions from Kinuseo campground: Drive back toward Tumbler Ridge for 600 m (660 yd) and turn right onto the Bulley Creek FSR. After 1.5 km (1 mi) turn right onto the Imperial Creek FSR and proceed 1.6 km (1 mi) to the bridge. The next significant feature is the footbridge across the river at km 6.5. Beyond here the trail climbs steeply to the Whale, a ridge of exposed limestone with a thin forest cover that allows views of the mountains and the Monkman Valley to the west.

Look for distant views of Horsetail Falls across the valley. At km 12 the trail descends steeply to the main campsite at km 13.5. This campsite has good water, two grubbed tent sites, a grate for cooking, ropes for a bear cache and an outhouse. It is a good base for exploring the Cascades with a day pack.

Beyond the campsite, the side trail to the two Moore Falls is at km 17.7, and the side trail to the various cascades centred on Monkman Falls is at km 19.5.

The Monkman Lake campsite at km 23.5 is an excellent location with numerous tent sites and great views southward beyond the lake to the Monkman Glacier and the high peaks of Mounts Barton and Vreeland.

The following approximate hiking times are for strong hikers and do not include breaks. Others may take considerably longer. My party came down from Monkman Lake in seven and a half hours.

Trailhead to km 6.5 (Murray River bridge): 1 hour 35 min

Km 6.5 bridge to km 13.5 campsite: 2 hours

Km 13.5 to km 17.7 (Moore Falls turnoff): 1 hour 5 min
 (down to Moore Falls: 20 min)

Moore Falls turnoff to km 19.5, Monkman Falls turnoff: 30 min
 (down to Monkman Falls: 10 min)

Km 19.5 to km 23.5, Monkman Lake campsite: 1 hour 15 min

211

Mountain bikes are allowed on the trail as far as km 12 (mi 7.5). Monkman Falls is 20 km (12 mi) from the trailhead at Kinuseo Falls, so this option does allow enough time to visit the Cascades in a single day without the necessity of carrying overnight gear. At present only 15 to 20 parties per year visit the Cascades.

Facilities: The full range of facilities is available at the BC Parks Kinuseo Falls campground at the trailhead. Beyond here there are primitive campsites at km 7 beside the Murray River, at km 13.5 and at Monkman Lake at km 23.5. There is also a possible camping spot at km 17 with good water and level spots for tents.

Highlights: To the accepted pantheon of BC's major waterfalls, Helmcken, Hunlen, Takakkaw, Kinuseo and Della, should be added a new star, the Monkman Cascades, also known as the Monkman Steps. This series of eight waterfalls aligned over 4 km (2.5 mi) of Monkman Creek are a magnificent, inspiring and totally unique part of BC's and Canada's waterfall heritage; indeed, there may be nothing comparable anywhere in the world. The Cascades' uniqueness is based not on their height, width, volume or fame, but on the fantastic sequence of consecutive waterfalls followed by jade-green pools. If Monkman Falls or Brooks Falls or any of the other individual cascades stood alone it would be notable, but for the sequence to be repeated eightfold is simply divine.

The wonder of the Cascades is made possible by the fortuitous juxtaposition of the karst geomorphology with a series of parallel fault lines that intersect Monkman Creek at right angles.

In sequence, moving downstream, the Cascades consist of:

1. Unnamed Falls. Al Tattersall of Tumbler Ridge appears to be one of the few people ever to have visited and photographed the uppermost of the Cascades. Monkman Creek divides around a small island as it drains from Monkman Lake with separate falls either side of the island. The location can be approached either downstream from Monkman Lake or by hiking 1 km (.6 mi) upstream from Chambers Falls, but both require bushwhacking as there is no trail.

2. Chambers Falls. This 2 m (6.5 ft) cascade is the least imposing of the eight Monkman cascades and is reached by either hiking downhill alongside Devil's Creek from the main trail, or by bushwhacking upstream along Monkman Creek from McGinnis Falls. It is about 750 m (820 yd) from McGinnis Falls to Devil's Creek and a further 250 m (270 yd) to the falls along the shore of the beautiful Chambers Pool. The falls can be viewed either from creek level or from a vantage point high above the cliff on the left bank.

A Guide to BC's Best 100 Falls

McGinnis Falls

3. McGinnis Falls. McGinnis Falls is 400 m (440 yd) upstream of Monkman Falls.

Monkman Creek flows into a horseshoe-shaped punchbowl before plunging 13 m (43 ft) to McGinnis Pool. At flood stage the creek covers the whole face of the cliff and flows around a treed island at the brink. McGinnis Falls is protected from human intrusion by the almost impregnable karst formations, and there seems to be only a single access route to the brink. To reach McGinnis Pool from Monkman Falls follow the bare limestone ridge to its obvious southern end and then cut down through the trees at 45 degrees toward the roar of the falls. This will deliver you to a rock bluff above McGinnis Pool, about 150 m (165 yd) from the falls, and with a magnificent view of the falls and the pool. To reach the brink of the falls bushwhack past both the pool and the falls at the foot of steep rock bluffs and ledges that appear inaccessible until you emerge at the lip of a dramatic sinkhole with cabin-sized blocks of limestone that have collapsed into the central pit. The Monkman Pass road builders who encountered a similar sinkhole in the vicinity christened it Hell's Half Acre. This particular sinkhole must be Hell's Whole Hectare. From here there is a route up the bluffs and along the ledges that still requires a little ingenuity and scrambling.

4. Monkman Falls. This triple segmented, 20 m (65 ft) plunge is at the heart of the entire Cascades experience. The main volume of water flows down the central falls in a 7 m (23 ft) plunge followed by a 7 m (23 ft) cascade through broken blocks

Monkman Falls

and slabs. The left and right falls are more purely plunges. Monkman Pool is the beautiful lake below the falls. The side trail delivers you to a viewpoint on an open limestone ridge that allows panoramic views of Monkman Falls, Monkman Pool and across to the spectacular mountains to the west, Shark's Fin (2,323 m/7,621 ft) and Castle Mountain (2,193 m/7,195 ft).

It is easy to visit the foot of the falls, but caution should be exercised on the wet, slippery rocks. The brink of Monkman Falls can be reached by walking upstream through the forest and doubling back along a bare ridge. The creek between Monkman and McGinnis Falls is a world of its own, a little Eden. The jade green creek flows placidly in two rock garden channels of rectangular slabs separated by a narrow treed island. At a bend in the creek the water circumvents a bluff as it flows in a rapids from McGinnis Pool. This stretch of the creek is absolutely magical. The scenery is unique, the beauty sublime, the solitude and peace absolute and the whole experience otherworldly.

5. Shire Falls. Helm reports the name is a reflection of Middle Earth ambiance. (Helm, p. 237) This segmented plunge is located between Monkman Falls and Brooks Falls. Surprisingly, it is not on the main channel of Monkman Creek, but falls from a short tributary drainage that runs parallel to Monkman Creek and consists of two small lakes and a short section of surface flow. The waterfall flows directly from a small lake over the same escarpment as Monkman Falls and into a large pool. This waterfall flows strongly even in late summer, and though the drainage has not been researched, it suggests the resurgence pattern typical of karst landscapes where stream flow is partly surficial and partly subterranean. The falls occupies a small part of the escarpment with a 400 m (1,300 ft) bare headwall to the west.

Brooks Falls

6. Brooks Falls. The highest of the Cascades is a 20 m (65 ft) block plunge that empties into Brooks Pool, the largest of the waterfall pools. Brooks Pool is confined on all sides by high cliffs and only the nearest portion of it is visible as it extends around a corner and down toward Upper Moore Falls about 1 km (.6 mi) distant. The trail from Monkman Falls to Brooks Falls is not marked, but is simply a matter of walking along the barren limestone for about 500 m (550 yd) and cutting through a few trees. The brink is high above Brooks Pool and a thrilling spot to lie on your stomach and watch the wild, hypnotic descent of the falls. After absorbing the attractions of this location the final destination is about 300 m (330 yd) away on the high bluff facing the falls. Here, with a splendid view of Brooks Falls, is the memorial plaque placed by the Brooks family to commemorate the Monkman Pass pioneers, and a short version of their story.

7. Upper Moore Falls. Upper and Lower Moore Falls have their own trail that drops down steeply from the main trail at km 17.7. Hiking time is about 20 minutes. Both falls can be seen from the main trail through a gap in the trees. At Upper Moore you can scramble out on wet slippery rocks into the spray zone of the 7 m (30 ft) plunge. This viewpoint is a residual mound from a previous incarnation of the falls that the creek now circumvents as it tumbles in a complex series of small steps into a pool, then cascades down a 45 degree slope into Upper Moore Pool.

8. Lower Moore Falls. This falls is a complex mix of plunges and cascades with a central 8 m (26 ft) plunge. At the brink a big slab has collapsed, points skyward, and now segments the falls. The base of the falls is a graveyard of fallen slabs and chunks. Lower Moore Pool is a carbon copy of Upper Moore Pool. Downstream of here Monkman Creek flows over a series of rapids confined by high canyon walls.

The long trail to the Cascades is enlivened by a profusion of the beautiful, deep blue-purple flowers of mountain monkshood. The flowers are named for their unique hoodlike shape that resembles the cowl of a monk. Contrary to their beauty, all parts of the plant are highly poisonous, especially to livestock. The tubers contain aconitine, an alkaloid that paralyzes the nerves and lowers temperature and blood pressure. The trail to Monkman Lake has the best display of the species that I have ever seen.

Snapshot: If I die tomorrow, I will die happy, for I have visited the Monkman Cascades. The Cascades, one of BC's and Canada's greatest natural wonders, are little known and little visited because of their remoteness in northeastern BC and the 20 km (12 mi) that separates them from the nearest car park. The series of eight waterfalls each with its own jade-green pool separating it from its cohorts is such an unlikely configuration that it almost defies human imagination. They must be the work of an artistically inclined deity who liked what he had created so much that he kept repeating himself. I believe this landform may be unique in the world.

On a sunny day at the Cascades you quickly realize that all the superlatives in the English language could never begin to convey the glory of this place. You are in the realm of religious experience. While I was sitting at Monkman Pool meditating on these things, a loon suddenly flew in, scudded along the surface of the green water and yodelled three times its uniquely haunting call that is the essence of the Canadian wilderness. In that moment I grasped the Holy Grail of the wilderness experience.

The Monkman Cascades were responsible for the single most amazing synchronicity in my life. I was having dinner in August 2002 with an old friend, Danny McGinnis, when I casually mentioned that I had to visit Monkman Provincial Park in connection with this book. Danny told me that back in the late 1930s his father had been in that area with Alex Monkman. Suddenly the bells began ringing in my head. I had been browsing Charles Helm's book, *Tumbler Ridge—Enjoying its History, Trails and Wilderness*, as I researched a visit to the Cascades. Subliminally, I vaguely recollected a reference to the name McGinnis. When I arrived home I consulted the book and immediately called Danny. "Was your father's nickname Shorty, by any chance?" I asked. He said it was, and I was able to inform him that his father was commemorated on a plaque at Brooks Falls. The plaque was placed in 1999 by the Brooks family and reads: "Named after Carl Brooks who in 1937 with Ted Chambers and Shorty McGinnis, led by Alex Monkman, blazed a trail thru the Monkman Pass for the Monkman Pass Highway Association."

Danny immediately suggested accompanying me on a trip to the Cascades and on August 30 and 31, 2002, we backpacked into the area. With Helm's book as a guide, it quickly became apparent that of the four men named on the plaque Alex Monkman had a pass, a park, a creek and a waterfall named after him, Brooks had a waterfall named after him, Ted Chambers had a ridge overlooking Monkman Creek named after him but Shorty McGinnis had been neglected. It also became clear that since only four of the eight cascades had names, one should be named after Shorty McGinnis. We explored the Cascades and Danny decided that the falls immediately upstream of Monkman Falls should be the one to name McGinnis Falls. Application was made to register the name with the Geographical Names Board of Canada and on December 1, 2003, the name became official.

In 2003 Danny and I reprised our 2002 visit, this time accompanied by his two sons, Loren and Ben, and I photographed the two generations backstopped by McGinnis Falls and pool.

96 RED DEER FALLS

Rating: ▲▲▲▲△
Type: Plunge
Location: 100 km (60 mi) SE of Tumbler Ridge
Access: Difficult. 15 km (9 mi) blacktop, 85 km (53 mi) gravel logging road, 10 km (6 mi) hike
Status: Provincial forest
When to go: Spring, summer, fall

Directions: From Tumbler Ridge drive south on the Heritage Highway for 14.6 km (9 mi) to where the gravel begins. Proceed 36 km (22 mi; odometer now reads 50.6 km), and turn right onto the Wapiti Forest Service Road. After 25.2 km (15.6 mi; odometer now 75.8 km) stay right on the Wapiti FSR and resist the temptation to turn left onto the misleadingly named Red Deer FSR. After a further 24 km (15 mi) you must ford a shallow creek (not a problem) and 300 m (330 yd) later turn right off the main line into a spur road. The Wapiti FSR has kilometre markers and the turn is at km 547.5. It is not recommended to attempt this long access when the road surface is wet as extremely slippery conditions prevail and the remoteness makes rescue unlikely in the event of a mishap.

Park 400 m (440 yd) along this spur at a turnaround that leads to a log cabin. This is the trailhead. Allow two to three hours one way for the hike to the falls. After 200 m (220 yd) the road is washed out. Proceed 200 m (220 yd) down the creek bed and take the uphill road to the right. Do not continue downstream to a

Red Deer Falls

second road. Follow the old road for 5 km (3 mi) to a point where it passes beneath imposing rounded cliffs. Beyond here the deteriorating road climbs steeply as it circumvents deep tributary ravines that drain down to the Red Deer canyon. After the road descends and begins to level out again watch for the obvious side trail that leads down to the falls viewpoint, five minutes distant. It is also possible to complete the hiking portion by mountain bike or ATV.

Facilities: None

Highlights: The scenery on the long drive into the trailhead becomes ever more impressive as you progress along the Wapiti FSR. You leave the foothills behind and enter the domain of the Rocky Mountains proper, with Mt. Becker dominating on the right. Much of the Red Deer drainage was burned in an enormous 1988 forest fire that began at a campfire adjacent to the falls. The conflagration, so devastating in its initial impact, is now ameliorated by the passage of time and by the regenerating forest of planted spruce and natural pine growing up beneath the sea of burned snags. Walking the trail you quickly come to appreciate the legacy of the burn as there are unimpeded views of the surrounding mountains and the spectacular Red Deer canyon.

Red Deer Falls is a major BC waterfall with a 20 m (65 ft) block plunge into a wide pool. At the brink of the falls, exposed strata that are close to vertical create a resistant barrier to the erosive forces of the stream. The falls can be observed from a rocky vantage point at the end of the trail, by clambering down a steep slope to the plunge pool or from an interesting spot where the water pours over the brink.

A flock of five harlequin ducks in the plunge pool on August 28, 2003, indicate a probable nesting area along Red Deer Creek. On the hike out, we saw three mule deer bounding through the regenerating trees near the aptly named creek and falls.

Snapshot: My party's hike into Red Deer Falls took on a new dimension when we missed the correct turn at the start of the trail and found ourselves bushwhacking for two hours through windfall snags, slide alder and steep canyons before relocating the trail. This experience brought to mind Prentiss Gray, one of the original explorers of this region, who in 1927 set out on horseback on a day trip to Kinuseo Falls that turned into a three-day slog through downed timber. In 1928 Gray was the first to describe and photograph Red Deer Falls and recorded in his journal: "Suddenly we came out on a rocky ledge directly above the river and there was seventy feet of sheer drop where the river plunged into a gorgeous pool, hemmed in by towering rocks. It paid for all the trip as we gazed at that silvery ribbon." (Helm, p. 313) It is instructive how little has changed at Red Deer Falls since 1928, including the sentiments of visitors to this blessed spot.

97 BELCOURT FALLS

Rating:	▲▲▲▲△
Type:	Plunge
Location:	120 km (75 mi) SE of Tumbler Ridge
Access:	Difficult. 15 km (9 mi) of blacktop, 105 km (65 mi) of gravel road, 3 km (2 mi) of trail
Status:	Provincial forest
When to go:	Spring, summer, fall

Directions: Prepare for a long drive on lonely gravel logging roads by filling your tank and checking the spare tire.

From Tumbler Ridge proceed south on Hwy 52, the Heritage Highway. After 15 km (9 mi) the Murray Forest Service Road to Monkman Provincial Park and Kinuseo Falls splits off to the right and the blacktop ends. Continue straight ahead here for 35 km (22 mi) and turn right on to the Wapiti FSR, which is marked at its junction by a forest of oil company signs. Be aware of logging trucks from here on.

Proceed 25 km (15.5 mi) on the Wapiti FSR to the Red Deer FSR junction. The Wapiti FSR, a.k.a. the 500 Road, is marked in kilometres. Watch for the Red Deer FSR to the left some distance after the 523 sign. At 1 km on this road there is a BC Forest Service Recreation Site and a crossing of the Wapiti River. The Red Deer Road is signed with markers and at R26 will cross the Red Deer River. After R32 stay right on the main road and immediately after R38 bear left. At R42.5 Hotslander bridge is signed. Stay left at the junction between R43 and R44 and proceed to the Belcourt bridge at R45. You are now 120 km (75 mi) from Tumbler Ridge.

Belcourt Falls

Cross the bridge and drive about 300 m (330 yd) around the bend in the road. On the left (north) side locate a road sign indicating a curve and the bridge; exactly at this sign look for a quad track. Follow this for about 2 km (1 mi), about 25 minutes walking time, until it peters out in a turnaround. Beyond here locate the hiking trail that continues along the canyon rim to the spectacular falls viewpoint, about 1 km (.6 mi) or 15 minutes hiking time. You can approach closer to the amphitheatre by walking along the rim but the view of the falls from here actually diminishes.

Facilities: None

Highlights: The long drive from Tumbler Ridge through the rolling eastern foothills of the Rockies is an introduction to the remote wilderness area of BC that borders on Alberta.

The trail to the falls hugs the rim of Belcourt Canyon and traverses a pine-spruce forest that in June is fragrant with wild rose, bunchberry and Labrador tea. Swallowtail, blue and fritillary butterflies flit about.

Just before you reach the viewpoint you will hear the familiar rumbling of a major waterfall. Soon after, you emerge at the rim of a high canyon with spectacular views upstream to the amphitheatre that collects both Belcourt Creek and a second unnamed creek. It is a rare feature, unique in BC, for two streams to share the same amphitheatre.

Belcourt Creek flows strongly and has eroded a deep notch through the strata. The discharge drops 2 m (6.5 ft) to a ledge before falling a further 10 m (33 ft) in a roiling plunge. The unnamed creek to the right drops about 40 m (130 ft) in a plunge–cascade–plunge sequence.

Downstream the canyon walls alternate strata of varying resistance, vertical rock alternating with loose eroded shale. It is strongly recommended to avoid walking along the foot of the canyon as fatalities have occurred when the loose material slides.

The main viewpoint offers a wonderful panorama of pristine, wooded foothills, a river canyon and the unique feature of two waterfalls tumbling into the same amphitheatre.

Snapshot: Belcourt Falls is one of the most remote in BC and is little known or visited. It is, however, a worthy destination for those who enjoy a day's outing in the wilderness exploring a distant corner of BC. Belcourt is at the opposite end of the spectrum from such high volume tourist destinations as Takakkaw or Helmcken, and it would be a surprise indeed if you were to share this destination with another party. To underline the wilderness aspect of Belcourt's setting, on my visit I encountered two separate black bears along the trail but both bolted as soon as I clapped my hands to scare them off.

ALASKA HIGHWAY

The three waterfalls in this vast region are spread over 1,200 km (745 mi). Sikanni Chief Falls, near km 256 of the Alaska Highway, is one of BC's major waterfalls, but you must then drive to km 840 to reach Smith River Falls. Liard Hot Springs Provincial Park at km 810 is a mandatory stop. Anyone with an interest in waterfalls will want to visit the unique ecosystem of this hot spring oasis lost in the vastness of the boreal forest. To reach the third waterfall of the region another long drive to km 1,350 is required, before turning off the highway and proceeding a further 100 km (60 mi) to the old gold rush town of Atlin. Atlin has one of the most spectacularly scenic locations of any town in BC and is well worth the drive. Pine Falls is a short drive from the town. Having reached Atlin and Pine Falls you are at the extremity of your search for BC's 100 best waterfalls. It is now about 2,750 km (1,700 mi) back to Vancouver.

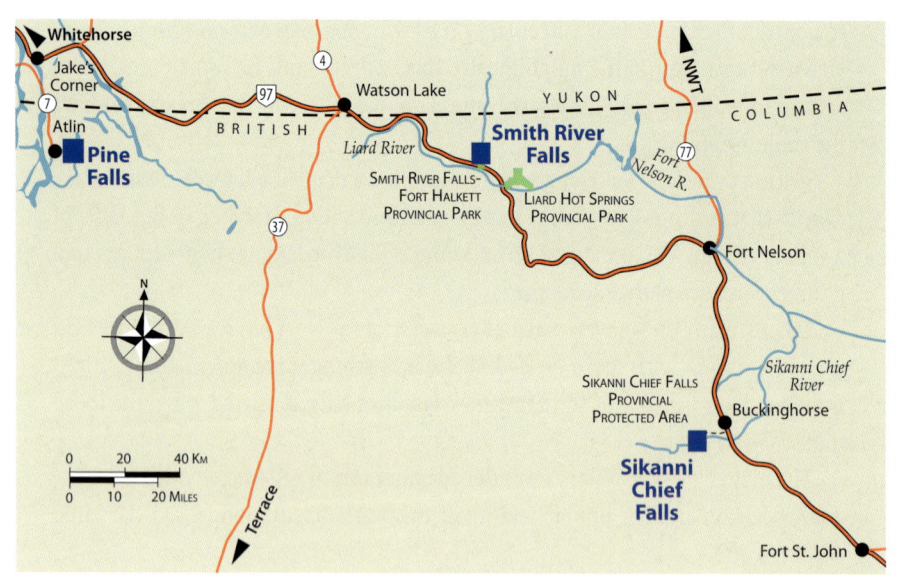

FALLS 98–100

98 SIKANNI CHIEF FALLS

Rating:	▲▲▲▲▲
Type:	Plunge
Location:	198 km (123 mi) N of Fort St. John, 200 km (125 mi) S of Fort Nelson, 7 km (4 mi) S of Buckinghorse
Access:	Moderate. Heavily gravelled road, 1.5 km (1 mi) trail
Status:	BC Parks Protected Area
When to go:	Spring, summer, fall

Directions: From Fort St. John drive north on the Alaska Highway to the bridge across the Sikanni Chief River at historic mile 162. Fifteen km (9 mi) north of the bridge (you are now 198 km/123 mi from Fort St. John) look for a sign indicating Mason Creek on a left-sweeping curve of the highway. Immediately beyond, turn left onto a gravel road with a marker "Sikanni River Ranch, Mile 171." Your next landmarks are a sign that reads "Sikanni Chief Falls Provincial Protected Area, 16K" and another that announces "This is a Radio Controlled Road. All vehicles must have a radio with frequency 150.815. Speed limit is 70 kph. Please drive defensively. Emergency phone 250-785-3085, or 1-888-878-3700." This is a private road and you travel at your own risk.

Proceed along the main line and just beyond the km 14 road marker take the left fork at the three-way junction for 2.5 km (1.5 mi). A sign at the trailhead marks the "Sikanni Chief Falls Recreation Trail." The hike to the canyon rim and the first view of the falls takes about seven minutes on a mainly level trail with a couple of short, steep sections. For the best views of the falls bear right at the canyon; a further seven-minute walk along the rim leads to a viewpoint above the great amphitheatre of the plunge pool. Another five minutes down a fairly steep trail brings you to the brink of the falls.

Facilities: The trailhead parking lot has a picnic table, a firepit and an outhouse. You will find a campground, store and gas at Sikanni Chief at mile 162, where the Alaska Highway crosses the Sikanni Chief River, and there is camping, gas and a café at Buckinghorse River, 7 km (4 mi) north of the turnoff.

Highlights: The trail to the falls winds through a spruce–aspen forest with bluebells, bunchberry and twinflowers beside the path and leads to the canyon rim. From here, views can be had of the rounded Rocky Mountain foothills to the west and good views down the canyon as the river heads east toward the Alaska Highway and the muskegs of the Fort Nelson Lowlands. Look for pearl crescent

Sikanni Chief Falls

butterflies nectaring on the yellow cinquefoil along the canyon rim and listen for Tennessee warblers in the woods. Mountain goats are reported to frequent the area. The second viewpoint is on the rim of the canyon directly above the amphitheatre of the plunge pool. Here at the rim flat slabs of rock are fractured and ready to fall, and caution is advised. The horizontal sandstone strata of the vertical amphitheatre walls are constantly undermined and shattered by erosional processes as the cliffs constantly spill detritus, which accumulates at their foot.

Above the falls the wide green river dawdles toward the precipice, picks up speed in a transparent green wave and then plunges 30 m (100 ft) in a terrifying maelstrom of white water and foam, first to a hidden ledge, then exploding down the main drop between a cleft in the strata and fanning out over a wide lower platform, before the final 5 m (16 ft) cascade to the plunge pool.

Snapshot: From the brink of the falls it is possible, with extreme caution, to look down into the maw while the rock on which you are standing vibrates disconcertingly from the thunder of the falling water. Immediately above the brink there is a tide line of debris deposited in the trees 2.5 m (8 ft) above the normal level of the river. One can only speculate and tremble at the thought of the mayhem at this spot when the river runs that high.

Sikanni Chief Falls is one of the major waterfalls of BC and, with its setting of untrammelled wilderness, should be better known and more widely visited.

99 SMITH RIVER FALLS

Rating:	▲▲▲▲△
Type:	Plunge/cascade
Location:	Km 820 of the Alaska Hwy, 340 km (210 mi) NW of Fort Nelson, 28 km (17 mi) NW of Liard Hot Springs Provincial Park
Access:	Easy. 2 km (1.25 mi) of gravel road
Status:	Smith River Falls–Fort Halkett Provincial Park
When to go:	Spring, summer, fall

Directions: The Alaska Highway crosses the Smith River on a major bridge 28 km (17 mi) northwest of Liard Hot Springs Provincial Park. Turn right onto the posted gravel access road to the falls 200 m (220 yd) beyond the bridge. The road ends in 2 km (1.25 mi) at a parking lot adjacent to the falls. The level trail from the parking lot down to the falls viewpoint takes less than five minutes. A steep wooden staircase with 70 steps descends all the way to river level within the plunge pool.

Facilities: Outhouse, picnic table, fire ring at the parking lot.

Highlights: The falls can be observed from the parking lot, but for a better, closer view follow the trail that leads to a viewpoint above the plunge pool. The trail through the spruce forest is flanked by an attractive flora of wild rose, horsetails, red osier dogwood, bluebells, northern bedstraw and bunchberry, with yarrow and cinquefoil around the parking lot. Along the trail listen for Swainson's thrush, yellow-rumped and Tennessee warblers, and watch for three-toed woodpeckers tapping on the spruce trees. Herring gulls, the common gull of this region, are often to be found within the plunge pool. Black bears and moose are frequent inhabitants of the park.

The viewpoint provides a good vantage of the river as it picks up velocity within a steep-walled canyon on its approach to the falls and plunges over consecutive ledges in a combined drop of about 35 m (115 ft). The upper falls is a steeply sloping cascade with water fanning out over successive ledges, while the lower one is predominantly a plunge. In the respite between the two falls the river has eroded a

Waterfalls of British Columbia

Smith River Falls

cave on the far shore. At the foot of the falls a huge, circular plunge pool with 20 m (65 ft) cliffs displays evidence of the complex geology of the site, where a fault plane separates a vertically inclined stratum of low-quality coal from the horizontal strata at river level.

   The Smith River is a major river and when it is running high, particularly in springtime, clouds of spray fill the plunge pool and drift away downstream through the canyon. On a late afternoon visit in mid-July there was a rainbow within the plunge pool.

The park combines the twin attributes of the Smith River Falls and the site of Fort Halkett, a Hudson's Bay Company trading post established in 1832 and closed in 1875, at the confluence of the Smith and the Liard rivers.

Snapshot: A late June visit to Smith River Falls was spoiled by clouds of voracious mosquitoes that were impossible to coexist with. On a scale of 1 to 10 this was a 12-bug experience! A local expert told me this is normal at this spot, so be warned.

100   PINE FALLS

Rating:	▲▲▲▲△
Type:	Plunge
Location:	5 km (3 mi) E of Atlin,
	180 km (110 mi) from Whitehorse, Yukon
Access:	Easy. 5.6 km (3.5 mi) gravel road,
	100 m (110 yd) level trail
Status:	Provincial Forest
When to go:	Spring, summer, fall

Directions: To reach the small, historic village of Atlin, turn south off the Alaska Highway at mile 866, Jake's Corner, Yukon. Hwy 7 traverses the Yukon for the first 40 km (25 mi), and then BC for the final 60 km (40 mi) before reaching Atlin. At the T-junction in Atlin, the townsite and services are to the right, but the falls are reached by turning left onto the Surprise Lake Road. Drive 5.6 km (3.5 mi) and bear right onto Spruce Road, where you will immediately see the bridge across Pine Creek. Parking is available here on the right side of the road. The short, level trail, only 100 m (110 yd) long, leads to viewpoints above the falls.

Facilities: None

Highlights: Pine Creek is a major stream, and was the source of the original gold rush to Atlin after gold was discovered in 1898. As the creek plunges over a series of ledges in a deepening canyon, the main feature is a triple segmented plunge waterfall with a height of 8 m (26 ft). The stream is segmented by gleaming, wet, black pillars of igneous material, a relatively rare substrate in BC waterfalls. The whole structure of this falls is redolent of Matthew Falls in the Cariboo, and not only because they are the only two triple segmented falls in this book.

After the falls the creek makes a right-angled turn as it cascades down a chute into a roiling circular cauldron with sheer, 30 m (98 ft) walls. Then it turns through another right angle before roller-coasting over more ledges as it disappears down the steep-walled canyon on its way to Atlin Lake. During the spring freshet much of the canyon is one long stretch of whitewater.

Waterfalls of British Columbia

The short trail and the dry forest adjacent to the falls host a variety of common wildflowers, including wild rose, yarrow, goldenrod, arnica, chamomile, fireweed, cinquefoil and alpine speedwell. Juniper, kinnikinnick and ceanothus flourish beneath the pine, spruce and aspen trees. From the falls the view to the west over Atlin Lake to Atlin Mountain (2,046 m/6,700 ft) allows good views of the rock glacier, which is the site of a wintertime snowmobile race to its top.

There is another view of the falls from a wide pullout on the Surprise Lake Road, immediately before making the turn onto Spruce Road. This gives a panoramic view of the whole canyon, but the main waterfall is hidden behind a bluff.

Pine Falls

Snapshot: Pine Falls is about 2,750 km (1,700 mi) from Vancouver and can only be reached by travelling through the Yukon Territory, which proves that those in search of BC's waterfalls will go virtually to the end of the earth in search of their quarry. If you do come in search of this waterfall, you will be blessed with the opportunity to visit Atlin, a remote gold rush town frozen in time since 1906, and located on perhaps the most stunning townsite in BC. It is well worth the trip

When I go from hence, let this be my parting word, that what I have seen is unsurpassable.

Rabindranath Tagore, *Gitanjali*

Glossary

Amphitheatre: the eroded and widened space downstream of the base of a waterfall.

Arch: where all or part of the waterfall passes through an eroded hole in the rock.

Basalt: lava that cools rapidly and solidifies into distinctive crystalline columns.

Batholith: a mass of igneous rock deposited below the earth's surface.

Breccia: a stratum formed by angular rock fragments.

Brink: the rim over which a waterfall plunges.

Caprock: a stratum that is more resistant to erosion than surrounding rock and protects an underlying softer rock, thus creating a cap.

Cirque: the amphitheatre created by erosion at the head of a glacier.

Ephemeral: a stream that flows intermittently, usually when the stream dries up after snowmelt and summer drought.

Fjord: a coastal valley eroded by a glacier and subsequently flooded by a rise in sea level.

Fluvial: relating to the effects of water.

Freshet: the increase in discharge in a stream when snow melts in the spring.

Geology: the science of the Earth's crust. Specifically refers to the arrangement of the various strata of rock.

Geomorphology: the science of the physical features of the Earth's crust. Specifically refers to the effect of natural processes such as erosion or glaciation on the landscape.

Grotto: the eroded cavern behind a waterfall.

Hanging valley: a tributary valley left at an elevated level after a main valley has been deepened by a glacier.

Headwall: the vertical wall of the plunge pool on each side of a waterfall.

Igneous: rock that originated as volcanic lava.

Intrusion: where lava extends into faults in sedimentary rocks.

Karst: landscape features specific to limestone geology.

Keyhole: a narrow canyon with vertical walls that resembles the shape of a keyhole.

Krummholz: wind-blasted dwarf trees in alpine environments.

Magma: volcanic lava.

Metamorphic: rock that is changed (metamorphosed) by heat or pressure and in the process becomes a different type of rock.

Misfit stream: a stream flowing in a valley that is too large to have been created by the present size of that stream. Indicates that the stream was much larger in the past, usually during a period of glacial melting.

Monolithic: an unstratified layer of rock.

Pleistocene: the most recent glacial epoch.

Plunge pool: the base of a waterfall where the erosive power of the stream creates a wide and deep spot in the streambed.

Pothole: a cylindrical hole eroded by rocks circulating within a depression in a streambed.

Roostertail: the plume of water created by an impediment in a streambed or waterfall that resembles the tail of a rooster.

Sedimentary: rock created by the deposition of sediment, usually sand, silt and mud, or by the accumulation of calcareous material that forms limestone.

Slot canyon: a narrow, sinuous canyon.

Spray zone: the cool, wet area constantly bombarded by spray at the foot of a waterfall.

Talus: the sloping mass of fragmented rock at the foot of a cliff.

Checklist of the 100 Best BC Waterfalls

LOCATION	DATE VISITED	COMMENTS

VANCOUVER ISLAND
1 Elk Falls		
2 Myra Falls		
3 Englishman Falls		
4 Little Qualicum Falls		
5 Stamp Falls		
6 Della Falls		
7 Tsusiat Falls		

COAST RANGE
8 Twin Falls #1		
9 Chatterbox Falls		
10 Harmony Falls		
11 Phantom Falls		
12 Chapman Falls		
13 Shannon Falls		
14 High Creek Falls		
15 Brandywine Falls		
16 Alexander Falls		
17 Soo Falls		
18 Nairn Falls		
19 Lizzie Falls		
20 Place Falls		
21 Keyhole Falls		
22 Bridal Veil Falls		
23 Rainbow Falls #1		

SOUTHERN INTERIOR
24 Nicoamen Falls		

Waterfalls of British Columbia

LOCATION	DATE VISITED	COMMENTS
25 Deadman Falls		
26 Weyman Falls		
27 Fintry Falls		
28 Rainbow Falls #2		
29 Sutherland Falls		
30 Cascade Falls		

SOUTHEAST

LOCATION	DATE VISITED	COMMENTS
31 Beaver Falls		
32 Deer Creek Falls		
33 Fletcher Falls		
34 Wilson Creek Falls		
35 Moyie Falls		
36 Perry Falls #1		
37 Marysville Falls		
38 Meachen Falls		
39 Bull River Falls		
40 Pedley Falls		
41 Lower Bugaboo Falls		
42 Morrissey Falls		
43 Josephine Falls		
44 The Petain Waterfalls		

YOHO-KOOTENAY NATIONAL PARKS

LOCATION	DATE VISITED	COMMENTS
45 Thompson Falls		
46 Wapta Falls		
47 Ottertail Falls		
48 Natural Bridge		
49 Hamilton Falls		
50 Takakkaw Falls		

LOCATION	DATE VISITED	COMMENTS
51 Laughing Falls		
52 Twin Falls #2		
53 Marble Canyon		
54 Helmet Falls		

WELLS GRAY PROVINCIAL PARK & AREA

55 Hendrix Falls		
56 Canim Falls		
57 Mahood Falls		
58 Deception Falls		
59 Sylvia Falls		
60 Goodwin Falls		
61 Spahats Falls		
62 Moul Falls		
63 Dawson Falls		
64 The Mushbowl		
65 Majerus Falls		
66 Helmcken Falls		
67 Osprey Falls		
68 Rainbow Falls #3		
69 Pyramid Falls		

CENTRAL

70 Odegaard Falls		
71 Hunlen Falls		
72 Matthew Falls		
73 Cariboo Falls		
74 Morkill Falls		
75 Rearguard Falls		
76 Overlander Falls		

Waterfalls of British Columbia

LOCATION	DATE VISITED	COMMENTS
77 White Falls		
78 Falls of the Pool		
79 Emperor Falls		
80 War Falls		
81 Bijoux Falls		

NORTHWEST

82 Cheslatta Falls		
83 Findlay Falls		
84 Nourse Falls		
85 Buck Falls		
86 Moricetown Falls		
87 Twin Falls #3		
88 Humphrey Falls		

TUMBLER RIDGE

89 Sukunka Falls		
90 Martin Falls		
91 Perry Falls #2		
92 Tepee Falls		
93 Bergeron Falls		
94 Kinuseo Falls		
95 Monkman Cascades		
96 Red Deer Falls		
97 Belcourt Falls		

ALASKA HIGHWAY

98 Sikanni Chief Falls		
99 Smith River Falls		
100 Pine Falls		

Selected Bibliography

Backroad Mapbooks Outdoor Recreation Guides, *Cariboo Chilcotin Coast, 2nd Edition*, Coquitlam: Backroad Mapbooks, 2006.

—*The Kootenay Rockies BC, 4th Edition* Coquitlam: Backroad Mapbooks, 2008.

—*Northern BC, 2nd Edition,* Coquitlam: Backroad Mapbooks, 2009.

—*Thompson Okanagan BC, 1st Edition,* Coquitlam: Backroad Mapbooks, 2007.

—*Vancouver, Coast and Mountains, 1st Edition,* Coquitlam: Backroad Mapbooks, 2007.

—*Vancouver Island, Victoria & Gulf Islands 5th Edition,* Coquitlam: Backroad Mapbooks, 2008.

Blier, R. *Hiking Trails III, Northern Vancouver Island including Strathcona Park, 9th Edition.* Victoria: Vancouver Island Trails Information Society, 2002.

Dodd, J. and G. Helgason. *Canadian Rockies, Access Guide.* Edmonton: Lone Pine Publishing, 1998.

Goward, T. and C. Hickson. *Nature Wells Gray.* Edmonton: Lone Pine Publishing, 1996.

Hanna, D. *Best Hikes and Walks of Southwestern British Columbia.* Edmonton: Lone Pine Publishing, 1997.

Helm, C. *Tumbler Ridge, Enjoying its History, Trails and Wilderness.* Tumbler Ridge: MCA Publishing, 2001.

Holmes, A. *Principles of Physical Geology, Revised Edition.* London, UK: Nelson, 1965.

National Geographic Society, *Field Guide to the Birds of North America, 4th Edition* Washington, DC: National Geographic Society, 2002.

Neave, R. *Exploring Wells Gray Park, 4th Edition.* Kamloops: The Friends of Wells Gray Park, 1995.

Patton, B. and B. Robinson. *The Canadian Rockies Trail Guide, A Hiker's Guide to Banff, Jasper, Yoho, Kootenay, Waterton Lakes, Mount Assiniboine & Mount Robson, 3rd Edition.* Banff: Summerthought Ltd, 1986.

Pojar, J. and A. Mackinnon. *Plants of Coastal British Columbia, including Washington, Oregon and Alaska.* Alberta: Lone Pine Publishing, 1994.

Pole, G. *Classic Hikes in the Canadian Rockies.* Vancouver: Altitude Publishing, 1994.

Pole, G. *Walks and Easy Hikes in the Canadian Rockies.* Vancouver: Altitude Publishing, 1992.

Schweitzer, W. *Beyond Understanding, The Complete Guide to Princess Louisa, Chatterbox Falls, Jervis Inlet.* Seattle: Eos Publishing, 1989.

Acknowledgements

I was a few years into this project when my good friend, Danny McGinnis, came on board. By that time I had visited most of the easily accessible falls, and when Danny and I had dinner together in West Vancouver on August 25, 2002, I was seeking a hiking partner to tackle some of the more remote sites that required backpacking and overnight camping. For details of the utterly unbelievable synchronicity that unfolded around this dinner see my description of the Monkman Cascades.

Somewhere along a wilderness trail amid magnificent scenery, Danny came up with the observation that "projects like yours shouldn't be allowed." I agreed that it was a dirty job, but someone has to do it. I would like to thank Danny for becoming a part of "the dirty job." Without his companionship on the trail this project would never have come to fruition.

When Danny and I first visited Tumbler Ridge we had the good fortune to make the acquaintance of Dr. Charles Helm. Charles, originally from South Africa, is a GP and author of the book *Tumbler Ridge—Enjoying its History, Trails and Wilderness*. This is quite simply the best local guidebook to the outdoor resources of any community in BC. In addition, Charles is a force of nature who inspires people to get out and enjoy their local areas. Largely as a result of Charles's interest, Tumbler Ridge is now the major centre of paleontology research in BC. The town is also one of the most important waterfall centres in BC. My thanks go to Charles for his book and his help in directing us to the waterfalls of Tumbler, and in some cases building the trails that took us there.

I would also like to acknowledge another excellent local guidebook, *Exploring Wells Gray Park*, by Roland Neave. Like Helm's guide to Tumbler Ridge, this book is a paradigm of the genre. Thanks also to Rand Rudland who accompanied me to Morkill Falls. Thanks also to all the photo contributors, including Mike Biro, Justin Coughlin, Michael van Dam, R.G. Daniel, B.D. Davis, Tim Gage, Thomas Gotchy, Phillippe Henry, John Humphries, Nathan Jantzen, Gareth Jones, Marc-Andre Leclerc, Jane Little, Michael Maughan, Edwina Podemski, Amanda Polson, Christopher Porter, Nick Riemondi, Olivier Robert, Rand Rudland, Tylor Sherman, Dianna Smith, Jeremy Staveley, Leon Turnbull, Ryan Van Veen and Jon Weaver, as well as the many other photographers who were kind enough to submit photographs not included in the final layout due to space constraints.

I am especially grateful to my editor, Margaret Tessman, for bringing her rigorous editing skills to this project, as well as to the helpful crew at Harbour Publishing including, Andrew Bishop for his photo research and Anna Comfort, production manager and cover designer. Thanks as well to John Lightfoot who created the many detailed maps in this book, to Patricia Wolfe for her eagle-eye proofreading, to Martin Nichols for an elegant page layout, to Erin Schopfer for creating the index and to Rafe Mair for writing the introduction found at the beginning of this book.

Index

Akrigg, Helen and Phillip, 141
Alaska Highway region, 11, 222–29
Alexander Falls, 58–**59**–60
Angel Falls, 10
Angel's Staircase, 123–24
Athabasca Falls, 15
Atlin, 11, 222, 227, 229
Azure Lake, 158, 159

Bamfield, 34
Banff, 129
Barkerville, 168, 170
Barrow Falls, 15
BC Hydro, 23, 54, 60, 98, 99.
  See also hydroelectricity
bears, 16–17
Beaver Falls, 85, **86**–87
Belcourt Falls, 197, **220**–21
Bella Coola, 11, 162, 164
Berg Lake Trail, 177–78, 181
Bergeron Falls, 14, 197, 205–**06**–07
Bergeron, P.O. John, 207
Bijoux Falls, 182, **184**–85
Blaeberry River, 111, 113
Blanket Creek Provincial Park, 82, 83
Blue River, 160
Bowron Lake Provincial Park, 170
Brandywine Falls, 55–**56**–58
Bridal Veil Falls, 69–**70**–71, 83
Buck Falls, 186, 191–**92**
Buckinghorse, 223
Bugaboo Falls. *See* Lower Bugaboo Falls
Bull Falls, 93, 98–99
Burns Lake, 188, 190
Bute Inlet, 37, 39

Cache Creek, 75
Canal Flats, 100
Canim Falls, 134, **136**–37
Canyon View Trail. *See* Elk Falls
Cariboo Falls, 168, **170**–72
Cariboo Mountains Provincial Park, 168
Cariboo River Falls, 171
Carp Lake Provincial Park, 182, 183
Cascade Canyon, 84
Cascade Falls, 83–**84**, 85
cascade waterfalls, defined, 14
Central region, 162–85
Chapman Falls, 40, **19**, 47–**48**–49

Chatterbox Falls, 15, **16**, 37, 40, **41**–43
Chaudiere Falls, 15
Cheslatta Falls, 186–**87**–88
Cheslatta River, 186, 188
Chetwynd, 184, 198, 200, 207
Chilcotin Plateau, 162, 166
Churchill Falls, 15
Clearwater Lake Tours, 159, 160
Clearwater Lake. *See* Osprey Falls
Clearwater River, 133, 139, 157, 159
Clowhom Falls, 45, 46, **47**
Coast Range region, 37–72
Columbia River, 85
Cranbrook, 11, 91, 94, 98

D'Arcy, 64
Daly Glacier, 122
Dawson Creek, 11
Dawson Falls, 134, 146–**47**, 149
Deadman Falls, 73, **75**–76
Deception Falls, 134, **138**–39
Deer Creek Falls, 85, 87–**88**
Deer Falls, 23, 88. *See also* Elk Falls
Della Falls, 20, 21, 30–**31**–34, 130
Dettifoss, 10
dipper, American, **29**
Douglas fir, 26, 28, 48, 141
Drinkwater Creek. *See* Della Falls
Drinkwater, Joe, 33

Egmont, 41, 43
Elk Falls, 20, 1–**22**–23
Elk Lake Provincial Park, 106
Elkford, 105
Emerald Lake, 117, 118, 120
Emperor Falls, 172, 177–78, 180–**81**
Englishman River Falls, 20, **25**–26

Falls of the Pool, 172, 177–78, **180**
Fay, Samuel Prescott, 200, 209, 210
Fernie, 11, 103
Findlay Falls, 186, 188–89
Fintry Falls, 73, 78–**79**–80
Fintry Provincial Park, 78–80
Fletcher Falls, 85, **89**–90
Fort Halkett Provincial Park, 225
Fort Nelson, 11, 223, 225
Fort St. John, 223
Fraser River, 175

237

Freil Falls. *See* Harmony Falls

Ghost Lake. *See* Matthew River Falls
glaciation, 12, 110
    Quaternary, 37
Goat Range Provincial Park, 90
Golden, 11, 101, 111. *See also* Yoho National Park
Goodwin Falls, 134, 139–**40**–42
Grand Falls, 15
Gray, Prentiss, 210, 219
Gray, Wellesley, 141
Great Central Lake. *See* Della Falls
Green River. *See* Nairn Falls

Hamilton Falls, 110, 118–**19**
hanging valley, 37, 52, 125, 127, 160, 206
Harmony Falls (Freil Falls), 40, 43–**44**–45
Harrison Hot Springs, 71
Harrison Lake. *See* Rainbow Falls #1
Hazelton, 11, 193
Helm, Dr. Charles, 236
Helmcken Canyon, 153, 156
Helmcken, Dr. John Sebastian, 153
Helmcken Falls, 9, 14, 111, 133, 134, **151**–**52**–**55**–56
    base of, 154–56
    south rim, 153–54
Helmet Falls, 110, 122, 129–**31**–32
Hendrix Falls, 134–**35**
High Creek Falls, 53–**54**–55
Homathko River, 39
Horseshoe Falls, 150
Hotham Sound, 43, 44
Houston, 188, 190, 191
Humphrey Falls, 186, 196
Hunlen Falls, 162, 164–**65**–**66**–67
hydroelectricity, 10–11, 21, 71, 80, 84

Ice Age, 12, 53, 127
ice
    climbing, 122, 194
    cone, 144, 151. *See also* glaciation
Iguazu Falls, 10
Independent Power Producer projects, 9–10

Jasper, 174, 176, 177
Josephine Falls, 85, 93, 105–**06**

Kaieteur Falls, 10
Kakabeka Falls, 15
Kamloops, 11, 73, 75, 133
Kelowna, 11, 78

Kenney Dam, 188
Kettle River, 83
Keyhole Falls, 37, 66–**67**–69
    base of, 68–69
Khone Falls, 10
Kicking Horse River, 114
Kimberley, 94, 95–96, 97–98
Kinuseo Falls, 197, 198, 207–**08**–10
Kitimat, 196
Knight Inlet, 37
Kootenay National Park, 111, 127, 129.

Lake Louise. *See* Yoho National Park
Laughing Falls, 110, 123–**24**
Lee, Robert, 150, 153, 209
Liard Hot Springs Provincial Park, 222, 225
Lillooet, 11
    Lake, 63
    River, 66, 68
Little Qualicum Falls, 20, 26–**27**–28
Lizzie Falls, **63**–64
Louise Falls, 15
Lower Bugaboo Falls, 93, 101–**02**–03
Lyons, Chess and Sylvia, 141
Lytton, 74

Macdonald, James "Mac", 42
Mackenzie Junction, 182
Mahood Falls, 136–**37**
Mahood, James Adam, 137
Majerus Falls, 134, 149–**50**–51
Majerus, Michael, 150
Marble Canyon, 110, 127–**28**–29
Mardelsfossen, 10
Martin Falls, 197, 200–**01**–02
Marysville Falls, 93, 95–**96**–97
Matthew River Falls, 168–**69**
McBride, 172
McDougall Falls, 150
McGinnis, Danny, 217, 236
McGinnis Falls, **213**, 217. *See also* Monkman Cascades
McGinnis, Shorty, 217
McLeod Lake, 182
Meachen Falls, 97–**98**
Meadow Falls, 150. *See also* Majerus Falls
Million Dollar Falls, 15
Monashee Provincial Park, 80
Monkman, Alex, 217
Monkman Cascades, 197, 198, 210–17
    Brooks Falls, **215**
    Chambers Falls, 212
    Lower Moore Falls, 216

McGinnis Falls, **213**, 217
Monkman Falls, 213–**14**
Shire Falls, 214–15
unnamed falls, 212
Upper Moore Falls, 215–16
Monkman Falls. *See under* Monkman Cascades
Monkman Provincial Park, 207, 210
Montmorency Falls, 15
Moricetown Falls, 186, **193**–94
Morkill, Dalby Brooks, 174
Morkill Falls, 172–**73**–74
Morrissey Falls, 93, 103–**05**
Moul Falls, 134, 144–**45**–46
Mount Robson, 178, 181
Mount Robson Provincial Park, 162, 174, 176, 177
Mount Waddington, 11, 39
Moyie Falls, 91–**92**, 93
Murtle River, 133, 146, 151
Mushbowl, The, 118, 134, **148**–49
Myra Falls, 20, 23–**24**–25

Nairn Falls, 61–**62**–63
Nairn Falls Provincial Park, 61
Nanaimo, 11, 25
Natural Bridge, 110, **117**–18
Nechako Canyon Protected Area, 188
Niagara Falls, 9, 10, 15
Nicoamen Falls, 73, **74**
Nicoamen First Nation Reserve, 74
Nimpo Lake, 164, 165
Nistowiak Falls, 15
Northwest region, 186–96
Nourse Falls, 186, 189–90
Nusatsum Falls, 163

Odegaard Falls, 162–**63**–64
Okanagan Lake, 78
Okanagan Valley, 80
orogenic forces, 11, 110
Osprey Falls, 15, 134, 157–**58**
Ottertail Falls, 110, 115–**16**
Overlander Falls, 172, **176**–77

Pacific Rim National Park Reserve, 34
Paint Pots Nature Trail, 29. *See also* Helmet Falls
Panther Falls, 15
Parks Canada, 35, 120
Parksville, 26
Pedley Falls, 93, 100–01
Pemberton, 61, 63, 64, 66,
Perry Falls #1 (Kimberley), **94**–95
Perry Falls #2 (Tumbler Ridge), 197, 202–**03**–04

Petain Waterfalls, 93, 85, 106–**08**–09, 132
Phantom Falls, 40, 45–**46**–47
Pine Creek, 227
Pine Falls, 222, 227–**28**–29
Pisew Falls, 15
Pissing Mare Falls, 15
Place Falls, 64–**65**–66
plunge waterfalls, defined, 14
Point Lace Falls, 123, 124
Port Alberni, 25, 26, 28, 30
potholes, 99, 129, 149
Prince George, 11, 172, 182, 184
Princess Louisa Inlet, 37, 41, 42, 43
punchbowl waterfalls, defined, 14
Pyramid Creek Provincial Park, 160
Pyramid Falls, 134, **160**–61

Qualicum Beach, 26
Quesnel, 11, 170

Radium Hot Springs, 100, 101
Rainbow Falls #1 (Harrison Lake), 71–**72**
Rainbow Falls #2 (Spectrum Creek), 78, 80–**81**
Rainbow Falls #3 (Azure Lake), 134, 158–**59**–60
Rearguard Falls, 172, 174–**75**
Rearguard Falls Provincial Park, 174
Red Deer Falls, 197, 218–**19**
Robson River, 177, 180
Rockwall Trail, 130
Rocky Mountains, 12, 85, 101, 110, 197

safety, 15–18
Salmon Inlet, 45
Sechelt, 45, 47
Shannon Falls, **12**, 37, 50–**51**–53, 58
Shannon, William, 52
Sikanni Chief Falls, 222, 223–**24**–25
Smith River Falls, 222, 224–**26**–27
Smithers, 186, 193, 194
Soo Falls, **60**–61
Southeast region, 85–109
Southern Interior region, 73–84
Spahats Falls, 133, 134, 142–**43**–44
Spences Bridge, 74
Squamish, 50, 53, 55, 58
Stamp Falls, 20, **28**–29
Stawamus Chief, 52
Strathcona Provincial Park, 30
Sukunka Falls, 197, 198–**99**–200
Sukunka Falls Provincial Park, 198
Sutherland Falls, 78, **82**–83
Swan, Bryan, 164
Sylvia Falls, 134, 139–**40**–42

Takakkaw Falls, 110, 111, 120–**21**–23
Tantalus Range, 46, 55
Tattersall, Al, 212
Teaquahan River. *See* Bute Inlet
Tepee Falls, 197, 204–**05**
Terrace, 11, 193, 194, 196
Tete Jaune Cache, 174, 176, 177
Thompson Falls, 110, 111–**12**–13
Thompson River canyon, 74
Thompson, David, 113
Thompson, Kelsey, **19**
Toba Inlet, 37
Tokumm Creek, 127, 129
Topley, 188
Trail, 11, 86
Trophy Mountains, 133
Tsusiat Falls, 20, 34–**35**–36
Tugela Falls, 10
Tumbler Ridge, 8, 11, 12, 13, 197–221
Tweedsmuir Provincial Park (South), 164
Twin Falls #1 (Yoho National Park), 123, 125–**26**–27
Twin Falls #2 (Teaquahan), 37–**39**–40
Twin Falls #3 (Northwest), 110, 186, 194–**95**
Twin Falls Chalet, 125
types of waterfalls, 13–14

Unna Lake, 171

Valemount, 11, 160, 174
Valley of the Thousand Falls, 178
Vancouver Island region, 12, 20–36
Vanderhoof, 186
Vermilion Range, 130
Victoria Falls, 10
Virginia Falls, 15

Wapta Falls, 110, 113–**14**
War Falls, 182–**83**–84
Wells Gray Provincial Park region, 12, 133–61
West Coast Trail, 34–36
Wet'suwet'en Indian Reserve, 193
Weyman Falls, 73, **77**–78
wheelchair accessible falls, 26, 52, 117, 122, 151, 206
Whistler, 11, 55, 58, 60, 61
White Falls, 162, 172, 177–**79**–80
Whitehorse, Yukon, 227
Wilberforce Falls, 15
Williams Lake, 164
Wilson Creek Falls, 85, **90**–91

Yoho and Kootenay National Parks region, 110–132
Yoho National Park, 111, 113, 115, 117, 118, 120, 123, 125
Yosemite Falls, 10

Request for Information

Anyone with information regarding the waterfalls of BC is encouraged to contact tony@whiskeyjacknaturetours.com. Such information might concern a waterfall that you feel may deserve a place in this book or any clarification you may have with regard to errors in the text. Trail access can change over time, particularly at those sites outside of parks, and updated information is welcomed.

Waterfall Tours

The author, Tony Greenfield, is the owner of Whiskeyjack Nature Tours. Tony offers guided waterfall tours of British Columbia. For information regarding waterfall and other natural history tours visit www.tonyswaterfallsofbc.com, www.whiskeyjacknaturetours.com or contact Tony by e-mail: tony@whiskeyjacknaturetours.com.